THE YANK

JOHN CRAWLEY is a former sergeant in the United States Marine Corps and a former Irish Republican Army (IRA) volunteer. Born in New York to Irish immigrant parents, he moved to Ireland as a young teenager and later returned to America to receive formal military training in order to join the IRA. John was imprisoned for ten years for taking part in a daring cross-Atlantic gun-running operation. Upon his release, he returned to IRA active service before being arrested in London for conspiracy to cause explosions. He received another thirty-five-year sentence but was released from prison under the terms of the Good Friday Agreement. John remains committed to the establishment of a united Irish Republic.

For all those who sacrificed their
lives for the Irish Republic,
and to those yet living who will
never abandon it.

JOHN CRAWLEY

THE YANK

THE TRUE STORY OF A
FORMER US MARINE IN THE
IRISH REPUBLICAN ARMY

MELVILLE HOUSE
BROOKLYN · LONDON

The Yank: The True Story of a Former
US Marine in the Irish Republican Army

Unless otherwise noted, all
photos are courtesy of the author

First Melville House Printing: September 2022
Originally published in the UK by Merrion Press

Melville House Publishing
46 John Street
Brooklyn, NY 11201

and

Melville House UK
Suite 2000
16/18 Woodford Road
London E7 0HA

mhpbooks.com
@melvillehouse

ISBN: 978-1-61219-984-9
ISBN: 978-1-61219-985-6 (Ebook)

Library of Congress Control Number: 2022938120

Designed by Euan Monaghan
Printed in the United States of America

1 3 5 7 9 10 8 6 4 2

A catalog record for this book is
available from the Library of Congress

PROLOGUE

I MOVED TO the bow of the *Valhalla* and inhaled a deep breath of sea air. The weather was mild with no rain and good visibility. Shore lights shimmered on the dark water and there was a gentle swell, but it wasn't bad. I had been on boats a lot during my time in the Marine Corps but never on a shrimping trawler trying to smuggle seven tons of weapons and ammunition across the wide Atlantic in hurricane season.

An initial taste of what might lie ahead occurred when we left the harbour mouth and ploughed into the first of the wild Atlantic swells. They were moderate, but the boat shuddered like a car going too fast over a speed bump. I braced myself and stood for a while longer at the bow. The lights from the American east coast receded behind us as the ocean before us grew blacker. In fourteen days or so, if everything went to plan, we would land the weapons and ammunition in Ireland.

I had left Ireland some months earlier with 9,000 pounds and instructions to build an arms network from scratch. I was returning with a quarter of a million dollars-worth of equipment and a boat and crew prepared to take it all the way. I had also acquired contacts and resources that would prove invaluable in the future.

The first few days at sea were routine and uneventful, but then we lost our autopilot. With the autopilot functioning, the steering wheel in the pilothouse could be set to a specific heading and maintain it despite strong winds and currents but, with it out of action, someone had to be at the wheel at all times to keep us on course. It was mainly Bob Anderson, John McIntyre and myself who took turns, in four-hour shifts.

About halfway across the ocean, we had a day when the sea was like glass. I never saw calmer water, not even on a fishing pond. The wake from the *Valhalla* caused the only ripple in the utter tranquillity of the benign Atlantic. I had no idea I was experiencing the proverbial calm before the storm.

That night the winds began to build and the sea churned. Bob grew concerned. He told me that a hurricane he'd been monitoring in the Bahamas was coming up the Gulf Stream and heading in our direction. Shortly afterwards, all hell broke loose.

The *Valhalla* wasn't designed for the battering it was about to receive. Enormous waves, forty to fifty feet high, dwarfed the boat, while ferocious winds, driving rain and crashing seas swept the deck. The boat reeled violently from side to side, its stabilising outriggers almost touching the surface with each roll. Walls of cold, dark water made endless attempts to swamp us.

Then, an enormous wave landed an almost knockout blow to the boat. There was the sound of a massive crash and I was thrown forward violently. It felt like a car collision. I stumbled from my berth to a chilling sight. Four of *Valhalla*'s seven tempered glass windows had been blown in. Bob was on his knees with blood gushing from a head wound caused by broken glass. He was trying desperately to hold on to the wheel while John rendered him assistance. Water had poured into the pilothouse and down into the forward engine room, causing a short circuit and starting a fire. Smoke poured up from the engine room where the guns and ammunition were stored. Seawater sloshed around my ankles. I knew at that moment we were doomed.

Blood was everywhere, but to my immense relief Bob was lucid and able to function. John did his best to clean and dress Bob's wounds while I took the wheel, trying to steer us into the waves so we didn't get broadsided.

There was so much damage to the boat and the storm was so fierce and persistent, I could not conceive of us evading catastrophe for much longer. I asked Bob if we should put on the survival suits we had brought along.

"There's no point!" he gasped painfully. "We're in the middle of the ocean. We have no communications. Nobody knows we're here. Go ahead and put it on if you want to, but it'll take you eight hours longer to die." None of us put them on.

I
RECON

"PAIN IS BEAUTIFUL and extreme pain is extremely beautiful." I was beginning to have my doubts about that. The US Marine sergeant, who assured us of this fact, sprinted effortlessly beside us. A dozen young Marines, who had just landed in Okinawa and volunteered for Recon training, were trying desperately to keep up with this loping gazelle of a man as he darted down narrow dirt tracks that took us over hill after hill after excruciating hill. Several recruits had already quit or collapsed in a pool of vomit. Despite three months of hard conditioning at boot camp and another month of hauling ass at Advanced Infantry Training at Camp Pendleton, California, this physical training was off the charts.

Hours earlier, I had stepped off a plane at Kadena Air Base outside Okinawa after a twenty-four-hour flight from California via Alaska and Tokyo. It wasn't supposed to be this way. I wasn't supposed to be in the Marines. I wanted to be a "Green Beret" like my cousin Ken Crawley, who had spent seven years in that outfit. When I signed up at a US Army recruiting station in Chicago, the contract certified that, after basic training, I would be given an opportunity to attend Jump School, Ranger School and the Special Forces Qualification Course or

"Q-Course." There was no guarantee I would make it through this training, of course. Most didn't. But they would permit me to try. However, while I had obtained the guarantee for assignment to Airborne, Ranger and Special Forces schools at the recruiting station, I had not yet signed the final enlistment papers when fate intervened.

I had originally flown to America in April 1975 from Ireland, where I had been living for the four previous years. I would turn eighteen in May and could then enlist in the military. After a stint with the Green Berets, I planned to return home and join the Irish Republican Army (IRA). No one sent me or encouraged me in this endeavour. I thought that one up all by myself.

While in Chicago, I stayed with my Aunt Alice and Uncle Mike. Mike Cahill was my mother's uncle. He had emigrated to America from County Kerry at sixteen years of age and worked for the gas company his entire life. Aunt Alice, of German-Dutch origin, was from a farm near Pontiac, Illinois. She was a lovely woman and our family adored her. The couple had no children and welcomed me in while I got sorted out for enlistment.

Uncle Mike was drafted into the US Navy during the Second World War. He fought in the Pacific theatre. He didn't talk about it much, but I remember the astonishment with which he spoke of watching Japanese kamikaze pilots slamming into American warships. Mike manned a 40-millimetre Bofors anti-aircraft gun on a troop transport carrying Marines into battle. He was at Saipan and Peleliu. Mike had a reverence for the Marines, and his experiences with them engendered a lasting affection and respect for Leathernecks. He told me if I wanted to join the military, if I really wanted to do it right and learn from the best, the Marines were my only option.

Partly out of curiosity and partly to keep Mike happy, I went to see a Marine recruiter. I told the recruiter that, although I thought the Marines were good, I wanted to go for Special Forces and the Marines had no such unit.

"Young man," he assured me, "we have the best Special Forces of all. The elite of the elite. The cream of the Corps— Marine Recon."

"Never heard of it."

"No shit. Recon doesn't flaunt itself like the Green Berets or Navy SEALS. It keeps a low profile. You won't see Recon chasing after writers and Hollywood producers to glamorise it. Being a Marine is enough for them. They don't want to be portrayed as better than their fellow Marines in the infantry. These guys are quiet professionals who prefer to remain in the shadows. 'Swift, Silent, Deadly' is their motto. They only accept the best."

That sounded interesting and challenging. "What kind of stuff do they do?"

"Recon parachute out of planes behind enemy lines to gather intelligence and carry out ambushes and raids. You could find yourself being shot out of a submarine torpedo tube to swim to some hostile beach to carry out an amphibious reconnaissance or to conduct a maritime infiltration. They get the toughest, most challenging and dangerous missions in the Marine Corps."

The recruiter could see he was pushing the right buttons. My soon-to-be-eighteen-year-old head filled with visions of swashbuckling audacity and derring-do. The recruiter leaned forward in his chair, as if sharing a secret he dare not breathe to another soul: "The only thing is, to volunteer for Recon, you gotta carry your balls in a wheelbarrow."

That clinched it. I asked to see the guarantee I would be sent to Recon training after boot camp. A contract similar to what the army was willing to offer me.

"Uh, we don't do that," said the recruiter. "We only guarantee you infantry. Once you're a Grunt, you volunteer for Recon at that point."

"But what if . . . ?"

The recruiter raised his hand to cut off the anticipated question. "Recon is always looking for volunteers. Believe me, you'll have no problem being accepted for Recon training. Whether you make it or not is entirely up to you."

The next day the Marine drove me over to the army recruiting office to pick up my papers. The soldier in the office had been expecting me to sign on the dotted line. Like all recruiters, he had a quota to reach every month. He was livid.

"What are you, a fucking idiot?" the soldier asked, answering his own question at the same time. I caught a glimpse of the Marine recruiter smirking beside me. "These jarheads won't guarantee you a fucking thing. Recon? You gotta be shittin' me! You'll end up in the cookhouse scrubbing out garbage cans with a toothbrush."

The next day I informed my cousin Ken I had joined the Marines. "What are you, a fucking idiot?" I presumed that was a popular question in the army. "The Marines will brainwash you, John. Their only tactic is to fix bayonets and hey diddle diddle straight up the middle. They haven't the sense to come in out of the rain. I think you fucked up."

I think I fucked up, I thought as the Recon instructor put us through a blistering pace. I had watched him perform thirty pull-ups back at camp. Perfect pull-ups. Hands facing out on the bar and coming to a dead hang at the bottom of each repetition. No bent elbows with this guy. He wasn't jacked up and muscular like a weightlifter. He was lean and hard as nails. His was all "go" muscle, not "show" muscle. Tall, handsome and quietly spoken, he did not spit fire and venom like the foaming-at-the-mouth drill instructors in boot camp. He politely asked you to perform a task. Either you could or you couldn't. Depending on your performance, you stayed for further training with Recon or were returned to an infantry unit.

We were taking part in what was known as the Recon Indoctrination Program or RIP school. I had never heard of it and didn't know what to expect. Recon was the only unit in the Marine Corps that allowed you to quit at any time, and that carried its own psychological burden. Knowing you could leave simply by asking only added to the mental pressure and stress.

Technically Recon wasn't Special Forces but special operations capable. The Marines preferred to keep Recon assets within the Marine Corps and did not want to share them with other branches of the service. Therefore, they wouldn't officially join the Special Forces community in the US military command structure until 2006, when a contingent of mostly Recon Marines was renamed Marine Special Operations Command or MARSOC. MARSOC is now an integral part of the Joint Special Operations Command.

In my time, just after the end of the Vietnam War, there were two types of Recon: Battalion Recon and Force Recon. The training was similar, and Marines would transfer between Battalion and Force regularly. Force Recon, however, was considered the more elite branch, with missions that took them deeper behind enemy lines than Battalion Recon. Force Recon had been disbanded in the 1st and 3rd Marine Divisions, leaving only the 2nd Force Reconnaissance Company at Camp Lejeune, North Carolina. Later, I would volunteer for the only Recon that existed in the 3rd Marine Division, the 3rd Reconnaissance Battalion based at a small camp called Onna Point on the western shore of Okinawa.

About halfway through boot camp at San Diego, we got a new drill instructor. He wore jump wings. I presumed he was ex-Recon, though I later learned this was not the case. I worked up the courage to approach him in the squad bay.

"Sir, Private Crawley, platoon 2059, requests permission to speak to Drill Instructor Staff Sergeant Smith, sir."

"Speak, freak."

"Sir, the private was wondering how does the private volunteer for Recon, sir?"

A recruit could only refer to himself as "the private." Pronouns such I, me or you were strictly reserved for human beings.

The drill instructor was apoplectic. "You fuckin' scumbag! You haven't even made it through boot camp, which you won't, and you want to get into Recon? It takes balls to jump out of an airplane, and you haven't got any. You got that, maggot?"

"Sir, yes, sir!"

"Get on your face and start pushing California further west!"

"Sir, aye, aye, sir!"

Performing push-ups at his feet, I realised I would have to come up with a Plan B.

After that incident, the drill instructors began calling me Ricky Recon. Whenever they wanted me for something, they would call out derisively, "Ricky Recon, front and centre!"

Because of my blunder in enquiring about Recon, I was

made a "House Mouse." A House Mouse was a recruit tasked with cleaning out the drill instructors' quarters at the top of the squad bay. There were three "House Mouses."

"House Mouse! Why are there ghost turds under my rack?" Ghost turds are small balls of dust or fluff on the heavily waxed and buffed floor.

"Sir, the private does not know, sir!"

"Get on your face, maggot!"

I was promoted to King Rat, which put me in charge of the House Mouses. This was a responsibility I could have done without. Attracting the attention of drill instructors at Marine Corps boot camp is never a good idea.

One day a Puerto Rican recruit named Hernandez approached the drill instructors to request an emergency phone call. Phone calls and visits were not permitted in boot camp. The only exception was in the event of the death of a close family member.

"Somebody die, Private?"

"Sir, no, sir. The private got a letter from his wife that she wants a divorce, and the private needs to phone her, sir."

We could all hear the conversation. I was amazed that such a young kid was married. The drill instructors ordered everyone to form a circle in the middle of the squad bay. The senior drill instructor opened an olive-green sea bag or duffle bag, the kind used to house and transport most of a Marine's personal belongings. He grabbed Hernandez by the back of the neck and shoved his head into the bag.

"You see a wife in there, cum bubble?"

"Sir, no, sir!"

"Everything you need is in that bag. If the Marine Corps thought you needed a wife, you'd have been issued with one."

"Sir, yes, sir."

"Disappear, maggot!"

"Sir, aye, aye, sir."

Another reminder, if one were needed, that if you were looking for sympathy in the Marines, you could always find it in the dictionary somewhere between shit and syphilis.

A bizarre incident happened while I was at boot camp. I was approached by a drill instructor and told to report to an office in an administration block. That never happens to a recruit. I was dumbfounded. I could only hazard a guess that my mother or father had been killed in an accident and they were going to inform me of it there. I couldn't imagine what else it could be.

Entering the office, I was met by a Marine Master Sergeant Whyte, the highest-ranking enlisted man I had met to date. I was astonished when he shook my hand with a warm smile.

"Have you ever heard of the Naval Security Group, Private?"

"Sir, no, sir."

The Master Sergeant invited me to sit down. He explained that I had the highest language aptitude of the 19,000 Marines who took the test as part of a battery of entrance exams. I had three years of Latin and four years of French under my belt from schooling in Ireland, so I had a good grounding in languages.

He asked if I would be interested in going to the Presidio in San Francisco to attend a fifty-week course in Mandarin Chinese after boot camp. I told him I had an infantry guarantee and hoped to get into Recon. He replied that I was being offered the chance of a great career in the intelligence community. If I decided to leave the military, I could get a job with the Federal Bureau of Investigation (FBI) or Central Intelligence Agency (CIA). It was a no-brainer as far as he was concerned.

But I had no intention, after my period of enlistment, of doing anything other than returning to Ireland and joining the IRA. While I neglected to mention that aspect of my projected career path, I turned down the offer. The Master Sergeant was disappointed in my decision but sent me back to my platoon with a warning to say nothing of what we had discussed. When I returned, my drill instructor demanded to know what it was all about. I told him I was ordered not to speak of it. To my surprise, he dropped it.

About two weeks later, I was woken from a deep sleep by the same drill instructor. He told me I had a phone call in his office. I thought it was some sort of trick. Recruits don't get phone calls. Slipping into my flip-flops, I warily followed the sergeant into his office wearing only my skivvies. I stood at attention and picked up the phone that lay on his desk.

"Private Crawley?"

"Yes, sir?"

"This is Master Sergeant Whyte. Would you consider learning Russian instead?"

"Sir, no thank you, sir." The phone went dead. I never heard from him again.

Being from Ireland sometimes caused me a problem during inspections. A loose thread is called an "Irish pennant" in the Marine Corps. We would cut them with nail clippers, but the eagle-eyed drill instructors still managed to find them. A typical encounter with a recruit would go something like this:

"You from Ireland, maggot?"

"Sir, no, sir."

"Then why are you wearing an Irish pennant?"

"Sir, the private does not know, sir."

"Assume the position and start pushing them out!"

"Aye, aye, sir!"

Except when it came to me. I missed a tiny thread just under the pocket button on the left breast of my utility uniform. The drill instructor looked at it in horror. He glared furiously into my eyes as if I had betrayed everything and everyone he'd ever believed in.

"You from Ireland, maggot?"

"Sir, yes, sir."

"What was that?"

"Sir, yes, sir! The private lives in Dublin, Ireland, sir!"

"Ireland! What part of Russia is that in?"

After boot camp, I was given ten days leave. I was one of a handful of recruits meritoriously promoted to Private First Class (PFC). I had earned my first stripe. I flew to Chicago and stayed with Uncle Mike and Aunt Alice. I then reported to Camp Pendleton, California, for Advanced Infantry Training (AIT).

Boot camp was a thirteen-week initiation into the Corps. AIT began the real training. On my first night in the receiving barracks, I was quite sick. I think I had a touch of food poisoning. As I lay on the rack looking out of the large windows at the brilliant stars twinkling in the moonless night, I heard the booming of thunder. It seemed as if there was quite a storm brewing. Then I realised there wasn't a cloud in the sky. It was my first time hearing artillery. They were carrying out a night-fire mission close by. It was a sobering sound.

At AIT, we were taught to move, shoot and communicate as individuals, as part of a fire team, and as part of a squad. A

Marine fire team consisted of four men. A squad consisted of thirteen men: three fire teams and a squad leader. A platoon contained three squads and a platoon leader.

Unlike boot camp, where we fired the M16 on the rifle range for qualification purposes only, we were now shooting live ammunition while conducting fire team rushes. Fully automatic fire from a shoulder weapon is of limited use. The Marines emphasise aimed fire.

"Don't spray and pray!" the instructors admonished. "Bullets don't go where you want! They go where you aim!"

We learned how to lay a base of fire while assaulting a position so other teams could frontally assault or manoeuvre around the enemy's flanks in what was known as an envelopment. Watching war movies, I never realised how the apparent chaos of the battlefield involved so much communication and choreography. Tactical radios and arm and hand signals play a major role in combat.

Our mission, we were told, was "to close with and destroy the enemy by fire and manoeuvre or repel the enemy assault by fire and close combat." Unlike the US Army, which had ceased bayonet training, we were encouraged to fix bayonets and follow up an assault with cold steel. The Marines emphasised attack and the offensive spirit far more than defence.

We threw hand grenades and fired the 66-millimetre disposable Light Anti-tank Weapon (LAW). We fired the M60 machine gun, the M203 grenade launcher and the flame thrower, and detonated the claymore mine. We learned first aid and how to navigate day and night using a map and compass.

We had one easy day sitting in bleachers observing the fire and effect of various company and battalion-level support weapons—the .50 calibre Browning M2 machine gun, the 60-millimetre mortar, the 81-millimetre mortar and the 106-millimetre recoilless rifle. We watched the splash of artillery rounds on hills in the distance and listened to the menacing buzz of a Cobra helicopter gunship firing its minigun and rockets.

Then, another unusual incident occurred. Once again, I was called out to an office to meet someone and had no idea why. When I got there, I was met by a young naval officer. He asked me if I would be willing to attend the United States Naval Academy at Annapolis. He explained that I would be required to participate in a nine-month prep school, spend four years in the academy, and give a minimum of six years guaranteed service after graduation. After two years in the academy, I could decide whether I wanted to be commissioned as an officer in the Navy or the Marines.

He was offering me the opportunity of a lifetime. It usually takes a recommendation from a State Senator or a Congressman to get into Annapolis. He was also asking me to sign away ten years of my life there and then. Despite gentle prodding from the officer, I declined. I was determined to play my part in ridding Ireland of British jurisdiction and establishing a truly national republic. I couldn't do that from Annapolis.

I asked again about volunteering for Recon while in AIT but was laughed at. One day, while on a force march climbing "Mount Motherfucker" with a full combat load, I watched a Boeing CH-46 Sea Knight helicopter pass overhead with eight men dangling from a rope beneath it. It must have been well over a thousand feet up. "There goes Recon!" I heard an instructor shout. That scared me. I hate heights. I thought the Recon men were simply clinging to the rope. I later learned that they were performing Special Patrol Insertion/Extraction (SPIE) rig training. This is used for inserting or extracting teams into terrain where a helicopter cannot land, such as a jungle. The soldier or Marine wears a harness and snaps himself onto a D-ring in the rope with a carabiner or snap link. Used by Special Forces worldwide, the US Marine's 1st Force Reconnaissance Company developed the technique in 1969.

After AIT, I had pretty much accepted that I was never going to get into Recon. No one had taken my enquiries about it seriously. I was ordered to report to the 3rd Marine Division in Okinawa, Japan. My Military Occupational Specialty (MOS) was 0311. I was officially a Marine rifleman or "Grunt."

On landing in Okinawa, we were marshalled into a room and given a lecture on Japanese customs and what to do and what not to do. We were shown a short film about Okinawa. I was given orders assigning me to the 1st Battalion, 9th Infantry Regiment, or 1/9 (One Nine). During the Vietnam War, 1/9 suffered the heaviest casualties of any Marine unit. They were nicknamed "The Walking Dead." Buses pulled up to take us to the large Marine Corps base at Camp Hansen.

As we filed out of the room, I hung back a little. The sergeant who had conducted the presentation was gathering his papers at the podium, preparing to leave. I thought, *Will I or won't I?* Asking about Recon again would probably lead to another insulting jibe. Besides, I had just been assigned to 1/9. I was the last man in the line waiting to file out of the reception area. Fuck it. I approached the sergeant.

"Excuse me, Sergeant. I was just wondering if you know how anyone volunteers for Recon?"

"You want to volunteer for *Recon?*" He sounded incredulous. That made me a little uneasy.

"Yes, Sergeant."

"Recon are looking for men. Wait here. Don't get on the bus."

The sergeant went out to the buses and asked if anyone else was interested in trying out for Recon. He returned with three men.

I was ushered into an office off the reception area, where a captain interviewed me. He had my military records in front of him.

"Why do you want to volunteer for Recon?"

"I'm told they're an outstanding unit, sir. I look forward to the challenge."

"All Marine units are outstanding units, Private."

"Yes, sir."

"Do you have a first-class PFT?" To be considered for Recon, you had to have a first-class Physical Fitness Test. Luckily for me, I did. To score a perfect 300 on the PFT, you have to perform twenty dead hang pull-ups, eighty sit-ups in two minutes and a three-mile run in eighteen minutes or less. I didn't have that perfect score, although I would eventually achieve it after some time with Recon.

"Are you a first-class swimmer, Private?"

"Yes, sir." That was a lie. My swimming was weak. I had done no swimming in Ireland. A first-class swimming score was essential because Recon Marines spent a lot of time in the ocean. I was gambling on the captain not bothering to notice that in my records. If he did, I'd be back on the bus for Camp Hansen and 1/9. Fortunately, he took my word for it.

A two-and-a-half-ton military truck pulled up. The three other Marines and I got into the back of it with our sea bags. We were dressed in our Service "A" uniforms. Green coat, green trousers and long-sleeved khaki shirt and tie. We wore a soft green cap with the black eagle, globe and anchor insignia. The cap was known as a "piss cutter." We wore black dress shoes. All were exhausted from the journey. We had left California over thirty hours earlier and had gotten little or no sleep. As I watched the Okinawan villages and rice paddies sail by from the back of the truck, I looked forward to changing out of this uniform and getting some rest before training commenced.

The truck pulled up beside a minor road. A sign announced "3rd Reconnaissance Battalion. Swift, Silent, Deadly."

"Get out of the truck!" We grabbed our sea bags and jumped onto the road. I could see no sign of the base.

"C'mon, let's go!"

We threw the sea bags over our shoulders and ran after a sergeant who was dressed in combat clothing and boots. It must have been two miles to the base. We were exhausted even before we began the run and dressed in inappropriate uniforms for exercise. I was soon drenched in sweat. My dress shoes were cutting into my heels. The sea bag was heavy and kept slipping off my shoulder. It was a short run but one of the most uncomfortable of my life.

The Recon base on Okinawa was located at Onna Point, on the opposite side of the island from the other Marine bases. It was quite small. We had it all to ourselves and liked it that way. My first meal at the mess hall was a pleasant surprise. It was the best dinner I had had in the Marines to date. I marvelled at the delicious selection and lavish portions. I had no idea it was Thanksgiving Day, as we didn't celebrate that holiday in Ireland. The next day, when I saw the greasy burgers and fries presented to us, I learned that Thanksgiving was a one-off.

Approximately a dozen Marines assembled for the RIP school. Where the others had come from, I had no idea. Some of them were huge—tall, well-muscled jocks and high-school wrestlers. I weighed 150 pounds. I looked around me at these Adonises and thought to myself with a sinking heart that I didn't have a hope, yet I never saw most of them again. Only three of us made it through the programme. It was an early lesson in the truism that what counts is not the size of the dog in the fight but the size of the fight in the dog.

The RIP school was a nightmare. Most nights we'd get two to four hours sleep. They would wake us up every half hour for push-ups. I began hallucinating from exhaustion. I saw little men, like Japanese leprechauns, jumping off the top of our racks and sliding down the bed ends to the floor. I lay down in a cold puddle during a short break on a jungle run and fell asleep in the mud. The six weeks were a blur of mental and physical torment.

"Remember, Privates! It's a simple case of mind over matter. We don't mind and you don't matter!"

They had ways of psyching us out. We were performing push-ups shoulder to shoulder while an instructor walked up and down our backs. "You're not going to do a hundred push-ups. You're not going to do a thousand push-ups. You're not even going to do a million push-ups. You're going to do push-ups forever and ever."

We ran up and down a soft, sandy beach carrying a rubber boat known as an Inflatable Boat, Small (IBS) on our heads. It weighed 225 pounds empty. An instructor then climbed into the boat. He made six of us place it back on our heads and begin running again. He casually announced, "You're going to run until *I'm* tired."

Sometime later, when I became a reconnaissance instructor myself, I learned this harassment was not designed to get people to quit but to get quitters to quit.

After RIP school, our training began in earnest. I was surprised at how cerebral a lot of it was. Trigonometry was required to adjust artillery fire, so big biceps were not nearly enough for Recon. We learned about camouflage, cover and concealment, not only for ourselves but also our weapons and equipment; how to conduct reconnaissance and photograph and sketch enemy targets; how to patrol quietly in the jungle; how to execute ambushes and counter-ambush drills. We had to identify the make and model of Warsaw Pact and Chinese ships, aircraft, tanks and artillery by observing their silhouettes. We were trained in potential enemy weapons such as the AK-47 and the RPG-7, and became experts in the use of maps and a compass. Tactical radio communications and procedures were drilled into us. We called in artillery and naval gunfire; we called in air support. I'd watch in awe as F-4 Phantoms dropped 500lb bombs during low-level tactical airstrikes. The accuracy and devastation were astounding.

Myself and two other men were sent to the Navy scuba school at Subic Bay in the Philippines. We flew down in a C-130 Hercules. On landing, it taxied to the end of a runway and lowered the tail ramp, and as we walked off the back of the aircraft, we discovered we were only yards from the jungle. I'll never forget the fragrance of tropical flowers carried on the soft evening breeze wafting in from the Pacific Ocean.

The scuba training was tough. I wasn't a strong swimmer, so I struggled to get through some of the evolutions, although I did so successfully. Treading water in a pool with twin steel tanks on my back was a challenge, as was swimming laps of the pool with a T-shirt in each hand. The weight of the water-soaked shirts made our shoulders burn. Drown-proofing took a cool head—we'd jump into the deep end of the pool with our feet tied, then our hands tied behind our backs and, finally, with both feet and hands tied. We would exhale and sink to the bottom, then kick off the bottom with both feet and rise to the top, gasping for a breath of air. Then, we'd exhale and sink to the bottom again, repeating this for at least thirty minutes. Anyone who quit or panicked would be sent packing.

We dived on ships in Subic Bay that had been sunk by the Japanese during the Second World War. We learned to navigate underwater using an attack board—a piece of plexiglass containing a watch, depth gauge and compass. We made many dives over a set distance to learn how far we would travel in a specific time. The watch gave us time and distance, the compass indicated our direction and the depth gauge's use was obvious.

We made night dives too. It is pitch-black underwater at night—the type of darkness that crawls to the back of your skull. We had to trust in the illuminated glow of the instruments on our attack board to get anywhere and back again. This was not long after the film *Jaws* had been released. I had seen it in the small movie theatre at Onna Point before we left for scuba school. I might have been better off not having seen it—it meant diving at night in the Pacific Ocean was not a relaxing experience.

I dreaded the final evolution: a half hour of harassment at the bottom of the pool in which the instructors would tear off our tanks, cut off our air supply and tie our hoses in knots. We were told that if we surfaced for air, we were out. We were expected to turn our air back on calmly and untie the knots. I passed and was awarded my scuba badge.

Not long after returning to Okinawa, a number of us conducted submarine lock-in/lock-out training on the USS *Grayback*. The *Grayback* was a diesel submarine designed for the covert insertion of Special Operation Forces into coastal regions. Its main clients were Navy Underwater Demolition Teams, Navy SEALS and Marine Recon. It had two chambers on its deck, one containing a Swimmer Delivery Vehicle or mini-sub and the other for personnel.

To conduct the training, about a dozen Recon Marines entered the lock-out chamber just before sunset. The *Grayback* was submerged at periscope depth. The chamber deck resembled an open grate and air hoses hung from pipes along the bulkhead. The white light was switched off and the red light came on. This would help preserve our night vision. Seawater poured in through the grates at our feet. The cold water reached our knees, waist and chest, continuing to rise until it filled the chamber. We breathed compressed air from the regulators attached to the hoses. The large convex door at the mouth of the chamber slowly opened upward. The red light from the chamber filtered only inches into the inky blackness of the ocean.

A navy diver waited by the exit. As each Marine reached him, the diver lightly punched him in the stomach to remind the Marine to expel air as he surfaced. Otherwise, the compressed air in our lungs would expand with the lessening water pressure as we rose to the surface, potentially causing an embolism. In other words, our lungs could explode. The submarine moved at about three knots. We had to hold on to a cable that stretched from the mouth of the chamber to the periscope. When we reached the surface, we grabbed a separate rope attached to the periscope. When all twelve men were present and accounted for, we let go of the rope. The *Grayback* returned to the depths of the East China Sea. We were alone.

Wearing wetsuit tops and fins, we surface swam several miles to Ie Shima island to carry out a reconnaissance of it. We dragged thick rubber bags behind us on six feet of rope that contained our dry clothing, boots and supplies. Our rifles and radios were tied to the top of the bags. These items were waterproofed in a manner that ensured we could still use the radio or fire our M16s if required. We were instructed to be back in the submarine before sunrise.

Returning to a submerged submarine while it is underway is quite an undertaking. On completing our training mission, we swam out on a compass heading a set distance of some miles. It was the deep darkness before the dawn. We carried a 100-foot length of nylon rope which we uncoiled. Six Marines gathered at either end of the rope and pulled it taut as if we were taking part in an aquatic tug of war. I held the Calypso sticks—two metal tent pegs which I banged together just under the surface of the water every ten seconds. I kept time by observing the tritium-illuminated minute hand of my military diver watch. The *Grayback*'s sonar would pick up the clanging tent pegs and fix our location. As the submarine neared, the night-vision capability of its periscope would fine-tune any adjustments.

I had been banging the Calypso sticks for some time, thinking about what I always thought about while swimming in the ocean at night—sharks. Suddenly, what looked like a massive telephone pole appeared, silhouetted against the night sky about twenty feet in front of me. My heart leaped into my throat. It took me a moment to realise it was the *Grayback*'s periscope.

The periscope caught the rope dead centre. As the *Grayback* steamed ahead, the six Marines on either end were drawn together until all twelve were being towed directly behind the submarine. Each man made his way to the periscope, searching for the cable that led to the lock-in/lock-out chamber. When my turn came, I took a great gulp of air. I had to hold my breath while negotiating my way to the entrance thirty feet below. The buoyancy of the equipment bag dragging behind me made the task that much more difficult. As I pulled myself down the cable, my lungs burned. I struggled to hold on as I looked frantically for the opening of the chamber. We were told that if we let go in wartime, we would be left to die. They would not risk an entire submarine and crew to rescue one man.

Just when I thought my lungs would burst, I caught sight of the red glow of the lights coming from the open hatch. The navy diver met me at the entrance and gave me a few breaths of welcome air. I swam to the back of the chamber and picked out the first available air hose. When every Marine had returned, the large door closed shut. Seawater was purged from the compartment. We were now able to reenter the main body of the submarine.

Although exhausted from the mission, we then engaged in an extensive intelligence debriefing about what we had discovered during our reconnaissance. An affable navy cook asked us if we wanted food. We were famished and expected a few sandwiches. He brought us a scrumptious roast pork dinner with all the trimmings. This was about 5 a.m.! I still class that as one of the best meals I ever ate.

While serving in Okinawa, I had been meritoriously promoted to lance corporal and then corporal. Shortly before my thirteen-month tour with the 3rd Marine Division was over, I was asked where I would like to be assigned next. The Marines would send you where they needed you but would sometimes ask if you had a preference. I requested to be sent to the 2nd Force Reconnaissance Company at Camp Lejeune, North Carolina. I wanted to remain in a combat branch and knew 2nd Force would send me to Jump School and Army Ranger School. Being Jump, Scuba and Ranger qualified in Recon was humorously known as the "Triple Threat." I was assured assignment to 2nd Force would not be a problem.

About a week before I left Okinawa, I was informed my orders had changed. The Marine Amphibious Reconnaissance School at Little Creek, Virginia needed an instructor with scuba qualifications. I was devastated. I did not want to become an instructor. I wanted to remain in the field. But the United States Marine Corps did not care what I wanted. I arrived at Little Creek in January 1977.

My first task was to complete the three-week Amphibious Reconnaissance Course successfully, which I did at a naval base at Key West, Florida. While I was an instructor at Little Creek, we expanded the course from three weeks to nine weeks and it formed the nucleus of the fifteen-week Basic Reconnaissance Course still used today to train Recon Marines.

Amphibious Reconnaissance grew out of a need identified during the Battle of Tarawa during the Second World War. Waves of Marine landing craft could not reach the beach at low tide because of coral reefs and other obstacles. The Marines were forced to wade ashore under devasting fire. The Japanese commander on Tarawa, Rear Admiral Keiji Shibazaki, boasted that a million men could not take the island in a hundred years. The US Marines took it in seventy-six hours but suffered heavy casualties doing so.

Our mission in Amphibious Reconnaissance was broadly similar to the navy's Underwater Demolition Teams. Our job was to go in preinvasion and scout out potential beach landing sites. We would slip ashore surreptitiously at night to take soil samples, so the weight of vehicles that the beach could support could be calculated. We conducted surf observations and assessed the currents. We carried out hydrographic reconnaissance, mapping the depth and slope of the ocean floor to determine if landing craft could safely approach the beach. We would pinpoint and record the location of mines, bunkers, obstacles and beach exits.

As an instructor, I, along with a team of other instructors, conducted amphibious reconnaissance training and small boat handling classes for Recon Marines, Army Rangers, Army Special Forces and even the British Parachute Regiment. SEAL Team Two was based in the compound beside ours at Little Creek. We did not train with them as they had their own assets and instructors, but we got along quite well and used their air compressors to charge our scuba tanks.

During my time as an instructor at Little Creek, I was sent to Jump School at Fort Benning, Georgia. The army cadre at Fort Benning were first-class professionals, although I found the army far more laid back than the Marine Corps. That wasn't true for the Airborne Rangers and Green Berets I met or worked with, who were highly motivated and consummate professionals.

Jump school consisted of ground week, tower week and jump week. During ground week, we learned how to don the parachute and carry out emergency malfunction drills. We practised countless parachute landing falls (PLFs). During tower week, we jumped from a 34-foot tower and a 250-foot tower, while jump week consisted of five jumps—one of them a night jump. We jumped from C-130 Hercules and C-141 Starlifters.

Nobody forgets their first jump. As the C-130 hurtled down the runway, I mused that I had never before taken off in a plane and not landed in it. Military aircraft are noisy. They have little of the insulation and soundproofing of civilian aircraft. When the plane's doors opened, I watched as brilliant sunlight bathed the jump masters overseeing the operation. The roar of the engines was deafening.

"Stand up! Hook up!"

The moment of truth had arrived. We snapped our static lines onto the steel cable that ran the length of the fuselage.

"Thirty seconds!" the jumpmaster roared, while simultaneously using arm and hand signals to confirm his verbal commands.

The red light came on. My stomach churned. I couldn't believe I'd asked for this. The green light came on.

"Go! Go! Go!" Each man disappeared in an instant. I shuffled towards the exit with mounting dread. I drew level with the door and assumed the jump position. Left foot forward, knees bent, both hands braced either side of the open door. The noise from the engines and whipping winds were shattering. I felt a slap on my rear.

"Go!"

I leapt into the void and watched the tail of the plane sail over my head. Everything seemed to be in slow motion, although it would all have happened in an instant. Seconds later, my parachute was open. I looked around and noticed that the C-130 I had exited seemed so high up and far away now. I marvelled at the calm and quiet that enveloped me. Four jumps later, I was presented with my jump wings. Shortly after, I was meritoriously promoted to sergeant.

My enlistment in the Marines ended on 29 May 1979. They tried hard to convince me to stay, offering me a long list of alternative specialties if I agreed to reenlist. One of them was Explosive Ordnance Disposal (EOD), but I was determined to return to Ireland.

I was discharged from the United States Marine Corps at 8 a.m. that fine May morning. By 2 p.m. the same day, I was on a plane for New York to catch a connecting flight to Ireland. I had done my bit for the American Republic. Now, I would do what I could for the Irish Republic.

2
VOLUNTEERING

HOW DO YOU join a secret army when you know nobody in it? The IRA didn't have recruiting offices. It is an illegal organisation in both Britain and Ireland. I soon discovered that getting into it would be a test of initiative and resolve. I believed I had revealed those qualities in Recon. But being a sergeant in the Marine Corps would not land me in prison. Being a volunteer in the IRA would.

There was another difficulty. Would the IRA accept me? Would they suspect I was a plant or a spy? Would they presume I was some dewy-eyed romantic or an adventurer? Someone searching for a sense of purpose, rather than someone with a sense of purpose?

I had to think things through. The Irish are a garrulous people. They love to talk. Even the most nebulous enquiry about joining the resistance could reach the wrong ears. I knew my first move could be my last. Where to even begin?

And, of course, the question I have been asked many times, why to begin? Why join the IRA? What compelled me to risk life, limb and liberty to engage in a struggle far more Irish people stood against than ever stood for?

I was born in Long Island, New York, on 6 May 1957. My

father, Brendan, an immigrant from County Roscommon, was serving a four-year enlistment in the United States Air Force. My mother, Josephine, an immigrant from County Kerry, was a homemaker. Both became American citizens. I was the eldest child and their only son. I have three younger sisters, Ann, Irene and Alice, all of whom were born in the United States and are American citizens. Irene and Alice now live in Ireland, my sister Ann lives in Chicago and my mother and father are deceased.

In 1959 we moved from New York to Chicago after my father's discharge from the service. He followed a familiar trajectory to countless Irish immigrants, beginning as a labourer on building sites and eventually becoming a general contractor. My mother worked for years at Stouffer's restaurant in the Prudential building in downtown Chicago. I remember her coming home in rapture one evening in 1968 after shaking hands with Bobby Kennedy.

In 1972, at the age of fourteen, I left Chicago and moved to Ireland. My father had longed to return home—in our house, Ireland was always referred to as "home." My dad and I had spent a month there the previous summer and I enjoyed every minute of it and loved every bit of Ireland. When asked would I be okay with moving there for good, I showed little hesitation. The following summer, I moved in with my father's sister Una and her family near Castlerea, County Roscommon, while my parents remained in Chicago to settle their American affairs. I went to school in Castlerea, the same school my father had attended. I even had some of the same teachers.

Fifty-nine years earlier, on 11 July 1921, my great-uncle Tom Crawley and fellow IRA volunteer Ned Campion shot dead Royal Irish Constabulary (RIC) Sergeant James King in Castlerea. The operation took place shortly before midday, when the ceasefire leading to the Anglo-Irish Treaty would come into effect. Had King come along a minute after noon, he could not have been touched. It is claimed they fired the last shots of the Tan War.

Sergeant King was what the Americans call a high-value target. He was directly responsible for the murder of IRA volunteers in the area. He scouted for English military forces on patrols as he knew the people and the terrain in a way the foreigners never could. King also handled a particularly dangerous informer by the name of Paddy Egan. This traitor was the IRA brigade intelligence officer for Tom's area. Egan did immense damage to the resistance in south Roscommon. The local IRA was desperate to get King to avenge their fallen comrades and to hold him to account for joining with the British in waging war on the government and army of the Irish Republic.

Tom was vice commandant of the 1st Battalion, South Roscommon Brigade, IRA when he shot King. He took the anti-Treaty side in the Irish Civil War but later became a sergeant in An Garda Síochána, the police force of the new Irish Free State government. My father and most of his family were lifelong supporters of the anti-Treaty party Fianna Fáil, founded and led by Éamon de Valera. De Valera's party would come to power in 1932 on a platform of republicanism and Irish unity but would deliver neither. Gradually, the party became as partitionist as their pro-Treaty Fine Gael rivals.

I met Tom Crawley briefly before he died. I held in my hand the Webley revolver that killed King. But as a young teenager, I regarded Tom's story as nothing more than an interesting historical anecdote. It did not influence me to join the IRA.

There's an old cliché that Irish rebels are nursed on their mother's knee. That could not be further from the truth in my case. My mother was from a Fine Gael household. This was the party that supported the Treaty, rescinding the Republic declared in 1916 and replacing it with a partitioned country containing two jurisdictions based upon a sectarian headcount.

Many in Fine Gael saw no problem with that. "Sure," I heard one elderly supporter say, "didn't we get the land back?" By resolving the land issue in the late nineteenth and early twentieth centuries, the British had succeeded in turning the bulk of a potentially rebellious peasantry into conservative proprietors. This did much to defuse constitutional issues concerning national sovereignty. For many Irish peasants, their farm was their country. From that position, it wasn't much of a leap to settle for twenty-six counties as enough Ireland for any man.

The Troubles in the North had no impact on our family. I can remember only two incidents that referenced the war in the Six Counties. The first was a news report in the mid-seventies of republican prisoners claiming they were tortured into making false confessions by a group of garda detectives known as the "Heavy Gang." A neighbour commented that the IRA were nothing but a bunch of gangsters whose godfather bosses would have ordered them to beat themselves up in their cells to discredit the gardaí. The other was a priest's observation during an RTÉ news report of a young man charged with IRA membership. He claimed that older men would groom young fellows by getting them drunk in a pub and then compromise them by involving them in a shooting or bombing so they became hooked and couldn't get out again. I remember thinking how horrible republicans must be to do awful things like that. How different the IRA of today must be from the "Good Old IRA" of the Tan War.

I lived in Ireland until I was almost eighteen, formative years in my transition from boy to man. After I had spent a year living with my aunt and her family in Roscommon, my parents and sisters moved back to Ireland. I joined them in Dublin and went to school at St Laurence's in Loughlinstown, which was hardly a hotbed of republicanism. I played on the rugby team there and we sang ribald songs that would make you think you were living in a place called West Britain rather than Ireland.

So, if I didn't get my republicanism from friends or family, from where did it spring? I can honestly say it was more a process than any one event that influenced me. There was no epiphany. I was a voracious reader, with a particular interest in history, and my education in the United States had made me naturally sympathetic to the concept of republicanism. After all, we began each school day by placing a hand on our heart, facing the Stars and Stripes and reciting, "I pledge allegiance to the Flag of the United States of America, and to the Republic for which it stands, one Nation under God, indivisible, with liberty and justice for all." Those words were not mindlessly recited. They would resonate with me my entire life: ". . . the Republic for which it stands . . . one Nation . . . indivisible, with liberty and justice for all."

As a young student, I believed that America had won its independence from England in a pure and noble fight against the hated redcoats. I later learned that the evolution from colonial status to that of a sovereign republic is never straightforward and often tarnished by elements of civil war. There is always a percentage of the population that remains loyal to the old order and wants no part of independence. Approximately one-third of Americans wanted nothing to do with an American Republic.

I was surprised to discover that thousands of Americans formed military units to help King George defeat George Washington and his men. Outfits such as the Prince of Wales' American Regiment and the Queen's American Rangers fought beside British regulars. At the Battle of King's Mountain, a stunning Patriot victory against American Loyalists in South Carolina, the only non-American on either side was the British officer commanding the Loyalist militia. While George Washington and his men froze at Valley Forge in that harsh winter of 1777–8, American Loyalists held balls for British officers twenty miles away in Philadelphia.

The British were as merciless to American prisoners of war as they were to Irish political prisoners. Nearly 12,000 American rebels died on British prison ships. And not only were Americans forced to kill Americans to achieve their republic, but a million American casualties were inflicted by fellow Americans to keep it during the Civil War of 1861–5. There is an echo of this reality in the enlistment oath I took when joining the Marines: "To support and defend the constitution of the United States against all enemies foreign and domestic."

Part of what inspired my burgeoning Irish republicanism was the Proclamation of the Irish Republic of 1916. It positioned national unity and democracy as core values calling for a "National Government, representative of the whole people of Ireland." It declared that "the unfettered control of Irish destinies" must be "sovereign and indefeasible" and called upon the Irish people to cast aside sectarian divisions "carefully fostered by an alien government." Not a word about two nations on one island. No mention of partition or of a twenty-six-county state.

The call of the Proclamation to break the connection with England and forge a joint civic identity in a united, sovereign and secular nation was overwhelmingly endorsed in an all-Ireland election in 1918. A thirty-two-county parliament, known as Dáil Éireann (Assembly of Ireland), was set up with its own army (the IRA or Óglaigh na hÉireann in the Irish language) and its own courts. Britain refused to recognise the legitimacy of the state, declaring the Irish parliament to be an illegal assembly. London rejected the Dáil's democratic mandate, opting instead to concoct its own version of democracy. In a blatant national gerrymander, the British unilaterally partitioned the country in 1920, turning a unionist minority in Ireland into an artificial majority in six counties which they now called Northern Ireland. Those Irishmen who accepted Britain's refusal to recognise the legitimacy of the Irish state were given guns to kill Irishmen who remained faithful to the national Republic.

The primary British condition permitting the South of Ireland, now called the Free State, to survive as a separate political entity was contingent upon them bringing a constitutional close to the republican project. This was accomplished by the Anglo-Irish Treaty and the acknowledgement of the legitimacy of Northern Ireland, the artificial polity the British had perfidiously established long before the Treaty negotiations had even begun.

After the 1916 Rising, an information sheet called *An tÓglác* (*The Volunteer*) was circulated to members of the IRA.

It described the political culture of constitutional nationalism which had dominated Irish politics since the mid-nineteenth century:

> All the dominant forces in Irish public life stood for coward-ice, compromise, and corruption. All faith in lofty ideals, in patriotism or self-sacrifice seemed to have vanished. A horrible cynicism reigned everywhere. The place-hunter seemed supreme . . . The British Government had set itself out to buy over Irish Nationalism . . . A weak, supine, corrupt Party seemed to speak for and have the confidence of the vast majority of the Irish people. The road seemed clear for hoodwinking whatever of National feeling was left in Ireland by passing off some trivial concessions on the Irish people as a satisfaction of the demand for self-government. It seemed as though the conquest of Ireland by England was at last to be accomplished.

That political culture did not disappear with the Easter Rising. It wholeheartedly supported the Anglo-Irish Treaty and became a key clientele class of the Free State government. Powerful, wealthy and deeply embedded in the national fabric, many of their grandparents had done well out of the Famine. Educated in elite Jesuit schools initially founded to provide middle-class Catholics with the education required to administer the British Empire, they effectively ran the Irish Catholic Church, dominated the business and legal professions and played a major role in shaping the confessional ideology and political culture of the new government.

This class viewed republicans as dangerous scoundrels and malcontents, even criminals, chasing a dream of national liberty, unity and democracy they neither shared nor embraced.

Republicanism jeopardised their golden circles and cosy cartels by threatening equality of opportunity (they believed God gave to them and not to others) and by riling up England and her unionist allies. They were the carrion crows of counter-revolution and would prove merciless towards Irish republicanism. The British could always rely on their support.

The Irish people of the twenty-six counties, who liked to believe they had won their freedom, actually bought whatever freedom they gained by abandoning their fellow countrymen in the Six Counties. They abandoned Irish nationalists to second-class citizenship and they abandoned Irish unionists to nurture the political culture of colonial squatters with its simmering supremacist, sectarian and siege mentalities. Reminding Dublin's political elite of this doesn't embarrass them. It makes them hate republicans all the harder.

Partitionist propaganda in the southern media increased exponentially after the Troubles broke out in 1969. Partitionists made it uncomfortable, even dangerous, for anyone with republican sympathies to express these. Strict censorship laws were brought in denying freedom of speech in Ireland to anyone whose speech was in favour of Irish freedom. Traditional songs extolling the struggle for nationhood were banned from the airwaves. Even contemporary music, such as Paul McCartney's "Give Ireland Back to the Irish," was banned in Ireland. A law was brought in by the Irish government automatically censoring anyone censored by the British.

I can't remember a single political discussion when I was in school that didn't end by blaming the Troubles on the IRA, even when the biggest atrocity of the Troubles occurred in May 1974. Four car bombs exploded almost simultaneously in central Dublin and the border town of Monaghan. Thirty-four men, women and children were killed, including a full-term unborn child. Nearly 300 people were injured. The bombings were carried out by the loyalist Ulster Volunteer Force, aided and abetted by members of British military intelligence and the Special Branch of the Royal Ulster Constabulary (RUC).

Both the Irish prime minister of the day, Liam Cosgrave, and the opposition leader, Jack Lynch, made statements pointing the finger of blame at the IRA for starting the Troubles in the first place, ignoring the fact that loyalists, determined to make no concessions on civil rights to nationalists, initiated the killing and bombing campaign. The garda team investigating the largest mass murder in Irish history was disbanded in July 1975, just two months after the bombings. All the files on the Dublin–Monaghan bombings mysteriously vanished from the Irish Department of Justice.

The British Ambassador to Dublin between 1973 and 1976, Sir Arthur Galsworthy, noted with approval a hardening of attitudes in the South against the IRA as a result of bombings carried out by British agents: "It is only now that the South has experienced violence that they are reacting in the way that the North has sought for so long . . . it would be . . . a psychological mistake for us to rub this point in . . . I think the Irish have taken the point."

The Irish had indeed taken the point. The South's political elite made their decision. If taking a national view of the national question put them in conflict with the British, they would adopt a firmer partitionist line. It takes time, however, for a state to shift its narrative into reverse gear. In 1960 the Irish Taoiseach (Prime Minister) Seán Lemass had said:

By every test Ireland is one nation with a fundamental right to have its essential unity expressed in its political institutions. The unit for self-determination is the whole country and we do not accept that a minority has a right to vote itself out of the nation on the ground that it is in disagreement with the majority on a major policy issue. We cannot and will not depart from that position.

Historical factors and years of hypocritical rhetoric from Irish politicians meant that, in the short term, it wasn't easy to increase security cooperation between Dublin and London to the extent the British would like. In due course, however, the British Ministry of Defence, Scotland Yard and the UK Security Service MI5 would increasingly, but quietly, train key members of the Irish Defence Forces and the gardaí, building an intricate web of close networks and alliances. Security collaboration between London and Dublin would become virtually seamless. British security chiefs noted with great satisfaction that when a senior RUC officer attended the Association of Garda Sergeants and Inspectors annual conference in the early 1980s, he was toasted by a Garda Special Branch delegate with the words, "We are the same force fighting the same enemy."

Despite this fraught atmosphere, I nurtured a simmering republican sympathy and a stubborn belief that the men and women fighting for the complete freedom of Ireland must have something going for them. Not for them narrow rationalisations based solely upon self-aggrandisement. While any part of Ireland remained under British rule, they would not be found "fumbling in the greasy till." The 1916 Proclamation reminds us that, "In every generation the Irish people have asserted their right to national freedom and sovereignty." If men and women of my generation were again asserting it, I would not stand idly by. I could not. I don't understand the people who ask me why I came to that conclusion. As far as I'm concerned, the question for me is, why didn't you?

I know that many are not happy with this explanation. They want to hear deeper, darker motives. Some believe IRA volunteers were inspired solely by revenge. The trouble with that theory is that I never laid eyes on a British soldier in Ireland until after I joined the IRA and was shooting at them. I had never set foot in the six counties of "Northern Ireland," so had not been discriminated against by that sectarian state. Crown Forces had never raided my home. The RUC hadn't beaten me up. I didn't possess the remotest motive or inclination for revenge. Revenge for what?

Years later, an Irish Special Branch detective believed he had hit upon the answer to my involvement. "You were probably a decent fellow from a respectable family, but somewhere along the way, some evil bastard got a hold of your brain." So, I was brainwashed. By whom? My parents didn't discuss politics and certainly had no sympathy for the Provos. My friends and broader family circle were no hotbed of revolutionary radicals. I never knowingly met an IRA man until I was in the IRA.

The simple reason, and the truth, is that, like many other IRA volunteers, I had the intelligence to form my own opinions and the courage to act upon them. As hard as it may be for some to believe, sometimes people do what they consider to be the right thing, without first reflecting whether or not it will line their pockets, affect their pension or save their skins.

I would have joined the IRA at eighteen years of age had I

known how to do so. The trouble was I knew nobody in the organisation nor did I know anybody who knew, or would admit to knowing, someone in it. The IRA wasn't called a secret army for nothing. So, instead, I had decided to travel to the United States to obtain professional military training. I would then return and figure out how to volunteer for the IRA. Even while boarding the Aer Lingus flight for Chicago in April 1975, I was sensible to the fact I might encounter circumstances that would alter my plans. Many factors could keep me from returning to Ireland. I might fall in love and get married or the gravitational pull of family and career could prevent me from ever swearing an oath to the Irish Republic. I hoped that would not be the case but understood it could be. I believed that if the motivation truly existed, returning to Ireland to see the thing through would indisputably demonstrate my commitment and resolve to help in the struggle to achieve Irish freedom.

Forty-four years later, my conservative mother asked in utter despair how someone of my education and background became "radicalised." When I was a teenager, she envisioned me becoming a doctor or holding some lucrative and respected position within society. The term "radicalised" grated on me, but she had been watching Fox News around the clock, so I had to make allowances.

I tried to explain that I had not been radicalised. I had never been indoctrinated to shift my opinions from one end of a political spectrum to another. I grew up being told and believing the best form of government is a democratic republic and that it had been a brave and honourable decision by the Founding Fathers of the United States to fight the British to achieve it. If anyone radicalised me it was the nuns at St Lucy's

Catholic school in Chicago who shoved my nose into those American history books.

Nor was I an extremist. I wanted to see a thirty-two-county national republic in Ireland. What's extreme about that? It's a reasonable and rational demand—a fundamental right that is constantly thwarted by the British government.

Perhaps where I differed from most was that I was prepared to risk life and take life to achieve that political goal. Not just talk the talk but walk the walk. If being prepared to risk life and take life as a US Marine in defence of the American Republic didn't qualify me as an extremist, why should it do so in defence of the Irish Republic?

My father didn't share my mother's concern regarding my republican beliefs, although it devastated him to see me in prison. He was sympathetic to the idea of an Ireland completely free from British rule but didn't want his son taking risks for it any more than I would want that for my own son. When I was a young teenager, my father had told me on several occasions to follow my heart and never look back with regret that I had not done something in life I wanted to do. He didn't mean that in a political sense but about life in general. It was good advice. Although I have many regrets about outcomes, I have none about my decisions.

When I arrived back in Dublin in May 1979, I didn't know where to begin to get into the IRA. Finally, through a long and convoluted process, I got temporary labouring work with a man renovating a house. I deliberately manoeuvred my way in there, knowing he had been a prisoner in Portlaoise Prison, where republicans incarcerated by the Dublin government are held. He rapidly guessed my intention and tried to talk me out of it. He said it could only lead to my death or imprisonment.

He didn't believe the IRA leadership in Belfast or Derry could be trusted. I didn't know what he meant by that and dismissed it as a throwaway remark by someone who wanted to justify his retirement from the struggle. I would find out what he meant the hard way many years later.

I persisted and, one day, a County Tyrone man approached me saying he had heard I was interested in joining the IRA. It took a few months of interviews and my family background was checked out but, finally, I was told to meet someone in John Joe McGirl's pub in Ballinamore, County Leitrim. John Joe was a highly respected veteran republican who had been imprisoned and interned in both the North and South. In 1957 he was elected a member of the Irish parliament while a republican prisoner in Mountjoy Gaol.

I was sitting in a small room between the pub and the kitchen when John Joe walked in smoking a pipe. He threw a book on my lap. "Read that," he said. It was the "Green Book," the IRA's manual of rules and procedures. It had to be studied before you could be sworn in as a volunteer. One passage read: "The Army as an organisation claims and expects your total allegiance without reservation . . . All potential volunteers must realise that the threat of capture and of long jail sentences are a very real danger and a shadow which hangs over every volunteer . . ."

Shortly after that, I met the Tyrone man again. He swore me into the IRA with the following oath: "I, John Crawley, promise that I will promote the objects of Óglaigh na hÉireann to the best of my knowledge and ability and that I will obey all orders and regulations issued to me by the Army Authority and by my superior officer."

Little did I know what lay ahead.

3
GOODBYE KANSAS

I OPERATED AS a full-time IRA volunteer between May 1980 and September 1984. Although I wasn't "on the run," I behaved as though I was, never being seen in the company of known republicans and keeping well away from republican haunts. I was often billeted in safe houses with volunteers who were genuinely on the run. Their example taught me how to cope with the hardships and dangers of operating along the border Britain had imposed on Ireland. They helped keep me sharp and I had a lot to learn.

Many IRA volunteers developed a bad habit of referring to me as "the Yank." I would tell them, "Jesus, lads, will you call me the Arsehole, the Eejit, the Wanker? I don't care what you call me but for fuck sake quit calling me the Yank! If somebody breaks during interrogation or mentions that name in a bugged location, you may as well be using my real name!" But it was no use; the name stuck, although one old man in a safe house used to refer to me "that lad with the white teeth."

It was quite a reality check to realise that I wasn't in Kansas anymore. Leaving a lavishly supplied, professionally trained outfit like the US Marines and joining a poorly trained and under-equipped guerrilla organisation like the IRA was quite a leap.

Not long after signing up, I was taken to an isolated field by two volunteers from a rural border unit, Pat and Dermot, and shown a Remington Woodsmaster rifle with an attached telescopic sight. They asked me if I thought I could hit a British soldier with it at 200 yards. My first reaction was that they had to be joking. We fired our M16s with iron sights out to 500 yards in the Marines. Two hundred yards was the closest we got to a target on the firing range. I thought it was a ridiculous question but could see they were serious.

I looked over the weapon. It was corroded and poorly maintained. The telescopic sight was an inexpensive Japanese import. It was attached to the rifle with cheap aluminium rings. I looked closer and couldn't believe my eyes. The rings were 30mm in diameter but the scope tube was 25.4mm or one inch. The difference was made up by wrapping the inner tube of a bicycle tyre around the scope—a completely unsatisfactory expedient that would play havoc with the rifle's precision. Accuracy is the ability to hit a target. Precision is the ability to hit it repeatedly.

I also noted that no scope covers protected the lenses, which were scratched and pitted. The lens coatings, which help transmit light into the shooter's eye and reduce lens reflection and glare, are only microns thick on a good quality scope. Ad hoc cleaning in the field with spit and the end of a shirttail damages this coating. The lenses must be cleaned with the proper materials. None of this was taught to IRA volunteers.

Pat and Dermot, the young men who brought the rifle to me were likable and sincere. I didn't want to come across as a "know-it-all" and launch into a harangue about the piece of crap they had handed me and had the affront to call a sniping rifle. They hadn't been properly trained, but they were keen to learn. I couldn't blame them if they seemed to know as much about sniping as a cat knows about its father. In my eyes, that was the fault of their leaders and not the men. As Napoleon observed, "There are no bad regiments, only bad colonels."

I firmly believe in the maxim that the best measure of a leader's performance is his men's performance. I often heard stories from senior IRA officers of trainees who could hit a matchbox at 400 yards on a training camp but would miss a British soldier at twenty yards on an operation. The implication was that some volunteers may perform well against paper targets but were too nervous to hit the enemy in actual combat. That may have been true in a minority of cases, but I never liked that excuse for poor results. I was uncomfortable with blaming the volunteers at the cutting edge.

Pat asked me to take a shot from the rifle.

"Okay, is it zeroed in?" I asked.

"What do you mean?" asked Dermot.

"I mean, is the scope adjusted, so the point of aim and point of impact coincide at a particular range. A hundred yards, maybe? Three hundred yards?"

The men looked at each other. "Uh, we haven't shot it like that."

I took the rifle, made the appropriate adjustments and fired at a target they put up 200 yards away. My bullet passed through the target dead centre. They were more astonished than I felt was warranted. It was an easy shot from a close range.

"What was that fiddling you were doing with the scope?" asked Pat.

"Okay," I replied, "the scope has to be adjusted or zeroed to hit a chosen spot at a particular range. In a nutshell, a bullet, when fired, begins to drop immediately due to the effects of air resistance and gravity. The drop becomes increasingly pronounced with range. The parabolic arc formed by its flight path is known as the trajectory. Looking through a telescopic sight at a target some distance away, you are looking in a straight line known as the 'line of sight.' The bullet does not follow the line of sight but crosses it twice, the first time approximately twenty-five yards from the muzzle on its way to the high point of the trajectory. It crosses it once more at the zero range, the range the weapon has been sighted in for, which in this case we'll say is 200 yards. From this point on, the projectile drops rapidly below the line of sight."

I pointed to knobs on the scope tube. "Do you see these turrets on the top and the right side of the telescopic sights?" The men nodded. "The top turret is for range adjustment— up and down. The side turret is for windage adjustment—left and right. Each adjustment increment moves the bullet impact one-quarter inch at 100 yards. That's half an inch at 200 yards, one and a half inches at 600 yards, two inches at 800 yards and so on. Knowing this, we can use a simple formula to adjust for the ballistic trajectory of a particular round of ammunition so that the scope's crosshairs and the point of impact coincide at any point along the bullet's path. The number of clicks or 'come-ups' that have to be dialled into the elevation turret for various ranges other than the zero range is placed on a ballistic data card. Once the sniper determines the range to his target, he examines the data card and dials in the adjustments required to hit dead on. It takes the guesswork out of aiming and is an extremely accurate system provided the range estimation is precise and the raw ballistic data is inputted correctly."

"Where would we get the raw data?" asked Pat.

"All the main bullet manufacturers in the United States publish ballistic tables."

"We thought you just put the scope on the rifle," said Dermot. The lads presumed it was like in the movies where a scope is simply attached to a rifle and the sniper fires a shot hitting his target every time. If it were that simple, the British Army in Ireland would have been on the endangered species list.

British soldiers had been shot by volunteers armed with scoped rifles, so the correct way to zero a scope was known to some in the IRA. The trouble was that training camps were not standardised throughout the army. There was poor organisational learning. A volunteer in one area could be told one thing and a volunteer in another area told the complete opposite. A talented sniper could appear in an area, but that skill and resource would suddenly disappear with the death or capture of the individual volunteer.

Joined-up thinking between operations, training and procurement did not exist. Other like-minded volunteers and I thought it would make sense to appoint a dedicated sniping officer in every IRA brigade area—someone thoroughly and expertly trained in sniping operations with real-world value. The sniping officers from different commands could then meet periodically to assess tactics and pass on tips, techniques and procedures to enhance the army's overall performance. Because of security implications, these officers would act more as managers than operators on the ground who should never learn who is carrying out attacks in areas outside of their own. They could oversee a professional and standardised training regime using joined-up thinking to develop best practice and resource the best equipment.

Such a competent and proficient team would have

debunked the many myths surrounding British Army capabilities and equipment, such as the almost universal and completely erroneous belief that the British infantry helmet was proof against high-velocity rifle fire. I heard this circulated by members of the IRA, from volunteers up to Army Council level, on many occasions.

Some claimed the "neck curtain" hanging from the back of the British Army helmet was also bulletproof. A neck curtain is a flap of flame-resistant synthetic material. Its sole purpose is to ensure that if a petrol bomb shatters on the helmet, the burning liquid flows outside the soldier's smock and not inside his collar, incinerating him. It is not bulletproof.

I recall a conversation I had with a senior Belfast IRA commander, in which we discussed the fact that British soldiers were driving around the city with their heads sticking out of the top of their armoured jeeps. This was done, in part, to counteract the possibility of IRA volunteers approaching with one of a range of improvised anti-armour devices developed by our engineering department. I made the point that the soldiers appeared vulnerable and queried why more were not being hit. He countered that there was little point in volunteers shooting at them because their helmets and neck curtains were bulletproof. The belief in these misconceptions had an extremely detrimental effect on our operational effectiveness and flagged the need for a qualified and proficient training cadre.

The obvious question was, where would we get this cadre? Over the years, the IRA had recruited a substantial number of volunteers who had served in professional armies. Many had served in the British military, the Irish Army, the American Army and even the French Foreign Legion. Some had been trained in elite units such as the British Parachute Regiment and the Royal Marines. A few had served in the British Special Forces and the Irish Army's Ranger Wing. We had school-teachers in our ranks who could write lesson plans and devise a course structure. We had artists who could design informative and effective training aids, yet few volunteers could zero in a rifle. Most weren't even aware they were supposed to. It took managerial ineptitude on an Olympian scale to achieve that level of incompetence, bearing in mind the pool of professional knowledge we had at our disposal. Either that or, as I began to suspect, subtle sabotage from within.

My first IRA operation was a revelation. I was part of a border unit that had taken possession of an M60 machine gun in transit from South Armagh to Derry city. We were told to keep it hidden until a safe method of transport to Derry could be arranged. No one present, except myself, knew anything about the weapon. Nothing. Not how to field strip and reassemble it, load it, lubricate it, zero the sights, nothing. There was certainly no training in its tactical application, for example, where to locate the machine gun in an ambush position for optimal effectiveness. They had no idea whatsoever of the classifications of machine-gun fire in relation to the ground, like dead space, danger space, plunging fire and grazing fire, and with regard to the target, such as flanking fire, frontal fire, oblique and enfilade fire. Neither had they knowledge of proper fire and control procedures nor easily understood fire commands. They looked upon the M60 simply as a bullet hose. Not because they were stupid—they most certainly were not—but because they weren't trained. I had heard so much from both the Brits and republican leaders about how highly sophisticated the IRA was that I found it hard to reconcile that narrative with the deeply disconcerting reality I experienced on a daily basis.

We decided to "borrow" the M60 for an attack. I was told that a two-car patrol of RUC men often travelled past a particular road junction on Sundays, but it was too close to houses to place explosives. They would be driving armoured Ford Cortinas, which landmine attacks had forced the RUC to adopt. The Fords resembled civilian cars, making it difficult for an IRA volunteer to confirm their identity. Close up, one could recognise them because of the weight on their axles and the thick, often tinted windows. Several hundred yards away, on the button end of a command-detonated mine, however, it was far more difficult.

These cars were thought to be impervious to rifle fire, but we hoped a sustained burst from the M60 on one of them would put the windscreen in and kill the crew. There was also the chance a British Army foot patrol would appear, as they were often on these roads.

Notwithstanding my training in Marine Recon, I had never been on an active military operation. I had never killed anyone, so I had a lot to think about. Despite this, none of my thoughts were second thoughts.

Five of us assembled in a byre on the southern side of the border that Saturday night. We were handed our weapons in the darkened shed. That was my first surprise—there was no opportunity to inspect the weapons in daylight, no notion of zeroing them for accuracy and no chance to test-fire them. As we left the shed and headed for the border, my second surprise was that there was no plan. It was a typical case of "join the IRA and see Ireland by night." We walked along in single file behind a volunteer who knew the way to the attack position. I wondered what we would do if we unexpectedly bumped into the British Army. We hadn't been briefed on this; we hadn't trained or rehearsed together as a team. The small-unit cohesion so critical to success in combat was nonexistent.

In a Marine Recon patrol, we would rehearse battle drills for a wide range of scenarios. Battle drills are standardised moves of how to react if you suddenly encounter the enemy or walk into an ambush—moves that give your team some chance to escape by concentrating maximum effective fire on the enemy without shooting each other. They enable everyone in the unit to move, shoot and communicate under stress, but they're useless unless practised until they become muscle memory. They must be performed without having to think about it and without direction from the unit leader. Hope is not a strategy. When the shit hits the fan, people don't rise to the occasion; they fall to their level of training.

For example, if a Marine Recon team ran into the enemy head on, the first man in the patrol (the point man) would drop down and fire on full-automatic to his front. The second man would throw a grenade as far forward as possible to disorientate the enemy and inflict casualties. The point man, when his magazine was empty, would reload while running to the rear, tapping the second man on the shoulder to let him know he was passing. The second man, who was now on point, would then fire on fully automatic and so on down the line until the team broke contact. We called this technique "the Australian peel." This might occur during the hours of darkness and people could get separated. So, on a regular basis, the patrol leader would designate "rallying points" along the route that team members would return to if separated or lost. We practised these drills day and night with live ammunition.

The IRA lacked the ammunition supply to conduct tactical live-fire training to any practical degree, but bolt converters to fire .22 calibre ammunition from Armalites and AK-47s were available in America and .22 ammunition was legal and plentiful in Ireland. Simulators and other devices were sold on the open market to replicate live fire for marksmanship instruction. There was a way around every difficulty that IRA leaders flagged up as an impediment or an excuse to rationalise our failure to train more proficiently.

I recall a conversation with one of the first training officers (T/O) I met in the IRA. I asked him how marksmanship training was carried out.

"Well, basically, we take the boys to a safe house and show them how to take the weapons apart and assemble them again. Then we go up to a forest before dawn to fire a few shots."

"Why before dawn?"

"We need to start shooting at first light and be away again very early before most people get out of bed, so nobody sees or hears anything."

"So, you're training to time when you should be training to standard. That's no use. You need to set a high standard of professional competence. Recruits should not be considered qualified until they meet that standard."

"That's easy to say, John. You don't understand. Training areas are hard to get and the noise from shooting is a big problem. We can't be as flexible as you seem to think."

"Why not use suppressors?" I asked. "You probably call them silencers."

"Because they fuck up the weapon," he replied.

"What do you mean?"

"They bleed off gas and slow the bullet down."

"Who told you that?"

"Everyone knows that."

"So, every special forces unit in the world uses sound suppressors but the IRA knows better? Listen, what happens to the propellant gasses when they leave the barrel and enter the suppressor has no effect on the bullet which has already left the muzzle. In fact, a well-made suppressor improves accuracy by lessening felt recoil and protects the shooter from enemy observation by reducing muzzle flash to near zero, especially at night."

"That's not what I've been told."

"Okay, leaving that aside. The real question is, are your trainers trained? Are they technically proficient on the weapon? Are they competent to coach? Can they recognise and correct faulty shooting techniques in the recruit?"

"We usually fire at paper targets in the forest and check for hits after the shoot."

"So, you don't examine the target after each shot to determine if the recruit is applying proper marksmanship fundamentals with every squeeze of the trigger and correcting him if not?"

"For fuck sake, we'd be running up and down all day from the shooting position to the target. We'd never get out of there."

"Then you have no feedback loop. You're not training them. You're just going through the motions. You don't need to run up and down if you buy a good spotting scope."

Most of the T/Os I met were doing the best they could with the meagre resources afforded them in an often thankless task. I later had the opportunity to observe a few training camps and noted they varied in quality and content.

For example, a T/O might tell the recruit his shots were high and to the left but could not explain why that was the case. Was the rifle firmly in the pocket of the shoulder? Did the recruit flinch at the moment of firing? Did he anticipate the shot by stiffening up? Did he snatch the trigger instead of squeezing it? Did he shift his focus from the front sight post to the target at the moment of firing? Observing, recognising and correcting these errors was essential to proper coaching.

Volunteers might be told to keep their rifles clean but not be told why or shown the proper method of cleaning and lubricating the weapon. All these issues could be easily overcome, but it wasn't helped by certain leadership figures who would invariably respond to suggestions for improvement with, "Even the Brits admit we're the best-trained guerrilla army in the world."

Before a Recon patrol commenced, we would jump up and down for the patrol leader to inspect us for noise discipline. No jingling change in pockets, no magazines bumping together, no sloshing canteens, no sling swivels slapping off the rifle. Everything is tied or taped down and quiet. We'd use arm and hand signals so we could operate in silence. Had I suggested any of this to our lads, I would probably have been laughed at for being eccentric. As our Active Service Unit (ASU) strolled along in the darkness, I was more afraid of being accidentally shot in the back by my own side than I was of the enemy.

I realised we had no first aid kit—not even a plaster in case one of us cut a finger crossing a barbed-wire fence. Shortly afterwards, I suggested to a senior IRA man that every volunteer on active service should be trained in first aid and know his blood type in case he was wounded. He replied that asking our men to find out their blood types would be counterproductive and demoralising as it implied they might get shot.

As we crossed the border—a nondescript hedgerow—the man in front of me, knowing it was my first IRA operation, turned and chuckled, "Welcome to England!"

Reaching the ambush position in a thick grove of trees

shortly before dawn, we settled down to wait for our target to appear. Every volunteer should have been assigned a sector of fire overlapping with the man on either side of him, otherwise you could have twenty Brits on the road with everyone firing at the same soldier. That didn't happen.

We had a long boring wait. The man beside me had an M1A rifle, the semi-automatic version of the M14, a powerful and accurate weapon. The others had a mix of AR-15 Armalites and M1 Garands. Nobody had brought a spare magazine and none of the magazines they did have were full. I had a 100-round belt of linked ammunition for the M60.

I told the volunteer beside me, who was armed with the M1A, that if a foot patrol appeared, I would open fire, but he would have to cover me as every Brit would be trying to take out the machine gunner. He nodded in agreement. He was a polite, laid-back, pleasant young man who addressed everyone as "lad." About halfway through the day, he nudged me and said, "Hi, lad, where's the safety on this yoke?" I was dumbfounded. He had been handed the rifle in the dark the previous evening. Unknown to me, he had never seen an M1A, much less been trained on it. Had the Brits arrived, he couldn't have covered me even if he wanted to. I showed him the safety on the front of the trigger guard and marvelled at the situation I found myself in. This was getting scary but for all the wrong reasons.

Late in the afternoon, we heard the hum of a helicopter. It came closer and closer. We hunkered as low as we could in the grove. The aircraft hovered almost on top of us. We could feel the prop wash from the twirling blades. The noise was deafening. I glanced up. It was a British Army Gazelle—a light utility chopper used chiefly for observation and reconnaissance. I stood up, the belt of machine gun ammunition draped over my arm, and prepared to pour fire into the belly of the machine no more than thirty feet above our heads.

"Get down! Get down! Get down!" The urgent cry behind me caused me to remove my finger from the trigger and drop to my belly. I thought that a foot patrol had appeared on the road and would have taken me out as I stood up to fire into the Gazelle. Perhaps the helicopter had been scouting the route for the patrol and that's why it was hovering over an obvious ambush position. The chopper moved away. There were no Brits on the road. Everything became quiet.

"What the fuck?" I exclaimed. "What happened?"

A volunteer behind me pointed skyward and said accusingly, "Don't you know those things are bulletproof?"

I was speechless. I couldn't believe what I was hearing. You could nearly put your fist through the light aluminium skin of a Gazelle. A hundred rounds from an M60 would have shredded it at that range. The rounds would have penetrated the fuel tank, cut fuel lines and hydraulics, severed cables and seriously injured or killed the two-man crew. The M60 would have taken it down. I never got over it.

No police or army patrol appeared that day.

My next eye-opener came when I was told we were to pull out that evening, even though we hadn't fired a shot. I had presumed we would stay until a target presented itself, but one volunteer had to work the next day, another had to sign on the dole and a third had cows to milk. It seemed glaringly obvious that this war could never come to a speedy and successful conclusion unless we formed well-armed, professionally trained and full-time ASUs. The M60 was subsequently captured in

Derry due to the treachery of Raymond Gilmour, an IRA volunteer who was an informer for the RUC.

My first operation was what the Marine Corps would call a complete clusterfuck from beginning to end. I could see that the volunteers were not a military unit but an unorganised group of armed civilians. They were poorly trained, badly trained and mistrained in relation to their weapons and also seriously misinformed about enemy equipment and capabilities. They weren't lacking in courage, but they were going up against lavishly supplied and highly professional British Crown Forces. I was proud of them and believed they deserved better from their leadership than this.

Shortly afterwards, I went to South Armagh to observe the local IRA test-fire a Browning M2 .50 calibre machine gun. They had received training from somewhere because they had a good knowledge of the weapon, including how to adjust timing and headspace. A .50 calibre machine gun is a loud weapon and I was astonished that they conducted the test in the North, an area saturated with British troops and air assets.

The South Armagh IRA's command of the ground was remarkable. The men never failed to conduct a thorough reconnaissance before moving in anywhere and engaged in meticulous planning. Every field and hedge was checked for Brits before approaching a position. A good dog was often the best defence against covert hides. Highly organised and disciplined, they had a cunning and multilayered system of communications using everything from coded CB radio chatter to flashing car headlights. They were exceptionally daring and courageous, and I was immensely impressed with them.

I began to realise that there wasn't one IRA but a dozen different IRAs depending on the area and the calibre of the local commander. My own IRA experience might be unrecognisable to a volunteer operating with another brigade or department. Overall, the IRA was an extremely ad hoc organisation. I believed the national leadership could change that if they were minded to do so.

IRA training in explosives was good, although quite different to the training I'd received in the Marines when I was sent to demolitions school at Camp Lejeune. While there, I learned how to safely work with TNT, C-4 and ammonium nitrate. I was taught how to use formulas in order to do the most damage with the least explosive; how to cut steel girders to blow a bridge; how to blow trees in one way to establish a helicopter landing zone and in another way, to cause them to interlock in an "abatis" to prevent vehicle movement on roads; how to use ammonium nitrate-based explosives to blow craters of a specific size and shape to cut roads and runways; and how to use, and if necessary, improvise a shaped charge.

The IRA were not trained to use formulas or in the precise application of explosives for tactical purposes. IRA training concentrated on the safe and correct use of improvised devices supplied by our engineering department. This department designed a wide variety of homemade mortars, rockets and booby traps that caused British forces in Ireland considerable difficulties. The movement had some very capable men and women developing these devices. Without them, the IRA would have been unable to inflict a fraction of the enemy casualties it did. Approximately half of the British soldiers killed between 1979 and the ceasefire of 1994 were killed in twelve bomb attacks. The training in this department was good because the IRA developed the devices themselves and knew them inside out. Our weakness was in the use of infantry weapons combined with little or no training in basic military tactics.

There were exceptions. The South Armagh Brigade was outstanding. One in six British soldiers killed during the Troubles was killed within three miles of the small village of Crossmaglen. If even one more IRA brigade area had approached South Armagh's level of effectiveness and tempo, the British Army in Ireland would have been stretched beyond its operational limit.

The Brits threw everything they had at South Armagh— every conceivable method of interdiction, detection and pursuit: spotter planes and helicopters, watchtowers, hidden cameras, eavesdropping equipment, active and passive night vision, thermal imagery, spectrum analysis, ground radar, seismic sensors, microwave intrusion detection, and mobile and static covert reconnaissance. Even, occasionally, satellite surveillance. Not to mention the thousands of troops in situ and on standby. Furthermore, the Brits knew that Dublin had their backs securing the southern side of the border that Britain had imposed on Ireland.

East Tyrone was another strong republican area with a proud history. It had been at the centre of Irish resistance to English rule for hundreds of years. Tyrone man Hugh O'Neill inflicted the heaviest defeat on an English army in Irish history when he crushed Sir Henry Bagenal's force at the Battle of the Yellow Ford in 1598, killing over 1,500 English soldiers, including Sir Bagenal himself. It was precisely because of the intense resistance put up by Tyrone that it was one of the areas chosen by England to be planted by loyalist settlers in an act of ethnic cleansing known as the Plantation of Ulster. Plantations formed a crucial role in England's counterinsurgency strategy.

County Tyrone had the highest level of Crown Force ambush activity in the North during the Troubles. Fifty-three Volunteers were killed in action, thirty-four of these between 1983 and 1992. In addition, loyalist death squads, armed and directed by British military and police intelligence, murdered forty-two people in Tyrone. Twenty-two of these killings were between 1987 and 1994, in a campaign designed to drive a wedge between the IRA and its support base. The overriding strategic consideration of British and loyalist attacks on Tyrone republicans was to destroy any potential opposition to an internal settlement on British terms.

Every command area contributed inspirational volunteers: Bobby Sands in Belfast, who died on hunger strike, epitomised the concept of leadership by example; Francis Hughes, who put manners on the Crown Forces in South Derry and who died with Bobby and eight other volunteers on hunger strike; Seamus McElwain, killed in action in a Special Air Service (SAS) ambush in County Fermanagh; George McBrearty in Derry, killed in action with Charlie "Pop" Maguire; and Jim Lynagh from Monaghan, killed in action with seven fellow volunteers in County Armagh. Another was Brendan Burns from Crossmaglen, one of the most experienced, able and fearless operators produced by the struggle, who was killed in an accidental explosion with his comrade and fellow top operator Brendan Moley.

Despite the high calibre of volunteers, the fact remains that no army can rise above the limitations of its leadership. The Brits knew that too. A large part of their counterinsurgency effort would be devoted to shaping an IRA leadership fit for purpose—their purpose, not ours, but few of us could see that at the time.

4
A LONE GUNMAN

SHORTLY AFTER THE operational nonevent with the M60, I was presented with an opportunity to participate in another IRA operation against Crown Forces. Jack was an IRA volunteer about thirty years of age who lived in a village not far north of the border. There was considerable British military activity in his area. He let it be known that he was keen to crack them.

I went up to his home, a small rural cottage. His father had died some years previously. His mother was in the hospital. I didn't know until I got there that his sister Sharon was temporarily staying with him to clean and cook until their mother returned. Jack spent most of his day farming and had no time for housework.

Sharon was beautiful. Slightly older than me but a stunner. She had long brunette hair and high cheekbones, perfect pearly teeth and sparkling blue eyes. I'd seen her once before when she came into a pub on the southern side of the border. I didn't frequent pubs but was waiting on a lift to go to a meeting. She had driven Jack down to catch the same lift and decided to stay there to wait for him. Our eyes met. My heart skipped a beat. I couldn't decipher whether there was something or nothing in her glance. I enquired about her and learned she was married but that they were in the process of separating. They had no children.

I knew I was no catch. I had nothing to offer a girl who might be interested in a proper relationship. I could manage to buy a few drinks and a one- or two-night stand, but anything other than that was problematic. No job, no car and no prospects. Even if we hit it off and formed a deeper bond, the trust required to seal the deal wouldn't be forthcoming. I could not confide in her about my activities because to do so would put her at risk if she was arrested and interrogated. She couldn't tell what she didn't know. What commitment could one give when death or prison loomed large over every move you made?

Jack's was an excellent safe house. He was completely unknown as a resistance fighter. His home had never been raided. Jack would tell his neighbours and anyone who cared to listen how much he loathed the IRA. Any operation the IRA carried out in his area would be met by Jack's loud opinion that "they didn't do it in my name." I learned that some of his neighbours, who secretly harboured republican sympathies, detested him.

Jack had organised the smuggling in of two rifles and these were hidden in a hedge near his property. They were an AR-15 and an AR-180 with a folding stock which the IRA called a "foldy butt." They had been driven into the North by Sharon and their sister Deirdre, in Deirdre's car. The rifles were broken down and hidden beneath the front seats. On the way in, the sisters were stopped by British troops. They asked Deirdre to step out of the vehicle and open the boot. She did as directed. A Brit searched while the others stood guard. Sharon was holding Deirdre's eighteen-month-old daughter on her lap. The soldier who rummaged in the boot opened the passenger door and asked Sharon to step out so he could examine the rest of the car.

Sharon pinched the child, who let out a roar and began crying hysterically. The soldier in charge of the patrol hesitated, then told the women to drive on. It was a close call.

The plan was simple. Jack and I would find a hide near the main road and open up on the army when they walked by. We would escape on foot, making our way by a circuitous route back to the cottage. The Brits would almost certainly presume any gunmen would head for the border. Jack knew the area like the back of his hand, so I was confident he knew what he was doing.

I spent the day in the cottage alone with Sharon as Jack had work elsewhere. She was lovely to talk to. I enjoyed her company and thought she enjoyed mine. She wasn't flirting or coming on to me in any manner that I could detect, but I was falling for her big time. She told me she was leaving her husband and going to live in Dublin. She wanted to get away from everything around here, including the intrusion of the Troubles into her life. I was sorry to hear that she was moving away from the area. I would probably never see her again. Not that seeing her would make a blind bit of difference—I knew she was out of my league.

Jack returned just before sunset that Saturday evening. We were meant to leave on the operation around midnight, but Jack was limping and in great pain. A heifer had kicked him and split open his shin. Sharon and I cleaned and dressed the wound and tried to convince him to go to the hospital, but he refused. He said we would have to call off the operation for now. I told him I would go on my own. Except for the fact I didn't know the lay of the land, what difference would it make?

They tried to talk me out of it, but I was adamant. Fortunately, I had brought along an ordnance survey map of the area and studied it carefully. Jack relented. He gave me a thorough briefing on the terrain, where to go and what to expect.

Shortly before midnight, I put on the camouflage jacket and trousers I had purchased in the Dandelion Market in Dublin the previous week. My officer commanding (OC) had given me forty pounds to buy some combat clothing for the unit. I also wore a pair of wellingtons. Nothing else was available. While slipping into the rubber boots, I heard the familiar racking of a firearm behind me. I turned and saw that Jack had locked and loaded the AR-180 I was taking on the operation. I didn't appreciate that. You never allow another man to load your weapon. Against my better judgement, I let it slide. I thought checking it might insult him.

Jack wished me luck. Sharon was subdued and anxious but said nothing. I left through the back door and strode the few yards to a gate into a meadow. I had about a mile to walk in the darkness to reach my firing position. As I started to climb the gate, Sharon ran out after me. "You forgot something," she said.

"I did?" I said, wondering what the hell I'd left behind. Sharon put her arms around me, kissing me full and long on the lips.

"Come back safe, John."

I was flustered and thrilled. "I'll do my best."

I clambered over the fence and disappeared into the night. The taste of her lips and the fragrance of her perfume stayed with me long afterwards.

The night was cold, but I was sweating heavily from my exertions and no doubt the stress of the situation. I travelled as close as I could to the hedgerows as the vegetation provided a degree of concealment from being silhouetted against the skyline. The odd tree afforded potential cover should I walk into a British Army ambush team and survive the initial contact.

I did not carry my weapon in the ready position, as a

conventionally trained soldier would do, but pointed down, close to my side in line with my body. I was advised to do this by an experienced volunteer who had explained that if I was scanned by enemy night vision, I might be mistaken for a farmer searching for a calving heifer or possibly a salmon poacher. Enough ambiguity, perhaps, for a challenge to be called out, giving me that half heartbeat of margin to dive out of the kill zone.

I strove to keep ground disturbance to a minimum. I carefully and quietly opened any gates I encountered between fields and closed them exactly as I found them. I tested electric fences with a blade of wet grass to determine if they were switched on or off. A tingle in the fingers would indicate they were live. I sometimes crawled under barbed-wire fencing and other times went over, ensuring no alteration was made in its tautness and no fabric was caught in the barbs. I knew that an Irish farmer could read his land like a ledger and some enterprising fellow might be tempted, for a small consideration, to translate what he read to the British.

A light rain began to fall. Reaching a drain beside the main road, I stopped and waited with constrained breath, listening carefully for the footfall of a British Army patrol. The moon glinted off the wet tarmac, making the road appear like a gilded ribbon winding its way to the horizon. It rendered visibility quite good, but that was a double-edged sword that would work for the British as well. The increase in ambient light would extend the clarity and range of their night-vision devices. I quickly crossed over.

Arriving at my firing position in a thicket of vegetation just over a football field's length from the main road, I nestled into my hide and settled myself for an indeterminate wait. There was little traffic in the predawn hours. All was quiet and still. From time to time, cattle lowed. In the distance, a fox yipped.

About an hour later, I could detect the hum of an enemy helicopter. I listened as the gunship buzzed and darted around the Irish countryside. The Brits were on the prowl. Eventually, I could tell that the chopper had dropped off an army patrol. Farm dogs barking in an ascending crescendo heralded the patrol's route as it moved gingerly down some country lane in the general direction of my position. The aircraft, probably a Lynx by the sound of it, would have a door gunner to provide covering fire. The soldiers would be shadowed by the helicopter at some distance so that the patrol's exact position could not be pinpointed. It wasn't long before the night settled and again became serene. No dogs barked. In the chill of the predawn darkness, all I could hear was the chattering of my teeth.

Where'd those Brits disappear to? I wondered. It was too quiet. I speculated that they could be holed up in some shed doing surveillance. I knew one thing for sure—I wasn't going to go looking for them.

I recalled an incident, relayed to me by a local republican sympathiser, that had happened outside a nearby village several months before. An old farmer, a bachelor, thought to be a bit simple-minded, was cutting a hedge with a billhook on a lane in front of his home. A patrol from the Parachute Regiment approached him and began asking questions. The farmer ignored them, just kept chopping at the hedge as if they weren't there. Finally, one of the Brits grabbed the old man by the back of his neck and growled, "Answer when you're spoken to, Paddy!"

The farmer spluttered, "W-what do youse want?"

"We're trying to find terrorists," said the Para.

"That's funny," replied the old man. "They don't seem to have any trouble finding you."

The farmer received a few slaps and kicks for that answer, but he didn't have to put his hand in his pocket in the local pub for weeks after.

A faint blush of crimson appeared in the east. The dawn chorus gathered pace with birds singing in the new day. I shivered in the cold. The sweat from my previous night's exertions chilled me right through. *A cup of tea would be nice*, I thought.

The air warmed as the day wore on. I struggled not to doze off. I had been up all night. The march to my firing position wasn't far, but it had been exhausting. Numerous fences and hedges had made it seem like an obstacle course. Around midday, I thought I might as well have a wee bite in case I didn't get a chance later.

I reached into the breast pocket of my combat jacket and let out a string of muffled curses, "Well, for the love of . . ." I looked at a sodden pottage of wax paper and dough that used to be an egg mayonnaise sandwich Sharon had made and shook my head in disgust. I had crushed it crawling under barbed wire. I reached into another pocket for the other sandwich with the same result. I felt disheartened, but luckily, I had a couple of Mars bars that were still edible. I produced a lemonade bottle full of tap water. That would do for now. Hopefully, I'd not be here long.

Traffic remained light that Sunday, with short surges in activity around Mass times in the local village. The previous two Sundays in a row, a foot patrol had set up checkpoints on this stretch of road. Although the British Army strove to avoid patterns, I was counting on them making it a third.

I rested my cheek on the synthetic stock of my AR-180 and

scanned the road and the fields beyond. I did my best to remain alert, but my eyes were heavy as my mind drifted to other things, not least the previous night and my moment with Sharon.

A thud from the road startled me. I peered from the hide to see that a British soldier had slammed shut the boot on a car directly in front of my firing position. Other soldiers were standing around the vehicle. One was bent over talking to the woman driver. My heart pounded. I had drifted off to sleep. While I was napping, a British Army foot patrol had strolled into the kill zone. They would probably have walked right by me unnoticed if they hadn't stopped to search the car. I had seriously screwed up.

My mind raced. I could only see four Brits. Where were the rest of them? If that's the front of the patrol, I'm okay, but if they're taking up the rear, then the other Brits have gone on ahead up the road. They could cut me off. I knew my escape route ran parallel to the road for a short distance. If Brits were ahead of me, I could be riddled by flanking fire.

I toyed with the idea of not firing. I could easily convince myself that some Brits had gone on ahead and would be blocking my escape. I could return reluctantly to base, cursing that I had to leave my firing position without pulling the trigger. Later, I would tell myself and others how disappointed I was, that I did my best and had put in a reasonable effort but circumstances had intervened; circumstances in which my courage could not be questioned. I could rest up in some comfortable billet, belly full and sipping hot tea, looking everyone in the eye and disregarding the secret whispers of the heart that would rejoice at the setting of another sun that left me alive and free for at least another day.

On the other hand, I hadn't got dressed up for nothing. I

decided to take the shot. I had no moral compunction about killing an armed British soldier on Irish soil. I saw it as my duty to remove a British gunman from Irish politics. What unnerved me was a feeling I hadn't anticipated. I would have to choose which soldier to shoot. Firing on the occupation forces was a military act rooted in a political decision. Setting my sights on a particular individual somehow made it personal. I wouldn't know the guy and could hold no personal grudge against him. (I should add here that I was not engaging in some inner philosophical debate. These thoughts were fleeting, random and unfocused.)

Two of the British soldiers began walking, continuing the patrol, while the two in the rear stood momentarily in conversation. I centred my front sight post on the chest of the British soldier who had slammed the car boot shut. I switched the safety into the fire position. A wave of nausea swept over me. I knew that nothing on earth could bring that bullet back once I pulled the trigger. It might set in motion a train of events that could lead to my own death.

Hang on, I thought. *If I open up now, the Brits might shoot the woman in the car.* I held my fire until the woman pulled away and drove off around a corner. Then I shook myself and concentrated on the BRASS rule the US Marines had taught me. Breathe—take in a breath of air. Relax—slowing exhale. Aim—keep focused on the front sight post, ensuring it remains centred in the rear sight aperture. Stop—hold the breath for no more than two or three seconds. Squeeze—gently touch the trigger with the tip of the index finger.

A muzzle blast startled the countryside. Birds scattered in a chorus of panic. Cattle ran wild-eyed in every direction. The soldier crumpled to the ground. No dramatic spinning or flailing like in the movies. He simply folded, as if every tendon in his body had been simultaneously cut. His SLR rifle bounced off the tarmac, landing some distance behind him. The other soldiers instantly disappeared, jumping into the drainage ditch that lined the road. I placed my sights on the soldier's chest to fire a second, confirming, shot into him.

Click. Nothing happened. Jesus fucking CHRIST and his Holy Mother! Thousands of rounds fired in the US Marines in training without incident and on my first gun attack as an IRA volunteer I had a malfunction on my second shot! Before this could sink in, and before I could perform an immediate action drill to clear the stoppage, bullets began whizzing around my ears.

I scurried backwards from the hide, rose to my feet and began to run. At least I tried to run. I was so stiff and sore from lying motionless on the cold ground that I could barely hobble the first twenty or thirty yards. I could hear the crack of high-velocity rifle rounds passing close by my head. Not a fusillade of bullets fired in panic but slow, methodical and aimed. Someone who knew what they were doing was trying to kill me. At least one British soldier had spotted me and grasped the opportunity to return the serve. I crashed headfirst through a hedgerow from one field into the next, disappearing from view. The shooting stopped. I would not feel the cuts and welts on my hands from the brambles and thorns for some hours.

At the far end of this field was a small river about twenty feet wide. Jack had assured me that a footbridge was located there but none could be seen when I reached the bank. The stream flowed slowly. It appeared deep and black as bog water.

I stared at the river like a rabbit caught in headlights. *The footbridge must be around that corner,* I thought, looking towards a bend about forty yards to the right. The sound of approaching helicopters announced trouble was coming, and fast.

I had no time to start searching for the bridge. I took a few steps back and ran as fast as I could towards the riverbank, making the longest jump of my life. I landed about four or five feet short of the far bank and sank into the icy blackness. Struggling to the surface, I kicked and thrashed my way the last few feet to the other side. My clothing was saturated. My wellington boots filled with water. They weighed me down to a degree I hadn't anticipated. The water was so cold it almost paralysed my breathing. I came within a hair's breadth of letting go of the Armalite and losing it. I could feel the first swell of panic rise in my throat as I reached the far side. I scrambled up the bank and lay on my back with my feet in the air to allow the water to pour out of my wellingtons. I must have presented a comical spectacle.

Three helicopters were closing in at a rapid rate. Now, I could make them out, two Lynx gunships and a Gazelle, coming in low over the trees less than a minute from my position. I grabbed my rifle and scrambled away from the riverbank. I was exhausted from lack of sleep, the run from my firing position and my flailing effort to swim the river.

Crossing a narrow road, I had just disappeared into a clump of bushes when the roar of the helicopters became deafening. I was convinced I had been spotted when a chopper hovered directly over my position. It couldn't have been more than twenty feet above me. The rotor wash from its powerful blades sent a torrent of hurricane-force winds roaring through the vegetation. I must have been observed while squelching across the road in my dripping clothing. I braced myself to be torn from gullet to gut by machine-gun fire from the door gunner. The realisation that there was no escape generated a numbing sense of hopeless and helpless abandonment.

My body stiffened as I anticipated the searing pain from the high-velocity bullets that would rip me to shreds.

Slowly but surely, though, the aircraft slid away from its hover and continued at low altitude to the next field on some sort of search pattern. I glanced up. I could see it now. It was a Westland Lynx multipurpose helicopter, a type used in a variety of roles, including as a troop carrier. It was armed with an FN MAG general-purpose machine gun, which fired between 650 and 1,000 rounds per minute. Another helicopter, the Gazelle, hovered high in the sky, keeping an eagle eye on the surroundings while the Lynx flew low, trying to spook me into moving and revealing my position. As soon as what they probably presumed to be an ASU of IRA men was flushed out, it would drop a British Army rifle section nearby to mop up. I couldn't see the third helicopter, the other Lynx, and surmised it had landed on the road near the ambush site to remove the casualty.

The helicopter search pattern appeared to be inching towards the British border between Southern and Northern Ireland. The border was roughly two miles away. Jack and I had banked on that when planning the operation. We knew the Brits would assume an ASU would jump into a waiting car and speed towards the frontier. Even if on foot, they would still be inclined to head towards a safe house in the South. Moving deeper into the North, I would have to keep my nerve, but I would be heading away from the heaviest of the security response. The ploy could only work if nobody spotted me. I found a thick growth of vegetation to scurry into and wait until nightfall. I could hear nearby farm dogs going ballistic. The place was crawling with Brits.

I examined my rifle to determine why it had jammed. I could see that I had a bolt over base stoppage. This was the

result of Jack loading my rifle. He'd placed the wrong magazine
into it. AR-15 and AR-180 magazines look identical and fire
the same calibre ammunition. However, the magazine engagement slot which holds the magazine securely into the rifle is
located on opposite sides of the magazine body in these weapons. The AR-15 magazine fit snuggly into my AR-180, but it did
not engage the magazine catch. After firing the first round, the
magazine was marginally too low for the reciprocating bolt to
load the next round into the breach and, consequently, the bolt
lay jammed over the top of the bullet. I pulled out the magazine
and ejected the jammed round. I put the magazine in my pocket
and chambered a single round of ammunition. If I ran into the
Brits now, I had only one shot. I may as well have had a musket.

I cursed myself for making such amateurish mistakes: first,
permitting someone else to load my rifle without inspecting
it; second, choosing a firing position concealed from enemy
view but not adequately covered from return fire; and third,
not reconnoitring my escape route and knowing exactly where
the footbridge was located.

Ironically, the rifle malfunction may have saved my life.
Had I been able to continue firing, the Brit shooting at me
might have had a better chance of hitting me had I not started
running. I made a mental note to bring in an ASU to line
the drainage ditch with explosives, so the next time the Brits
jumped into it they'd be in no condition to fire back.

I wondered if the soldier I shot was dead. I didn't feel anything in particular about it—certainly no triumphalism or
gloating, which would have repelled me. Neither did I feel any
hypocritical remorse. It was simply a fact. The operation was
completed. I would either escape, be captured or be killed. If I
got away, I would immediately meet with members of my unit

to begin planning our next operation against British forces in Ireland. These were the only matters that concerned me now.

A seasoned IRA volunteer had advised me that it took a high degree of mental toughness, what he called "psychological resilience," to operate in this environment. He said that in a conventional war, the enemy are usually objectified shapes and shadows—fleeting and anonymous. In Ireland, you would see photographs of the man you killed that night on the evening news or in the following day's newspaper. You would learn his name, perhaps the names of his wife and children. You might watch them trudge behind the hearse at his funeral. Every drop of blood would be parsed and analysed. Every tear followed in its track. He would invariably be a paragon of virtue murdered by cowards with no justification whatsoever. And the world would be reminded once again that an Englishman who fights for his country is a hero, while an Irishman who does so is a criminal. The IRA man said, "You'd better know what you're fighting for and never forget who you are or what you represent. It's too fucking late when you're being led into the interrogation suite to discover that your heart's in the right place but your balls aren't."

Night came. Clouds darkened the landscape. No moonlight or stars could be seen. Heavy rain began to fall. I was happy about that. High winds, darkness and rain. We called it "Provo Sunshine." It would help conceal my noise and movement.

I was beyond exhaustion and ravenous. My circuitous escape route took three miles of crawling, walking and running. I had only a mile to go to reach the safe house, but it took me five hours. I stopped often to listen to the night and tread carefully in case the British Army had put out ambush teams. Reaching the farmhouse at dawn, I waited another two hours, observing the cottage and the surrounding area, before approaching the door. I lightly tapped a coded knock. Jack hobbled to the door and opened it.

"You made it!" he exclaimed.

"Yeah, I made it." I wondered why he sounded so surprised. Sharon bounced out from the sitting room and threw her arms around my neck. She had been crying. Jack seemed taken aback by her display of affection towards me.

"We thought you were dead," she sobbed.

I was tired and confused by their reaction. I wanted to find out what had happened to the soldier I fired at.

"What did the news say about it?" I asked.

"Nothing," said Jack.

"Nothing?" I spluttered. "What do you mean nothing?"

Jack and Sharon outlined their version of events. They had continued with normal activity the previous day. Shortly after noon, they heard a shot. They froze. Jack said the colour drained from Sharon's face. Moments later, they heard a volley of shots. They were desperate to know what was happening and decided to jump into Jack's car and drive towards the local village. If stopped by the Brits, they would say they were going for groceries. Turning onto the main road, they watched a military helicopter land in a nearby field. In a gap leading into the field, they witnessed a group of soldiers gathered around a casualty. They could see the upturned boots of a figure lying on the ground. Sharon presumed it was me. She forgot I had been wearing wellingtons. She thought that I had been ambushed and shot by the British Army. By the time Jack and Sharon returned from the village, checkpoints had been set up. They were not allowed to pass for a second look. When Jack observed British Army helicopters scouring the countryside, he assured Sharon that I must have escaped or the Brits would not be searching for me.

I found the whole thing disconcerting. I'm good with a rifle. I qualified as an expert shot in the Marine Corps for several years running. The range was slightly over a hundred yards. I saw the soldier go down and lie still on the road. Jack and Sharon saw what they saw. Yet, there were no news reports of the incident and certainly no admission of a casualty. I was at a loss to explain it.

I leaned my rifle against a wall and sat down heavily upon an old brown leather two-seater sofa that faced a solid-fuel cooker warmed by a turf fire. I looked at myself in a mirror. I was shocked at how dirty and dishevelled I appeared. My face was deeply scratched and scarred from struggling through branches and brambles in the dark. The aches and pains from my exertions bore down on me. Steam rose from my clothing. I watched gratefully as Sharon placed a frying pan on the cooker and removed eggs and bacon from a small fridge. Light shone fitfully through a scullery window opaque with grime.

A week later, I met with two senior IRA commanders south of the border. They heard about the incident and quizzed me about it. I told them what happened. Neither seemed surprised. They said that the Brits had hidden casualties in the past. If the soldier had no family, or perhaps came from a military family that would cooperate with the authorities, and provided there were no civilian witnesses who would come forward with the truth, they might deny us the propaganda value of a successful operation. The news might later report a soldier had been killed in a car accident in Germany or during a training mishap in Cyprus when a mortar exploded prematurely in the tube.

As I left the meeting, one of the IRA officers shook my hand and grinned, "Good effort. You can claim the next one."

5
A FIVER FOR BOSTON

I CONTINUED TO operate full-time as a member of an IRA ASU throughout the early 1980s. The results were rarely as ambiguous as the sniping operation in Jack's area.

The term ASU was a flexible concept—any group of volunteers on an operation was given this moniker. While membership of such units could be relatively stable, in some command areas, it fluctuated widely. One might never operate with the same team twice.

When the time came to assemble for an attack, volunteers who were not on the run would have to make credible excuses to family, friends and, in some cases, employers as to why they would be missing and incommunicado for anything from a day up to a week. This disappearing act was one of the more challenging aspects of planning and organising an operation. It was where the lack of full-time professional units was most keenly felt.

During the Tan War, the IRA had used "flying columns" to roam the countryside and attack Crown Force bases and patrols at carefully selected times and places. These columns were made up of full-time volunteers armed with supplies captured from the enemy and trained to a higher standard of competence by Irishmen who had served in the British Army during the First World War. I read a farcical article in some Dublin rag that the modern IRA's inability to use flying columns proved we did not have the same support from the people as the "Old" IRA. The reality was the invention of the tactical radio, covert surveillance cameras and troop-carrying helicopters made the use of large roaming units redundant.

We fought, and many suffered imprisonment and died, as proud volunteers of the IRA. We believed and had every right to expect that the term "republican" was not merely a suggestion but a statement of intent. An old man who had fought in the Tan War and on the republican side of the Civil War reminded me that there were only two possible outcomes to this struggle. "One is the Irish Republic," he declared, "the other isn't."

Although we may have articulated it in different ways, most volunteers understood what was meant by "The Republic." It was Ireland unfettered by foreign control or by domestic divisions cultivated by the foreigner. It did not defer to Britain for terms and conditions regarding its unity and independence. The Republic was a thirty-two-county sovereign and secular state to which Irish citizens of all traditions gave allegiance. It stood for freedom, civic unity and social justice. For 200 years, it had been worth fighting for. Nothing had changed to alter that.

The British are acutely aware that while the Union is existential to unionism, the Republic is not so to nationalism. You cannot be a unionist without the Union, but you can be a nationalist without the Republic. Many Irish nationalists, especially those keen on leveraging themselves into positions of office and influence, have few qualms about British rule that cannot be squared with their conscience or their ambitions. If the Brits squeeze hard enough, most will happily settle for a compromised authority, an accommodation falling short of national sovereignty. Nationalists amenable to this approach, whom the British call "moderates," then convince the electorate there's no alternative if they desire peace. It happened with the Anglo-Irish Treaty in 1922, which cemented partition. We could not foresee it would happen again in 1998 with the Good Friday Agreement.

Whenever the Irish Republic raised its head, the British nurtured a nationalist leadership to stomp it down. In fairness, the Brits don't mind the Irish challenging them. They will even pay Irishmen salaries and expenses to oppose them, provided they do so within constraints defined by London. These arrangements are designed to tantalise and entice a clientele class of political careerists with the allure of salary, status and autonomy, while withholding complete independence.

During the first half of the nineteenth century, Daniel O'Connell, a landlord and lawyer, claimed sovereignty didn't matter. Irish Catholics required only equality within the Empire. He was christened "The Liberator" because he helped achieve Catholic Emancipation in 1829. This permitted affluent Catholics to attend the British Parliament and hold most public offices. O'Connell must share another legacy. He refused to challenge the British government in any meaningful way. A million Irish people perished during the Great Hunger, which began on his watch. In the words of a Tipperary peasant recorded by Alexis de Tocqueville: "Emancipation has done nothing for us. Mr. O'Connell and the rich Catholics go to Parliament. We die of starvation just the same."

In the early years of the twentieth century, John Redmond, leader of the Irish Parliamentary Party, said sovereignty didn't matter. He declared the 1916 Rising to be treason against the Irish people. He longed for a "brighter day when the grant of full self-government would reveal to Britain the open secret of making Ireland her friend and helpmate, the brightest jewel in her crown of Empire."

Redmond promised that joining England against Germany in the First World War would result in Home Rule—a devolved parliament loyal to Britain. More than 35,000 Irishmen died for what James Connolly called "the deferred promise of a shadow of liberty." One of them was Martin Crawley, a brother of my grandfather and my great-uncle Tom, the man who shot dead RIC Sergeant King in 1921. Martin was killed in Flanders in October 1916, serving with the so-called "Irish" Guards.

Now, we had the Social Democratic and Labour Party (SDLP) claiming sovereignty didn't matter. "You can't eat a flag," they would boast, though content to swallow partition. Republicans referred to them as the "Stoop Down Low Party." It was run by mainly middle-class Catholic professionals and those who aspired to that rank. The party was strongly endorsed by the Irish Catholic hierarchy, who came primarily from the same socio-economic and educational background. The SDLP called themselves nationalists, but they rarely took a national view of the national question. They were happy to play the game within the political constraints defined by Britain. They condemned armed resistance to the occupation, advocating a gradual trajectory towards Irish unity through cooperation and collaboration with the British government. Ultimately, they wanted their slice of the pie and cared little whether it was baked in an Irish or a British oven.

There is a popular narrative, bolstered by the ubiquitous rebel songs, that the Irish people fought bravely for their freedom over the course of many centuries. Tom Barry, the legendary IRA leader of the West Cork Brigade during the Tan War, disputed this:

> I have always attacked people boasting about it, that we had a seven-hundred-year struggle for independence. We had not. We had every sixty or seventy or a hundred or a hundred and twenty years an effort made by a small handful of men. And these handful of men, the real patriots . . . were a very, very, limited crowd. They weren't more than twenty thousand of our nation.

While I was on active service, I had no contact whatsoever with Sharon. We had begun an intense and passionate relationship shortly after she left the border area and moved to the capital. On the rare occasions I made it to Dublin, I would stay in her one-room flat in Rathmines. This was between 1980 and 1984. I would appear on her doorstep without notice at irregular intervals. An occasional weekend was the best we could do, although perhaps I'd stay a while longer over the Christmas holidays. She worked in a retail outlet in Dublin that paid very little. We lived on the margins of poverty, never having the money to go to the pub or out for a meal. Time alone in her tiny flat was our only luxury. I didn't drink or smoke, but she would sometimes purchase an inexpensive bottle of wine. When I'd leave, we had no idea if we'd see each other again. All we had was the moment. We could imagine no future that ended well.

I never had money. An IRA volunteer on full-time active service was supposed to be given ten pounds a week by the organisation to buy cigarettes or toiletries. I rarely saw that tenner. I felt guilty asking for it, especially after so many men died on hunger strike. Like most volunteers, I neither experienced nor expected the incentive of salary.

The life of an IRA volunteer could be nasty, brutish and short. Most volunteers knew only those in their immediate circle. They rarely knew who was in the leadership. You were never told that. You didn't join the IRA and hear, "Oh, by the way, now that you're in, the Chief of Staff is so-and-so." You only knew what you read in the papers or heard from loose talk—unless you needed to know. The Brits, of course, knew who was who at all times. In a number of cases, they helped keep them there.

Shortly after joining the IRA, I was told by my OC that the army was, for the most part, a largely unobtrusive organisation, that much of what I could do would be down to my own initiative and I wouldn't be burdened by meddling oversight or excessive discipline. "You'll hardly know the IRA is there," he said, "until you fuck up."

Like most military organisations, IRA personnel ran the gamut from intelligent and highly capable operators to incompetent bluffers. Poor training, inept leadership, faulty intelligence and sloppy tradecraft sometimes led to operations that went tragically wrong, causing unintended casualties. From time to time, British agents would tamper with IRA bombs so they would explode prematurely. This not only led to innocent civilians being killed, which rebounded on the IRA, but to volunteers being blown up by their own devices—what the British gleefully referred to as "own goals."

The IRA's supreme decision-making authority was the General Army Convention. It elected a twelve-man Executive, which, in turn, selected seven of its members to form the Army Council. For day-to-day purposes, authority was vested in this council. At a regional level, the organisation was divided into Northern and Southern Commands. Northern Command comprised the six Irish counties under British jurisdiction, as well as the border counties of Louth, Cavan, Monaghan, Leitrim, and Donegal. Its primary responsibility was to conduct military operations against the British occupation forces and their agents, allies and collaborators. Southern Command was made up of the other counties of Ireland and mainly provided logistical backup, organising most of the training, engineering, arms procurement and finance activities for operations in the North of Ireland and in England.

When I joined the IRA, there were close to 30,000 Crown Forces in the Six Counties pitted against a few hundred volunteers. British military culture has long been strongly influenced by its wars in Ireland. Britain's first standing army was organised to fight the Irish. As Brigadier General Frank Kitson, their foremost authority on counterinsurgency warfare, noted: "It may be of interest to recall that when the regular army was first raised in the seventeenth century, 'Suppression of the Irish' was coupled with 'Defence of the Protestant Religion' as one of the two main reasons for its existence."

The forces we faced during my time included regular British troops, the Ulster Defence Regiment (UDR) (a locally recruited militia of Irish unionists integrated into the British Army) and the RUC. Our principal opposition at the tactical level was directed by the Tasking and Coordination Groups (TCGs) set up in the late 1970s to coordinate and integrate intelligence and live action. Intelligence from various military and police agencies was sifted and assessed by these TCGs.

The RUC Special Branch took the lead role in counterterrorism, with MI5 and the Ministry of Defence in a subordinate position. There were also three specialist British Army units that operated out of the TCGs—the Force Research Unit (FRU), which recruited and operated agents among both loyalists and republicans; 14 Intelligence Company or the "Det," which carried out static and mobile surveillance; and the SAS, the trigger pullers, tasked with carrying out killings in intelligence-led ambushes against the IRA. The vast resources of the British state were at their disposal in their battle to defeat the Irish republican movement.

Opposed by this array of highly trained and well-armed British combatants, I continued to operate as a full-time volunteer, doing the best I could within the constraints imposed by our organisational, leadership and logistical limitations. One day in early 1983, I was asked to report to John Joe McGirl's pub for a meeting. There I met Martin McGuinness for the first time. Martin was a legendary IRA leader from Derry, whom the British conceded was of exceptional character and ability. I was star-struck. I felt deeply honoured and proud to meet the man even our enemy acknowledged was a formidable opponent.

Martin asked me if I would go to America to set up a new arms network there, as there had been setbacks with arrests in New York and other areas. He told me they needed a man with an American accent to go into gun stores to buy weapons. He said an Irish accent attracted too much attention.

I was crestfallen. I thought I was being asked to go because I had military experience and might know something about weapons, but that was never broached. As far as McGuinness was concerned, the only thing I had going for me was my accent. That was my first clue, repeatedly confirmed over the years, that joining Marine Recon had been a complete waste of time. No one I met at a leadership level had the slightest interest in anything I had to say about improving our organisational, logistical and training skills and abilities. While the men on the ground were very keen on this and I got a terrific reception from active service volunteers on these matters, it was invariably a damp squib at a leadership level.

Two exceptions were Army Council members from East Tyrone and South Armagh, both of whom had a sympathetic ear. They were willing to listen and seemed genuinely interested in exploring ideas to improve our military capabilities. However, I had a sense that they could not get past others in the leadership who had a different agenda. What that agenda was, I could not begin to imagine.

After thinking about it for a few days, I asked John Joe McGirl to relay a message to McGuinness that I was declining the offer to go to the States. I had three principal reasons. First, if they needed someone with an American accent, plenty of people already there would be suitable. Second, I didn't want to leave Sharon. I saw little enough of her as it was. Third, I'd been informed by my OC that I was being reassigned to Jim Lynagh's unit. I was keen to join Jim and his men and had been ordered to report to him in Monaghan town the following week.

Jim Lynagh was a highly motivated and courageous operator. I met him on several occasions. We got on well. I was impressed by his keen intellect and sense of humour, which could be irreverent and self-deprecating. I always found this a good sign in a man, especially humour in the face of adversity. I detest imperious arseholes full of their perceived self-importance, men who can laugh at others but never themselves. The Provos had their share of that type too.

Jim possessed that dynamic charisma that resistance fighters look for in a leader. He could inspire men of calibre and competence to follow him. Republican supporters who provided crucial financial and logistical backup respected him. Though lacking in military training and professional development, he displayed that "follow me" tip of the spear leadership no bluffer could emulate. Having worked with the Special Operations community in the United States, I understood what type of man made a Special Forces soldier. I recognised those qualities in Jim Lynagh. He had the potential to become an IRA leader of inspirational significance, if he managed to live long enough.

I received a message from John Joe to call to his pub at the earliest opportunity. When I arrived, he was smoking his pipe. He looked at me and said simply, "You're going." I knew at that point that McGuinness was not taking "no" for an answer. If I wanted to remain in the IRA, I would have to go to America to complete this mission.

Before I left Ireland, I was handed half a five-dollar note that was torn in an erratic manner. I was informed that my contact in Boston had the other half of this note. I was told nothing else. Were they Irish or American? Was it a man or a woman? Nothing. I was also handed 9,000 Irish pounds—a derisory amount to set up a new arms network. I was unpleasantly surprised that I was given no instructions whatsoever on what type of weapons to spend this on. I had expected to be briefed on what to purchase, as I presumed the IRA leadership had a strategy and wished to organise and equip the army to implement it.

Strict orders were given to me to have nothing to do with the Irish Northern Aid Committee (NORAID). This was an American prisoner support group that raised funds to help the families of Irish republican prisoners of war. The British were attempting to blacken NORAID by tying it in with the purchase of arms. I was to do nothing that would directly or indirectly connect the group with funding IRA activity. As I didn't know anyone in NORAID, that was an easy one to follow.

My principal contact in Ireland for this mission remained Martin McGuinness. I met him regularly while planning the operation. Our usual spot was the Botanic Gardens in Dublin. He was polite and avuncular. I liked him. We brought peanuts and fed the squirrels. He always arrived by bus and wore a tweed walking hat and sports coat. I'm not sure if Martin was chief of staff at this stage, but he was definitely on the Army Council and played a significant leadership role. At meetings with senior IRA officers in attendance, I noted that Martin was generally deferred to.

Martin could be humorously direct. One morning I was in a tizzy over a newspaper report that the Irish Taoiseach Garret FitzGerald was considering implementing joint Garda–RUC patrols along a border corridor.

"Jesus, Martin, what'll we do if FitzGerald goes ahead with that?"

"Well," said Martin matter-of-factly, "we can't blow up half a police car."

I couldn't help but laugh at the way he said it. Not because I thought the death of anyone was funny. I would never think that. But because his reply was so unexpected and given with such a deadpan delivery that it created a dislocation of expectation in me that manifested itself in a nervous laugh. Clearly, as far as Martin was concerned, if members of An Garda Síochána wished to volunteer as human sandbags for Her Majesty's constabulary in South Armagh, that would be their misfortune. As a matter of policy, the IRA did not attack the security forces of the Dublin government. If, however, those forces entered the occupied territory to adopt an active posture on behalf of the British war effort, that would alter the dynamic. I don't know if Martin actually meant this or was simply honing his hardest of the hard men rep. I later learned the Irish police baulked at the plan and it was quietly scrapped.

Martin McGuinness had an enormous reputation as our finest military thinker. I recall a senior British Army officer claiming he was so capable that he could have been trained at their academy at Sandhurst. As time went on, however, I found no evidence of this. In fact, I became increasingly frustrated by his military illiteracy. I couldn't blame him for not having professional training but some of the stuff he came out with was baffling. I began to see a different side to him, a side that gave me my first niggling concerns about our prospects for victory.

I had recently spoken to an IRA quartermaster who witnessed a container of weapons being unloaded. It came from the United States. My heart fell as I examined the hodgepodge of deer hunting rifles, shotguns and bolt actions that had been inscribed into his notebook. The next time I met Martin, I asked him about it.

"Was that a junk load, Martin?"

"Junk load?"

"Yeah, bits and bobs gathered up to test the route before the good stuff is sent over?"

I could see a flash of annoyance in his eyes.

"No, that was the shipment. Why?"

"It was crap. Few of the weapons were military grade and there was a muddle of various calibres. One of the rifles was a Swiss Stgw 57 in an unusual calibre, which we almost certainly don't have in stock. Furthermore, it came with only one magazine."

"What's your point?"

"Every gun shop in America sells the AR-15 rifle (a semi-auto version of the M16), and most sell the HK91 (a semi-auto version of the G3). It would be just as easy to buy military-grade weapons and standardise our logistics as it is to do what we're doing now. Also, standardisation would greatly simplify training."

Martin regarded me for a moment as if I had special needs. "A variety of weapons shows the people that the IRA can obtain a wide range of arms and get them into the country. It's good for morale."

I was incredulous. Clearly, the dolly-mixture of bolt actions and deer hunting rifles was part of an ingenious strategy that intellectual pygmies such as myself could not comprehend.

"But, Martin," I protested, "take sniping camps, for example. You might have four rifles on a camp. Each a different make and model and each a different calibre. The same with telescopic sights. All different. Some are fixed power, others are variable power and most have vastly different characteristics making training a nightmare. It would be a very simple matter to standardise this stuff. For example, we could

exclusively buy the Austrian SSG sniper rifle and the Leath-
erwood ART II scope. Sniping ammunition should be match
grade."

"Match grade?"

"Bullets specifically designed for shooting matches in the
United States. They're engineered for exceptional accuracy.
The Sierra MatchKing, for example, can be easily bought
over the counter in the States and has been used in Olympic
competitions."

Martin seemed singularly unimpressed. "I don't hear
anyone else complaining about this, John." I could sense
Martin was trying to wrongfoot me onto the defensive. So,
I was "complaining." What was I thinking? How could anything be wrong in an organisation run by the greatest of all
leaderships?

At another meeting with Martin in the Botanic Gardens,
I was reading a newspaper article reporting on an IRA attack
the previous day in Belfast which killed a British soldier. The
soldier was in a concrete sangar, or sentry post, that had been
hit by an RPG-7 rocket.

"Good job in Belfast yesterday," I commented.

"It was surely," said Martin. "The rocket didn't explode,
though. The warhead went straight through the concrete and
hit the soldier in the chest." It took me a moment to digest
this. I thought he was pulling my leg. I soon realised he was
deadly serious.

"Uh, Martin, the rocket exploded." The newspaper reporting the attack carried a photograph of the aftermath. I pointed
out the small hole made by the shaped charge just under the
observation slit. A hole far smaller than the eighty-five-mil-
limetre diameter of the warhead. I pointed to the concentric

blast rings around the hole caused by the explosion. I referenced the broken windows in a building just beside the sentry post shattered by the concussion. I told Martin that an RPG-7 warhead does not penetrate a target by kinetic energy but by the chemical energy of its shaped charge. A copper cone focuses the explosive energy at the point of impact. This is known as the "Munroe effect." An RPG warhead could not possibly penetrate a reinforced concrete fortification unless the explosive jet performs as designed.

Martin went silent. I could see he was seething, but he said no more about it. I shut my mouth. The last thing I wanted to do was alienate him. I wanted to help the IRA beat the Brits. I wasn't there to criticise him personally, although I believe that's how he interpreted it. My heart fell into my boots. I had expected to be led by skilled professionals, men who were technically and tactically proficient. A true professional would value the correction and pass it on to the men on the ground but not this fellow. He took it as an insult.

Because of his status and prestige in the movement, I knew that if Martin McGuinness said the rocket didn't explode then, as far as the IRA was concerned, it didn't explode. Nobody was going to listen to what I had to say about it. It didn't matter to me personally whether or not I was believed, but the real damage was to volunteers' confidence in the weapon.

As a US Marine instructor at the Amphibious Reconnaissance School, I was under strict instructions to never make anything up or disseminate information I wasn't 100 percent sure was factual and according to doctrine. If asked something I didn't know, I was to reply, "I don't know, sir, but I'll find out." I would visit the Tactical Training Library that evening, research the question and deliver the correct answer in the following day's class. So it was a shock for me to discover that some IRA volunteers, particularly leadership figures, did not like admitting they did not know the answer to a question. When asked something they didn't know, they might guess an answer or make one up. I found this deeply disturbing.

A mish-mash of disinformation, misinformation and wrong information was damaging our effectiveness as a guerrilla army. I was repeatedly told that the RPG-7 had separate warheads for steel and concrete—complete nonsense. Several volunteers insisted that the launcher had to be discarded after firing three rockets. I was mystified as to where this bullshit was coming from and marvelled at how it had gained such currency throughout the movement. The list was endless. Some of it was so damaging it had to have emanated from agent provocateurs.

I made up my mind that, instructions or not, if I got to the States and set up an arms network, we would buy the best we could get and work towards standardising our arsenal.

6
WHITEY

WHEN I ARRIVED in Boston with my torn five-dollar note, it brought me to an old man called John Connolly, who hailed originally from County Galway. John was a sincere and dedicated republican without a criminal bone in his body. But, having lived a lifetime in Southie (the local vernacular for South Boston), he knew who some of the major criminals were. There is a saying that "needs must when the devil drives." We needed money, guns and false driving licences to buy more guns. Law-abiding citizens are a poor source for these items.

I first met Jim "Whitey" Bulger when I was taken to Triple O's tavern by a son-in-law of John Connolly. I had another IRA man called "Mark" with me. I had met Mark through the IRA support network in America. He had been wounded while on active service in Ireland and was recuperating in the States. It was a fortuitous encounter as I needed reliable help and there was no better or more enthusiastic candidate than this brave volunteer from East Tyrone.

Mark was a tall, blue-eyed blond, more Germanic in appearance than Irish. He had what would have been called in another age a bit of dash about him. He was highly intelligent with a quirky sense of humour and a remarkable ability to mimic accents which, combined with his good looks, made him popular with the ladies. In his free time, he enjoyed nothing better than the leisurely read of a good book in a neighbourhood coffee shop. He referred to it as "cultivating my ennui." More than one waitress bade him a sad farewell, never realising her partner for the night was not, indeed, a Danish aristocrat.

Mark and I were shown a short film on the Irish Troubles in a back room of Triple O's. We were then brought to a dingy upstairs office to meet Jim Bulger. I can't remember when I first heard the name "Whitey," but I recall being advised not to call him that to his face.

Whitey shook hands with us. He was polite and respectful without being fawning. We reciprocated but gave false names. Whitey projected an air of calm but unalloyed authority and was casually but immaculately dressed, sporting a short, expensive-looking brown leather jacket, top-of-the-range designer jeans and cowboy boots, which were in style at the time. He was freshly shaven and impeccably groomed with clean, manicured nails. He carried himself well—chest out, shoulders back. In future meetings, I never saw him with a hair out of place. His image meant a lot to him and he managed it with care. I was twenty-five years old at the time; Mark was twenty-three. Whitey would have been around fifty-four but was lean and energetic. You could tell he worked out. We paid our respects and left.

Shortly after that, Whitey Bulger and a group of men I later learned were Steve Flemmi, Kevin Weeks and Pat Nee met Mark and me in the Southie apartment where we were staying with republican sympathisers. We sat across from each other in the living room, sizing each other up. Everyone was courteous. It occurred to me that my accent might seem unusual, even suspicious, as it was more American than Irish. I hoped it would not cause them to doubt my bona fides as an IRA volunteer or even suspect I wasn't who I purported to be.

It didn't take a genius to determine who was the boss. Whitey did most of the talking on behalf of his team. I didn't know Jim Bulger from a crow and I knew nothing about his criminal activities or operations, nor did I want to know. I had a vague notion he could help us acquire guns, but little more than that, and I didn't really want to work with criminals. When I told Martin McGuinness that I was extremely uncomfortable with this operation, his succinct reply was, "Little old ladies in NORAID can't get us M60 machine guns."

In calling them criminals, I am not making a moral judgement. They referred to themselves as criminals. They didn't employ euphemisms or tiptoe around the subject. They engaged in organised crime for a living and made no bones about it. They were refreshingly honest on that score. They were bad boys. If I didn't like it, I could fuck off back to Ireland. Otherwise, it was what it was.

Whitey spoke knowledgeably about the Troubles. He knew more about the topic than many people in Ireland living south of the border. He read a lot and asked sensible questions. Whitey wasn't emotional about it like some Americans. He struck me as being intelligent and professional. I rapidly deduced that whatever criminal activity this guy was involved in, he wasn't snatching handbags off grannies.

To say I didn't trust him and his men was an understatement. It takes time to build a relationship. I also didn't know what they could do for us or how far they were willing to go, but I doubted Whitey would jeopardise his own enterprise for our benefit. Still, any help they could give would be appreciated.

After an hour or so of conversation, Whitey handed me a wad containing $5,000 as a donation. I thanked him and placed it on the table in front of me. I took out a notebook and noted it down. I asked Mark to witness it. Pat Nee later told me that Whitey was impressed with this. Pat said that if I had taken the money and put it in my wallet, we would never have gotten another penny.

I couldn't help glancing at a sea bag they had brought into the room. It was similar to the ones we used in the Marine Corps. I was curious as to what it contained. After handing over the money, one of Whitey's men opened the bag and emptied it of weapons. There were at least a dozen pistols, including semi-automatics and revolvers. There was also an M1 carbine and a Chinese AK-47 with an under-slung folding stock. Pat Nee said the AK-47 was brought back from Vietnam by someone who had fought there. He told me he, too, had been "in-country" with the Marines. I was tempted to tell him that I had served in the Corps but decided to bite my tongue until I knew him better.

Mark and I thanked them for the money and weapons. For all we knew, this could be the extent of their support. Nevertheless, we were grateful. It was far more than most gave. I decided to push the boat out and ask them if they knew of any way we could get false driving licences. We needed them to purchase weapons from gun stores. A New York state licence was best because, at that time, it did not include a photograph. However, a good forgery from another east coast state would suffice.

Whitey seemed animated by this and eager to help. He told me he would get someone to steal a driver's licence-making machine from the Massachusetts Registry of Motor Vehicles. *This guy's motivated!* I thought. That particular resource, however, never materialised.

Whitey eyeballed us. "You guys look like a couple of Micks just off the boat. You gotta blend in around here." He handed Pat Nee a wad of cash and told him to have us looking like Southie boys by the next day. So Pat Nee took me and Mark shopping. We were fitted in classic '80s gear—Members Only jackets, Calvin Klein jeans and cowboy boots. We certainly looked the part by the end of that day.

Whitey may have given the nod for his men to help us out, but it was Pat Nee who took us under his wing. Pat was the principal driving force behind our Boston operation and looked after us in many ways. While I could never discern Whitey's true motives or intentions, I never doubted that Pat had a genuine love for Ireland and was keen to help the struggle for Irish freedom.

Drinking tea in the kitchen of Pat's childhood home in Southie, I could hear his parents in the next room converse in rapid and fluent Irish. Pat was born in Rosmuc, an Irish-speaking district in County Galway. He had emigrated to America at an early age and no longer spoke the native tongue, but his heart remained in the right place. Although he was a patriotic American and cherished his Marine Corps service, Pat never forgot the land of his birth.

Pat was proud that his neighbourhood of Southie had a reputation for stepping up to the plate. He lived in an apartment on East Broadway, directly across from M Street Park. One day, he took me across to the park to show me the memorial to the twenty-five Southie boys who died in the Vietnam War. Fifteen of them were Marines. Southie was your quintessential working-class Irish neighbourhood. When America called, you didn't debate the wrongs and rights. You stood tall and took your place in the line. When Ireland called, we got a lot of help there too.

During my visit to the States, I made numerous trips to New York on Amtrak. The journey took a little over four hours. My primary contact in New York was Liam Ryan, from the Moortown-Ardboe area of East Tyrone. I usually stayed in his apartment in the Bronx. Liam would have been about thirty years of age at the time and was working for the electric power company Con Edison. He was funny, down-to-earth and accommodating. He was proud to be an Irishman and prouder still to be an East Tyrone man. He had tremendous respect and admiration for the volunteers of the IRA and a special place in his heart for the courageous fight put up by the men and women of his home area. He was particularly proud of his cousin Pete Ryan, who, along with seven other IRA men, shot his way out of Crumlin Road Prison in Belfast in June 1981. Pete was a highly motivated volunteer with extensive operational experience. He would be killed in action in June 1991.

Around this time, I also hooked up with Lawrence McNally, another Moortown man. I had last seen him in County Monaghan in the company of Jim Lynagh. Lawrence was in New York with his partner, trying to put together a little money to return to Ireland and buy a home. He was living in the same apartment complex as Liam Ryan and had a job tarring roofs in the stifling New York summer heat. He had also taken up jogging and I went for a few runs with him around Van Cortlandt Park. He looked fit and well, having lost over two stone in weight since the last time we met. Lawrence had taken part in numerous IRA operations and cheerfully offered his full support in any endeavour we undertook to supply the republican movement with weapons. He would later be killed in the same action that took the life of Pete Ryan.

Liam, too, was destined to die in the struggle. He was killed in County Tyrone in November 1989 by a loyalist death squad armed, trained and directed by British military intelligence and the RUC's Special Branch. As Liam, Lawrence and I sat planning arms purchases over cups of coffee in a small corner restaurant in the Bronx, these impending tragedies remained mercifully unimagined by us.

Liam had contacts all over New York and Philadelphia who bought and stored guns for the IRA. Philadelphia had a large contingent of Tyrone men living and working there and Liam was eager to help in any way he could. He proudly showed me the "comms" he had received from his cousin Pete while he was incarcerated in Crumlin Road. Comms were tiny messages written on fragile cigarette paper and wrapped in cellophane. They were smuggled out of prison and these ones had made their way to Liam in New York. The comms spoke of a planned escape and the urgent need to acquire tiny pistols that could be secretly carried into the prison. Liam duly obtained a few small automatics, .25 calibre if I recall correctly, and sent them to Ireland where they made their way into "The Crum" to allow the escape to proceed.

I made it clear to Liam that I wanted to ensure that we followed a coherent plan in procuring arms. As I had pointed out to Martin McGuinness, it was as easy to do this the right way as the wrong way. Few of our sympathisers purchasing weapons in gun shops had military training or experience. They could end up buying almost anything and often did. There was little or no direction from the IRA leadership and no discernible strategy that I could see. I was determined to put that right.

Buying weapons in retail gun stores is a tedious process. No more than one rifle at a time should be purchased to avoid suspicion. It involves a lot of travel between stores. The rogue arms dealer who can supply any amount and type of weaponry to the highest bidder is a myth reserved for thrillers. No substantial arms dealer could operate without government sanction. That sanction might be secret or clandestine for deniability purposes, but it would be there. Otherwise, the dealer wouldn't last a day without being arrested or assassinated by some intelligence agency for eventually supplying the wrong people.

I lost track of the number of times someone in the States told me they knew a fellow who could "get us anything." I was well aware that the only people who could get us anything were the FBI. If someone claimed they could supply arms, I wanted to know how they got them and why they were willing to sell to us. You cannot buy a man-portable surface-to-air missile from some guy on a bar stool.

While in New York, I was told that an Irishman had a contact who claimed to have a large number of M16 assault rifles for sale—brand new in the boxes. The inventory numbered around 900 weapons. I was immediately suspicious, so I sent a communication asking how the rifles had been acquired. A week later, a message returned with a cover story that seemed tantalisingly plausible.

Apparently, the weapons were stolen from a railway car that had been part of a freight train held up in or near an Indian reservation in upstate New York. A small gang of Native Americans occasionally robbed a stalled freight car if they could break into it. The weapons were being transported from the Colt factory in Hartford, Connecticut. Military rifles, I was told, were often shipped under the radar as nondescript freight in trucks and trains because it was more secure to transport them this way than in openly marked containers that advertised their contents. The robbery was strictly opportunistic; the thieves hadn't known the shipment contained rifles. There was severe heat from the Feds and they were keen to get rid of them at a reasonable price.

It seemed too good to be true. I returned to Boston and asked Pat Nee to organise a meeting with Whitey Bulger. I understood that Whitey had excellent police contacts at local, state and federal levels. I told Whitey the story and asked whether he could use those contacts to verify if such a theft of M16s had taken place. He got back to me three days later and informed me that the scenario was a complete fabrication—the robbery never happened. I was being set up. It wouldn't be my last close shave.

Despite the assumption of many republicans in Ireland, the Troubles made little impact on the general public in America. When they were covered on the news, it irritated me to hear the mantra in the American press about the religious war in "Northern Ireland" between Catholics and Protestants. They often referred to the "Catholic" IRA. It was a sectarian line the Brits spun to make the conflict appear irrational in foreign eyes. It gained great traction in America because Britain was their principal ally and rarely challenged on anything.

However, the situation was not that simple. The Irish republican movement had been founded by Protestants 200 years previously. These patriots did not accept that being Protestant meant they were British. Wolfe Tone and Thomas Russell didn't accept it, nor did Henry Joy McCracken. Robert Emmet, the Protestant who led the 1803 rebellion, didn't accept it either, and neither did the Protestants who founded the Young Irelanders, the Protestants who helped establish the Irish Republican Brotherhood, nor Thomas Davis, the Protestant who wrote "A Nation Once Again."

I found the level of ignorance on the conflict in the States demoralising. An American woman once asked a friend of mine, "Hey, who won the Black and Tan War anyway? The Blacks or the Tans?"

There remains a widespread misconception that the struggle for Irish freedom is simply about reuniting Ireland. When I joined the IRA, the border had existed for less than sixty years. Historically, the struggle for freedom was about achieving independent nationhood. For the prior two centuries, it had been based on the concept of a sovereign republic. We were, after all, the Irish Republican Army not the United Ireland Army.

Until they unilaterally partitioned the country in 1920, the British had always treated Ireland as one political unit. Up to that point, they had no problem with a united Ireland. They had governed a united Ireland for centuries. However, the Brits did have a major problem with the establishment of a sovereign Irish parliament. Britain wanted to preserve a bridgehead in the strategically placed island on her western flank and partition permitted that. It allowed them to retain a military garrison in our country. The British considered

Ulster unionists to be what they were initially planted there to be, their civic garrison in Ireland. London rejected the concept of majority all-Ireland opinion and was determined to ensure that the principle of democratic consent applied only to unionists, who today form a majority in only two of Ireland's thirty-two counties. What amounted to a unionist veto over Irish independence was calculated to be a permanent dagger aimed at the heart of our national cohesion. So, regardless of what IRA activity I and others were engaged in, the political and historical context of Ireland's fight for complete independence influenced everything we did.

Meanwhile, back in Boston, I struck up a good relationship with Pat Nee. I moved into his apartment on East Broadway in Southie, sleeping on a fold-up army cot in his sitting room. When I eventually told Pat that I, too, had served in the Marine Corps, we formed a bond that ex-Marines everywhere will understand.

Pat showed me how to purchase military goods by mail order, such as rifle magazines, telescopic sights and even night-vision equipment. Much of the material was sent to the Columbia Yacht Club in Southie as Pat had a contact there who signed for it. I was buying accessories I believed were needed. We had only one magazine for many of our rifles in Ireland. I bought a thousand synthetic magazines for our Armalites: high-quality, rust-free and self-lubricating. I had never seen a volunteer wear an ammunition pouch on an operation. In the rare case they had a spare magazine, men would sometimes drop it or lose it from their coat pocket while running, so I purchased a couple of hundred rifle magazine chest pouches.

I got a bit of stick over this from a Belfast IRA leader. He thought it a waste of money because they weren't necessary in the city. But I knew from experience that operating in a rural environment was a different matter and that the volunteers on the ground would appreciate them. Furthermore, I felt there was a tendency to think more in terms of killing as opposed to soldiering. You can kill a man with a single blast from a sawn-off shotgun. You don't need accoutrements. However, fighting a sophisticated war against the British Army would necessitate a more studied and robust approach towards weaponry and ammunition supply.

I made infrequent trips back and forth to Ireland to brief the IRA on developments. These would have taken place primarily in the last half of 1983 and early 1984. I would see Sharon fleetingly and disappear again. It was emotional torment for us both. During one of these trips home, I had another tense meeting with Martin McGuinness in the Botanic Gardens in Dublin.

Martin maintained a rigorously mechanistic view of military equipment, emphasising quantity as opposed to quality. I told him I wanted to purchase a substantial number of Swedish Aimpoint sights for our rifles. Many IRA operations took place at night or in conditions of low visibility. Volunteers couldn't aim because they could not see their sights in these conditions. The Aimpoint was battery operated. It had no magnification but projected a red dot onto the target allowing the operator to shoot with both eyes open day or night. It didn't matter if it was so dark you couldn't see your rifle; you still acquired a distinct point of aim. Furthermore, the Aimpoint was parallax-free which, without getting bogged down in technical jargon, meant that once correctly zeroed, the target was getting hit if the dot was on it.

"So, it's a laser?" asked Martin.

"No, it's not a laser," I replied. "It uses a light-emitting diode to produce an aiming dot which is reflected off the front lens back towards the shooter's eye. The projection of the dot on the target is an optical illusion. The enemy can't see it. We could put them on Armalites, AKs and even the RPG with the proper mount. Any weapon, really."

Martin asked me the price. I can't remember what they cost, but it was by no means prohibitive. Besides, the IRA wasn't coughing up the money. I was getting most of it from supporters in America. I emphasised that, in my opinion, Aim-points would drastically improve our operational effectiveness.

Martin seemed lost in thought for a time but finally shook his head. He told me not to buy them, to concentrate on guns. I could not comprehend his reasoning or even if he had a reason. I knew there was no point in arguing my case. Martin was used to getting his way. He could be quite forceful when challenged.

I then told him I had acquired a Litton M845 Third Generation night-vision weapon sight and had mounted it on an accurised Armalite rifle with a sound suppressor (more commonly known as silencers). Suppressors are illegal in America unless bought from a dealer with a Class 3 federal firearms' license and registered with the government. Whitey knew a guy who made superb ones and didn't ask for paperwork, only money.

I explained that the Litton night sight was "passive." It emitted no radiation like an "active" infrared device so could not be detected by the enemy. The Litton made it possible to view targets and terrain in the darkest conditions. It had a red dot reticle for aiming. I suggested that in South Armagh or East Tyrone, the combination of night vision, accuracy and sound suppression would pose a severe difficulty for British troops on night patrol.

"We could buy five Armalites for the price of that one Armalite," said Martin.

"I know, but what's going to be more effective? This sniping package or five Armalites where we'll probably lose three of them before they fire a shot?"

"Just stick to buying guns. And forget about silencers. They screw up the weapon."

Christ, I thought, *I'm hearing this shit about suppressors everywhere!*

While I instinctively respected anyone in a leadership position, this was beginning to piss me off. I could see there was no point in pursuing this line any further. My instructions were clear. No Aimpoints, no night vision and no suppressors. I left the man the British claimed was our greatest military thinker feeling depressed and demoralised.

Back in Boston, I had regular conversations with Whitey Bulger. When I say conversations, I mean he did most of the talking. I would be out all day, often in the company of Pat Nee, trying to put things together. Mark had gone to New York to manage our operations there. I was tired by evening and ready to conk out on the army cot. Whitey was a nocturnal predator. He would come over to Pat's apartment around ten or eleven o'clock, usually in the company of Stevie Flemmi, and hold court until two in the morning.

Flemmi was the son of Italian immigrants. He was a former paratrooper who fought during the Korean War and had been awarded the Silver Star and the Bronze Star for valour. His nickname was "the Rifleman." He maintained a respectful silence while Whitey talked. I never got to know him beyond forming a superficial opinion that he was polite, intelligent and reserved. Years later, when I learned he would pull the teeth out of corpses he and Whitey had murdered, I was reminded of a lesson I should have remembered from my experiences in the IRA: never, ever judge a book by its cover.

Whitey would offer his opinion on how the IRA should operate and suggest ways and means of fighting the Brits. I struggled to keep my eyes open. I knew that if I yawned or nodded off, he would be intensely insulted. That could have repercussions. It's not that he was boring, we just had different sleep cycles. His day infringed on my night.

In his book *A Criminal and an Irishman*, Pat Nee speaks of Whitey Bulger suggesting that the IRA use time pencils attached to incendiary material to destroy British Airways jets. I remember that conversation. Time pencils are delay devices that use acid to burn through a wire holding back a striker. When the wire eventually snaps, the striker hits a primer that detonates a blasting cap. Whitey suggested they could be planted on the plane by a departing "passenger" and millions of dollars' worth of aircraft would go up in flames. In fairness, he intended this for use on the ground when the jet was parked. He didn't suggest it be used in flight. I nodded and said, "Great idea, Jim. That's the type of thinking we need."

It was a crazy suggestion. Something would inevitably go wrong. A device could malfunction and fail to go off on the ground but detonate later, in flight, killing hundreds of innocent civilians. There was no way we would contemplate risking that.

As time went by, I got to know Whitey better and began to hear stories about him from some of his men. He could be impulsively generous but just as impulsively deadly. One story

I heard was that he needed a man killed but didn't want any suspicion to rebound on him. So he entered the man's apartment, placed a blow torch, sleeping pills and a bottle of whiskey on a coffee table and told the man to choose his method of murder. Whitey made it clear there was no way out—it was going to be one way or the other. After a few hours of crying and begging, the man eventually downed the pills and whiskey. His death was classed as suicide. The story may be apocryphal, but something about Jim Bulger made me believe he was capable of it.

I had to walk on eggshells. Whitey asked me to show him how to make an under-car booby trap bomb used by the IRA. This was an improvised explosive device that was attached under a target vehicle with a magnet. It contained a mercury tilt switch. The bomb would detonate when the car moved or hit a bump in the road.

I had to think quickly. We could not have Whitey Bulger killing people in Boston with technology linked to the IRA. I lied that I had no idea how to make one, that our engineering department manufactured them and all our volunteers had to do was place them on a target and remove the safety peg. I kicked the can down the road. I told him I would find someone in Ireland who would fly to Boston and show him how to make the booby trap. I knew that would never happen, but it gave me breathing space to work on other things.

Whitey suggested he could arrange for IRA men on the run to move to Boston, where he would supply them with false identifications, work and places to live. I knew what he was getting at. He saw himself with a small army of IRA hitmen indebted to him and under his control. That could never happen either.

Jim Bulger was giving us crucial help, but he thought like a criminal not a patriot. He didn't grasp the political considerations we had to factor in when planning or conducting military operations. Nor did he have the type of personality that would tolerate all that aid going in one direction for long. I knew that if my Boston mission dragged on without something in it for him, I would eventually wear out my welcome.

I sometimes had the feeling that Whitey was sizing me up, that he didn't quite know what to make of me. On more than one occasion, it crossed my mind that gun-running activities on his patch could one day cause him difficulties he would need to resolve. Pat Nee was sincere and highly invested in our project, which took him away from work more profitable for Whitey. I wondered what would happen if my mission ever seriously conflicted with Whitey's operation. I suspected I could end up in a lobster pot at the bottom of Boston harbour. Eventually, the IRA would send someone looking for me. All Whitey had to say was, "Jeez, I gave John $200,000 to bring over to you guys. Ain't you seen him?"

I never trusted him and could never relax in his company. I was a soldier, but Whitey Bulger was a killer.

7
BLT

BY NOW, WE had been acquiring weapons for a period of about nine months. But, how to get them home? The answer to this question appeared in the form of Joe Murray from Charlestown.

Joe was involved in organised crime, although I didn't know the precise nature of his activities. The Boston underworld did not brief me on what they were doing or keep me informed of their movements. Likewise, I never told them what I was doing or where I was going once I left Boston. We didn't inhabit a world where an inquisitive mind was a healthy attribute.

I knew that Charlestown criminals had a reputation for robbing banks and armoured cars. Joe alluded to bank robberies on several occasions, not just armed hold-ups but digging tunnels in and clearing out the vaults. I had no reason to doubt the veracity of this but no way to confirm it either. All I knew for sure was that Whitey Bulger told me Joe Murray was exceptionally wealthy and would be an invaluable asset to have on board.

Joe owned the Celtic Tavern on Sever Street in Charlestown. I learned that among his many business interests, he also owned an oil storage facility and had access to boats. Whatever Whitey said to him, Joe agreed to work with us. He supplied our first boat, the *Surge*. This was a 150-foot steel fishing vessel. It looked like a small freighter in bad condition. Joe said he was going to have new engines fitted and he maintained that while it would look like a rusty Volkswagen Beetle on the outside, it would drive like a Porsche.

Pat Nee implied that Joe was wary of Whitey Bulger, even afraid of him. I didn't understand the dynamics between Whitey and some of his collaborators, such as Joe. There was no internet in 1984 and it was more than twenty years before Facebook. I had no way to check someone out or research their lives and connections. I could only go by what I was told or saw with my own eyes.

Joe was a big man—six feet four inches tall and heavyset. He said he had been in the US Army Special Forces—the Green Berets. He was an instructor at the Recondo (Reconnaissance Commando) School at Fort Carson, Colorado. He told me he kept a holiday home in that state and promised that he would take me there after we got the weapons to Ireland. He also said we'd get some pack horses and rifles and hunt bear and elk in the mountains. That sounded good to me.

A friendly man, Joe also had a good sense of humour which, I noticed, was always directed outward and never inward, and often directed at me in fact. I didn't mind as long as the help kept coming. He christened me "BLT" (Boston's Littlest Terrorist). He told me this was because of my dogged determination to complete my mission. He said I reminded him of the story of the Littlest Train chugging uphill and panting, "I think I can, I think I can." I remember Joe coming up to Pat Nee's apartment and laughing at the rising pile of assault and sniper rifles under my army cot in the living room. Pat grinned, "I'm glad John's on our side and not after us. He's fuckin' relentless."

I went to Joe's house not far from the Bunker Hill monument, where I was introduced to his wife, Susan. He told me they met in Las Vegas when she was a showgirl dancing in one of the casinos. He was crazy about her. They were touchy-feely and all over each other to an embarrassing degree. I felt a little uncomfortable when I was alone in their presence. I recalled that feeling ten years later when I read that Sue put five .357 Magnum bullets into Joe's chest, killing him.

Shortly after meeting Joe Murray and his wife, I took a trip down to the Bronx to learn how things were proceeding in New York. Liam Ryan showed me a brochure for the Barrett Light Fifty sniping rifle. It was the first time I became aware of this weapon. I could hardly believe civilians could buy a semi-automatic .50 calibre rifle. I had fired the M2 Browning machine gun in the Marines and knew that a .50 calibre bullet would penetrate the British Army's ceramic jacket, hardened undercover vehicles and armoured patrol jeeps.

It took the IRA a while to figure out that the Brits were wearing the ceramic jacket. Not surprisingly, South Armagh was the first place the British Army tried them out. The Brits referred to it as "Improved Northern Ireland Body Armour." The IRA called it the "hard jacket." It was worn beneath the soldier's combat smock where it couldn't be seen. It contained layers of Kevlar fabric augmented front and rear by ceramic plates known as Small Arms Protective Insert (SAPI) plates. The portion of the jacket protected by the plates was impervious to rifle fire up to .30 calibre armour piercing. The rest of the jacket would stop low-velocity pistol and submachine gun rounds.

A few of our lads around Crossmaglen hit Brits dead centre in the chest or the back at ranges of under 100 yards. They could clearly see they'd hit them, but the Brits landed on their arses and got up again. The volunteers couldn't figure it out. The boys were told they must have missed but insisted they hit. Other volunteers on the operation confirmed the hits. Some speculated our ammunition was faulty or had been sabotaged. Eventually, the IRA discovered the truth about the hard jacket.

Unfortunately, they didn't discover the whole truth. A misconception gained traction that the entire jacket was bulletproof. True, the entire jacket would stop a standard pistol or submachine gun bullet, but only the parts protected by ceramic plates could stop a high-velocity rifle round. So, even though an Armalite or AK-47 would penetrate the sides of the jacket and substantial portions of the front and rear, many volunteers were discouraged from shooting at the Crown Forces at all. The true value of the jacket to the British Army was the attritional function it performed on our operational flexibility and effectiveness.

When I returned to Boston from the New York trip I spent some time working on the *Surge*, mostly painting the crew quarters. There, I met John McIntyre, a fisherman and amateur marine engineer. He was good with his hands and could fix anything fixable. I was taken aback when McIntyre spoke to me of our gun-running mission. While Joe may have earmarked him to come on the trip as a crewman, I felt there was no need to tell him anything until the guns were already at sea. I hoped he would keep his mouth shut.

Once the *Surge* was about 50 percent ready, I took a trip home in March 1984 to brief the IRA on developments. I had a meeting with three members of the Army Council in a safe house near Ardee. One of them, from Belfast, who I believe was chief of staff at the time, chaired the meeting. A capable and dedicated republican, I was impressed by both his demeanour and the intelligent and professional manner in which he conducted the meeting. He would later be marginalised by more devious elements within the movement who didn't share his unqualified commitment to achieving a complete British withdrawal from Ireland. The two other Army Council members were from rural parts of the North. Martin McGuinness did not attend.

I briefed them about the boat and our progress to date. I was surprised when the Belfast man asked if I thought we could move Libyan arms shipments from Malta to Ireland. I replied that I was no skipper but was confident if the *Surge* could cross the North Atlantic, it could certainly manage the Mediterranean.

I didn't get too excited about this suggestion. Acquiring military equipment from a government was the holy grail of logistics, but I had heard so much talk and speculation over the years about big weapons deals and game-changing arms shipments that I took it all with a pinch of salt.

The Belfast man asked me to write out a list of weapons I thought it would be useful to look for. Martin McGuinness had never sought my opinion on that. The wish list was ready for our second meeting a week later. I believed we were chasing the rainbow, that we'd probably never get any of this stuff, but there was no harm in writing it down.

The first item on my list was the 106-millimetre recoilless rifle. I had recently read that when the Italian Army adopted the Tube-launched, Optically tracked, Wire-guided (TOW) anti-tank missile, it sent its 106s to its former colony of Libya.

No one in the IRA leadership had heard of the 106. I had fired it in Japan and Pat Nee was a 106 gunner in the Marines; in fact, it was Pat's Military Occupational Specialty (MOS). Pat knew the recoilless rifle far better than I did—I had merely fired one for familiarisation purposes as part of my Recon training, but Pat could field strip the weapon and knew how to zero it in.

The 106 is an anti-tank gun that fires a shell weighing ten kilograms out to a maximum range of over 7,000 yards, although its optimal range is approximately a mile. The barrel is a shade over eleven feet long. Because it is recoilless, the 106 is much lighter than conventional artillery, weighing in at less than 230 kilograms. It can be fired from the back of a jeep permitting the gunners to shoot and scoot. The shell's shaped charge can penetrate 400 millimetres of armour plate. The acquisition of 106-millimetre recoilless rifles would have given the IRA direct fire artillery. They could have demolished British Army watchtowers in South Armagh, sunk Royal Navy patrol vessels in Carlingford Lough and heavily damaged British military and police installations throughout the North.

Other items I put on the list were AK-47s, 12.7 heavy machine guns, 81-millimetre mortars, RPG-7 anti-tank rockets, hand grenades, flame throwers and SAM-7 man-portable surface to air missiles. If we obtained arms of that nature, I firmly believed that, provided the right men were professionally trained and secrecy maintained, the IRA could have attacked any barracks in the North, killing or capturing the garrison and relieving it of weapons, supplies and intelligence files. In a well-planned and highly coordinated assault, adjacent IRA units could have used 81-millimetre mortars to destroy enemy Quick Reaction Forces and their helicopter transport on the ground. Potential helicopter landing zones in the vicinity of an IRA withdrawal could have been preregistered for rapid mortar and machine-gun fire should Crown Forces attempt to cut them off. Simultaneous attacks by IRA units throughout the North using mortars, recoilless rifles and 12.7 heavy-calibre machine guns could have damaged or destroyed command, control and communications infrastructure critical to a British counterattack.

I knew that only South Armagh could handle anything approaching that level of military performance—perhaps East Tyrone if they were trained up to it. I couldn't imagine handing out recoilless rifles to units whose maximum operational reach to date had been to shoot an off-duty UDR man, or 81-millimetre mortars to volunteers who didn't know how to use a map and compass. How was that going to work? It's a crude mechanistic view of war to believe equipment alone is the answer. Training would have to reach a hitherto unimagined level, not just in terms of weapons and tactics but also advanced operational planning. We'd have to change our entire organisational culture. I was confident we had the required calibre of leadership within the IRA to accomplish this. Whether or not we had that leadership within the leadership was a different question. Time would tell.

One of the first responses from the London and Dublin governments to such an assault would have been internment, the detention without charge or trial of IRA suspects. Both governments had used it in the past with varying results. We'd lose some good men, but it would also hoover up a lot of dead weight holding us back. By that stage, the gloves would be off. People would be forced to choose sides in the starkest of terms as had happened in the aftermath of the 1916 Rising.

British aggression or Irish resistance. It would be go big or go home. Would the leadership permit that? Their necks would be in the noose with everyone else's. That didn't deter Patrick Pearse, Tom Clarke or James Connolly. It didn't faze Bobby Sands or Francis Hughes. But then, isn't leading by example what leadership is all about? Why seek out all this equipment unless we intended to use it?

During this trip to Ireland I also met separately with a senior IRA commander in South Armagh, showing him the brochure Liam Ryan had given me on the Barrett .50 calibre rifle. This commander exemplified the calibre of leadership we needed. I wished there were more like him. He was impressed by the Barrett and, like me, incredulous that private citizens could purchase such a weapon through normal channels. You just needed to have that state's driver's licence and no criminal convictions.

The commander asked me if I thought a .50 calibre bullet would penetrate the hard jacket. I replied that the Brit jacket would be equivalent to American models of a similar design. These were rated to stop a projectile striking with between 3,000 to 4,000 thousand foot-pounds of energy. That included all rifle rounds in our inventory at the time. In contrast, a .50 calibre bullet strikes with up to 14,000 foot-pounds of energy. I was confident it would rip through both the front and rear of the jacket and penetrate both ceramic plates. He told me he wanted to run the brochure by a few people and we agreed to meet again the following week.

At our next meeting, the South Armagh man told me he was keen on obtaining these weapons, but a Belfast IRA commander had said to him that, in his opinion, it wouldn't work because the Brits wore a bulletproof jacket. The .50 calibre round was a bullet, so that was that. I assured him that there was no such thing as a completely bulletproof jacket. Jackets are bullet-resistant to a degree, depending on the projectile's design, velocity and energy. As a result, he told me to go ahead and purchase a few Barretts for testing.

I returned to Boston to help prepare the *Surge* and procure more weapons. I decided to take a trip to the West Coast to see what could be organised among sympathisers in California and some of the states in between. Mark came along. He had contacts in Arizona and San Francisco who might prove helpful. I also wanted to determine whether there were any checkpoints between states if we needed to move guns cross-country.

Shortly before we departed, Mark and I had a conversation with Whitey Bulger. Mark had a contact in Florida who might be able to acquire small arms. I hadn't been to Florida since I went to Key West as an instructor with an Amphibious Reconnaissance Mobile Training Team in 1978. Whitey mentioned that he might like to come down to the Sunshine State with us. We joked for a while about Miami Beach and the beautiful women there. I wouldn't cheat on Sharon but joined in the "boys will be boys" banter. It was all light-hearted and jovial until, suddenly, Whitey's demeanour turned to stone. "I'm not a pimp," he hissed coldly.

The temperature plummeted to below zero. Mark and I instantly wiped the smiles off our faces. You could have heard a pin drop. Finally, I said, "We know that, Jim. We never meant to imply that. We're grateful for the help you're giving us. The lads back home appreciate all you're doing. I can't begin to tell you how highly they think of you and value you." My arse-kissing seemed to placate the mercurial psychopath, but I wondered why he would put us on the spot like that and embarrass us. We resolved to be extra cautious in anything we said around him in the future.

Mark and I headed out from Boston and drove south on I-95, stopping in New York to see Liam Ryan and catch up on developments there. Then we headed to Philadelphia and down through Virginia. We spent the night in a B&B that had served as a Confederate hospital during the American Civil War. We crossed the Mississippi at St Louis and drove through Missouri and Oklahoma into Texas, where we had a terrifying night driving across the Texas panhandle with local radio stations announcing the approach of tornadoes all over the place. We were extremely concerned as we drove for mile after mile through torrential thunder and hailstorms with no refuge in sight. Finally, we were able to get off the road and hunker down in a cheap motel in some nondescript Texas town.

In Arizona, we stayed with friends of Mark for a couple of weeks' rest and recuperation. We were taken to a small cabin in the White Mountains that they used as a holiday home. It was about as in the middle of nowhere as it is possible to get. Mark agreed that it would prove an excellent location to train snipers. The owner knew who we were and would allow us to use the place any time we wanted.

I planned to approach someone in the IRA leadership whose judgement I trusted to propose sending sniper candidates to Arizona to train them. We could supply them with top-of-the-range scopes, rifles and unlimited match ammunition. It would be expensive, but the lads could shoot thousands of rounds without looking over their shoulder like they had to in Ireland. We'd start by training the trainers. We could devise a selection course in Ireland to ensure anyone who came to the States would have the aptitude and fitness to pass the sniper course—perhaps four men three times a year. That would rapidly build up a highly proficient and effective sniping cadre within the IRA. If the arms network worked the way we hoped, the *Surge* could take men in and out of the States without the hassle and the intelligence profiling of going through official channels. We could supply the volunteers with fake IDs so they could move around America on public transport.

We also had access to a cabin in Maine that could be used to teach courses on rifle and pistol marksmanship, small unit tactics, such as ambush and counter-ambush drills, close-quarter combat, camouflage, communications, land navigation, fieldcraft, first aid and the use of Aimpoints, sound suppressors and night-vision devices, which I fully intended to continue buying. I knew that when this equipment reached the hands of IRA ASUs, the clamour for more would drown out the objections of even Martin McGuinness. In addition to their own gear, it was essential volunteers learned the capabilities and vulnerabilities of British vehicles, helicopters and their personal protection equipment such as helmets and body armour.

When these volunteers returned to Ireland, they would be fit to train and equip the rest of our people to a professional standard. We could never train people in everything or for every possible scenario. Still, if we concentrated on developing a mission-essential task list, we could achieve brilliance in the basics. The improvement in our operational effectiveness would be striking.

Mark and I stopped near Pinetop, Arizona, with another of his contacts. While there, I purchased a Colt Python .357 Magnum revolver from a private dealer. I intended to keep this for personal use in Ireland. Keen to try it out, I drove into thick woods to fire a few shots. Mark came along to observe and fire some himself.

I placed a paper target on a tree and moved back about thirty yards. We took turns shooting. We had been firing for about twenty minutes when I heard a vehicle rapidly approaching on the dirt road beside us. Looking over my shoulder, I was startled to see a pickup truck full of Apaches. Two were in the cabin and two more in the back of the pickup. The Apaches in the back were carrying rifles. They motioned for us to approach.

Now what? I thought. I placed the revolver in a protective cloth case, removed the paper target from the tree and walked towards the Native Americans with Mark close on my heels. Because I had an American accent, I would do the talking.

I approached an Apache who was cradling a Winchester rifle. A red bandana topped his long black hair. I noticed he wore a badge on his vest. He identified himself as a Fort Apache reservation policeman and asked what we were doing there.

"I just bought a pistol and me and my cousin were firing a couple of shots."

"You're on a reservation. You're not supposed to do that here. It's a federal offence."

"Oh, we're sorry, officer. We're just down from Chicago visiting relatives. We're strangers here. I had no idea this was reservation property." Unknown to us, we were just inside the boundary.

The policeman eyeballed us. He saw that I had a regulation paper target and the gun was safely cased. We were polite and respectful. We weren't a couple of drunken yahoos firing blindly into the woods. Neither of us could afford to be arrested or fingerprinted. I had a false ID and Mark was wanted by the British. Our entire operation would go down the tubes if they took us in.

The Apache was calm and courteous. "Okay, go on your way. Be more careful in future."

"Thank you, officer."

It was a close call—a reminder of how precarious our situation was and how things could go tits-up in a heartbeat.

I was surprised to come upon a permanent checkpoint on the Arizona/California border. It was there to check for banned agricultural products to protect California's vital fruit-growing industry. I was concerned we might get searched or interrogated, but they just asked if we had any banned produce and waved us through.

After contacting IRA sympathisers in Los Angeles and San Francisco, we drove back across the continent to Boston. We stopped in a gas station in Wyoming at about 3 a.m. The national maximum speed limit was fifty-five mph at the time—a frustrating constraint on endless straight roads that carried almost nobody else at that time of night. Still, I couldn't afford to get pulled over for speeding with Mark in the car.

The old man filling our tank wore a cowboy hat. "Pretty frustrating," I said, making light conversation, "only fifty-five miles per hour in country like this."

"Hell," drawled the old man, "go any speed you like. This ain't no chicken shit state."

We got back to Boston and began accumulating more guns. A contact in Philadelphia gave Liam Ryan twenty-fire Ruger Mini-14 rifles which we moved up to the New England area for storage. The RUC used this rifle and I wasn't a fan. Firing the same calibre bullet as the Armalite, they used a different magazine, causing a logistical problem we didn't need. They also required different training and zeroing procedures. I wouldn't buy them, but I certainly wasn't going to refuse when offered them for nothing.

I gave Liam Ryan $7,000 to put a down-payment on two Barrett .50 calibre rifles. There was a three-month waiting list for them at the time and I wanted to get the ball rolling. Pat Nee and I bought a thousand rounds of .50 calibre machine-gun ammunition from a dealer in New Jersey. I intended to source far more accurate match ammunition for the Barretts later.

By late summer 1984, everything was falling into place. The only hiccup was that the *Surge* was taking longer to prepare than anticipated. It now looked as though we would have to wait to make our maiden voyage in the spring of 1985. She needed to be fully outfitted and John McIntyre had told us that, understandably, he wasn't keen on crossing the Atlantic in the upcoming hurricane season. Then, I received a message that would alter our plans and change the course of my life.

8
ASSEMBLING
AN ARSENAL

AS OUR ARMS network developed and spread, I was amazed at the level of support we could garner in America. Politicians, police officers, judges—the types of people who were likely to be our enemies at home—were firm allies among the Irish and Irish-American communities in the United States. Insulated from the incessant anti-republican propaganda of London and Dublin, they took a stubbornly national, as opposed to a partitionist, view of Ireland. Many citizens of Irish descent, who had thrived in the American Republic, were giving something back in memory of ancestors washed up on her shores in squalid destitution.

That help wasn't always one way. The Irish contributed enormously to the American War of Independence. In 1784 the future Lord Mountjoy stated: "America was lost by Irish emigrants . . . I am assured from the best authority, the major part of the American Army was composed of Irish and that the Irish language was as commonly spoken in the American ranks as English, I am also informed it was their valour that determined the contest . . ." The nineteenth-century British historian James Anthony Froude wrote: "Washington's Irish supporters were the foremost, the most irreconcilable, and the most determined to push the quarrel to the last extremity."

By 1860, as a result of the Great Hunger of 1845–52, more native-born Irish resided in New York City than in Dublin. There had been starvation in Ireland, but there was no famine. The country was full of food and only one crop failed—the potato. The Irish peasant was forced to live on that single foodstuff so other produce could be used to pay the rent to landlords whose English ancestors had confiscated Ireland in a genocidal policy of conquest and colonisation.

A million Irish died during the Great Hunger. Another million emigrated, freeing congested land for cattle to graze and feed a voracious English appetite whetted by the industrial revolution and the expansion of Empire.

At the outbreak of the American Civil War, an Irish nation over a million strong lived in the United States—a nation irrevocably hostile to England yet beyond the reach of Crown jurisdiction and reprisals. The British were alarmed these Irish were learning bad habits, not least experiencing life in a democracy within an independent republic that had thrown off the shackles of British rule. Many Irish were prospering and amassing money and resources denied them in their native land. Furthermore, by the end of the Civil War, tens of thousands had received military training and combat experience. They would not ignore the injustices visited upon the Emerald Isle forever.

An apprehensive British government concluded that the Irish people had to be shielded from what *The Times* of London called "the despicable ideas" inspired by "American democracy." Since that time, Britain has invested massive resources into nurturing a loyal nationalist opposition to lure the people away from the republican ideal and divert and deflect Irish Americans from supporting that ideal—the establishment of an independent, sovereign all-Ireland republic.

Since creating the twenty-six-county Irish Free State as a dominion of the British Commonwealth in 1922, London enjoys the collaboration of an indigenous regime it had legislated into existence and armed to fight the IRA. In endorsing the Anglo-Irish Treaty, the Free State government renounced the Irish Republic proclaimed in 1916 and conceded that, in partitioning Ireland, Britain had a legitimate right to determine the parameters of Irish democracy. Southern separatists in Dublin, Northern unionists in Belfast and Tories in London turned as one to face down their joint enemy, that small minority of Irishmen and women who didn't get the memo that the Republic had been consigned to the dustbin of history.

In 1948 a Fine Gael Taoiseach (Prime Minister), John A. Costello, declared on a visit to Toronto that the Irish Free State would become the Republic of Ireland—a republic that would tell the world Ireland is Ireland without the Six Counties. In the future, when any Dublin politician would proudly assert, "I stand by the Republic," they were referring exclusively to the twenty-six-county Republic of Ireland announced by this former Blueshirt in 1948 and not the thirty-two-county Irish Republic proclaimed in 1916.

When the Troubles broke out in 1969, republicans in the North had no national government to organise their resistance. To challenge the British occupation and pursue republican objectives, they had no option but to volunteer as guerrilla fighters in the IRA. And for those guerrilla fighters to have any chance of success, the IRA relied on substantial support in money and arms coming from various sources at home and abroad, much as it had done throughout the long history of Irish resistance.

Continuing our work in Boston and New York, I learned that Liam Ryan was returning to Tyrone for a brief holiday. I asked him to take some messages to the IRA. I told him to tell Martin McGuinness that Whitey Bulger had a contact who said he could provide M60 machine guns for $8,000 apiece. I also asked Liam to organise a meeting for me with the head of the engineering department when I got home.

I discovered that the only part of the AR-15 rifle required by law to be registered with federal authorities by the manufacturer is the lower receiver. This is made from 7075 T6 aluminium and I had acquired blueprints on how to manufacture it. I knew that if the IRA could make the lower receiver, all the other parts of the weapon could be legally purchased in bulk with no paperwork required. In other words, we could have an almost unlimited supply of untraceable Armalites without the need for identification or any trips to gun stores.

In the meantime, I convinced Whitey Bulger to get me ten rounds of armour-piercing Teflon-coated ammunition from a licensed arms dealer who would do him the occasional favour—nothing big that would lose the dealer his licence and certainly nothing that could be traced back to him. That was fine by me. I wanted to carry out trials on its effectiveness and I could worry later about where to get substantial stocks of the specialist ammunition if the tests proved successful.

I removed one of the bullets from its cardboard box and examined it carefully. I noted it was made of hardened steel and covered with a black Teflon coating. The Teflon round was in .308 calibre, equivalent to the 7.62 NATO rounds used in the M14, G3 and FN FAL rifles. A common misconception is that the Teflon coating was applied as a lubricant to enhance target penetration. In fact, its principal purpose was to reduce barrel wear caused by the passage of the steel projectile through the barrel.

I had a lot of questions about the round. I wanted to know how many of these rounds could be safely fired before the rifling was functionally degraded, but the Boston gangster couldn't answer that. I realised, however, that Whitey Bulger was not a man to be pressed. I did not know who the arms dealer was, so I couldn't ask him myself.

I thanked Whitey for procuring the bullets and asked him no further questions. I would contact the bullet manufacturer at a later date. The name of the company was on the box that contained the rounds. I could pretend to be a university student studying ballistics. Most firms are proud of their products and keen to provide any unclassified information that may increase sales. They are not anticipating a phone call from the IRA.

I ordered a bullet-resistant jacket from a company called Second Chance Body Armor. It duly arrived at the Columbia Yacht Club. It was their top-of-the-line model consisting of thick layers of Kevlar fabric with steel plates front and rear. It had what was known in the industry as Level IV protection. The plates were rated to stop multiple hits from 30.06 armour-piercing bullets at a range of only three feet. The IRA had large stocks of these rounds, which they used in their M1 Garand rifles. In the early 1980s, this was our most powerful rifle ammunition. The black-tipped 30.06 armour-piercing round would effortlessly pass through the British Army's flak jacket. However, it would not penetrate the ceramic plate on their hard jacket, nor would it penetrate their armoured Cortinas or hardened jeeps.

Myself, Mark and Pat Nee took the ammunition, the jacket and several rifles to a clearing in upstate Maine. We draped the body armour over a thick post. I took an AR-15 rifle from the car's boot and chambered a standard 5.56-millimetre round. Advising everyone to take cover in case of a ricochet, I flipped the safety off and fired a single shot into the chest area. Examining the jacket and the steel plate, it was as if nothing had happened—there wasn't even a dent. I was impressed.

I picked up an HK91 loaded with 7.62-millimetre, full-metal-jacket rounds and fired a few shots into the same area of the body armour. We examined the jacket carefully. No penetration—not even close. We got the same result with an M1 Garand loaded with armour-piercing ammunition. Multiple hits from just a few feet away failed to make any significant impression.

Finally, I took one round of Teflon ammunition and loaded it into the HK91. The bullet penetrated the front steel plate of the jacket, all the layers of Kevlar, the rear steel plate and the thick wooden post the jacket was tied to. I removed the steel plates from the jacket for inspection, noting that they were almost too hot to handle.

Mark and I immediately understood the significance of this. The ability to penetrate the Brit's hard jacket with a bullet fired from a standard rifle would send shock waves through the Crown Forces in Ireland. It would substantially increase their casualties and damage their morale. I believed the Teflon round would also penetrate the armour used on undercover vehicles and be effective against the hardened jeeps used by the British Army and Crown constabulary. I looked forward to reporting this to the IRA.

One evening not long afterwards, Whitey Bulger drove me to an apartment he owned in a salubrious suburb of Boston. Upon entering, I was introduced to his girlfriend. I can't remember her name, but she was gracious and welcoming. I was in my mid-twenties, Whitey in his early fifties; she fell somewhere in between. She was an attractive woman and you could tell she worked out. Her short skirt revealed shapely, toned legs. Her makeup and hair were immaculate, her clothes the best that Whitey could buy.

"Take John upstairs and fuck him." For a moment, I couldn't believe what I was hearing. I looked at Whitey in disbelief. At the same time, I knew the wrong facial expression could hang me. Neither the woman nor I replied. She wore a faintly pained and embarrassed smile.

"Go on," urged Whitey, "fuck this guy."

He was playing with us, humiliating us both. I didn't know where to look. I froze with an inane grin plastered on my face as my mind raced, trying to figure out what the gangster thought he was doing and how to respond without this pantomime spiralling downward out of control. Thankfully, before I could say anything, which would almost certainly have been the wrong thing, the woman politely excused herself and went upstairs. Whitey dropped it and carried on as if nothing had happened. My heart pounded for some time afterwards. I knew I had worn out my Boston welcome with Whitey Bulger.

Shortly after this, Pat Nee took me out to dinner in Little Italy in the North End. I enjoyed Pat's company and we had a lovely meal. I didn't mention the episode with Whitey's girlfriend. Pat might have said something to him, leading to a dispute that could only have complicated my mission.

Pat caught me glancing at a couple of guys at a far table with olive skin, slicked-backed hair and wearing expensive suits.

"You think those guys are mobbed-up, don't you?" he grinned.

"I was wondering."

"Those assholes come in from the suburbs and eat in places like this pretending to be Mafia. They enjoy the stares they get from the tourists."

"Like me?"

"Yeah, like you," laughed Pat.

Shortly afterwards, Pat pointed out two men walking on the street past the restaurant window. They were casually dressed in worn jeans and T-shirts.

"See those guys?" said Pat.

"Yeah."

Pat knew them and named them. "They're made guys. The real thing."

I glanced again at the two posers sitting across the restaurant and recognised the type. Experience led me to believe that only a minority of IRA volunteers wanted to be IRA men—quiet operators carrying out their duty at the risk of life, limb and liberty to end British rule in Ireland, men who sought neither reward nor renown, happy to remain forever in the shadows. In contrast, far too many volunteers wanted to be known as IRA men, especially during periods of political tension and increased support, such as during the hunger strikes. They craved the reflected glory that emanated from being a resistance fighter or being assumed to be one. It was no use being an IRA volunteer, with all the status and distinction that gave to a young man within some communities, if nobody knew you were in it or at least suspected you were in it. And there were plenty of ways to court that suspicion, even if one wasn't involved. Some were even capable and courageous operators who simply became egotistical and fond of the limelight when it eventually shone on them. Others swaggered in the background, acting the bully. They might kneecap a petty criminal or intimidate some poor fellow who was not getting with the programme, but they would never face down a British Army foot patrol or cross the water to England.

When Liam Ryan returned from Ireland, he informed me that Martin McGuinness had decided that $8,000 for an M60 machine gun was extortion. I was told not to buy them. This from the man who sent me to Boston because few little old ladies in NORAID could get us M60s. Now that I could get them, he didn't want them!

Liam also handed me the number of a public phone kiosk in Ireland and I was told to ring it at a specific time, at which point a representative of the IRA leadership would give me further instructions. It was an unusual practice to use phones in this manner.

I rang on the appointed day and hour. I did not recognise the voice on the other end. I was instructed to cross the Atlantic immediately with anything I had. I was given a stark and explicit command: "You, be on the boat!"

I hung up and wondered what the hell was going on. What's the rush? And why was I to be on the boat? I wasn't afraid to go, but I was no sailor. I would be dead weight—a passenger. Besides, I had all the contacts in America and was the only one who knew the entire network we had painstakingly put together.

Not to mention the work that still needed to be completed on the *Surge* to prepare her for a potential run to Malta to pick up Libyan weapons, weapons that, in trained hands led by competent commanders, could shift the strategic balance in favour of republican forces. I was mystified, but orders are orders.

This was around July 1984. The *Surge* would not be operational this side of Christmas. We still had a lot of guns and ammunition to get hold of. I was hoping to procure at least a dozen Barrett .50 calibre rifles and 10,000 rounds of Teflon armour-piercing bullets, not to mention a large quantity of AR-15 and HK91 assault rifles, SSG sniping rifles, top-of-the-range telescopic sights, Aimpoints, night-vision scopes and goggles, bullet-resistant jackets and millions of rounds of ammunition. But this would all have to wait because someone in the IRA leadership hadn't the patience to hang on for a few more months.

When I relayed my new orders to them, Pat Nee and Joe Murray sprang into action. In surprisingly short order, they convinced a fisherman called Bob Anderson from Gloucester, Massachusetts to agree to move guns and ammo across the Atlantic for a fee of $10,000. John McIntyre would also get ten grand. In addition, Bob would be given money to pay for 8,000 gallons of fuel, thirty tons of ice and over 7,000 pounds of bait. He could keep all the profit from the sword fishing he intended to do on the way back from Ireland. His boat, the *Valhalla*, was smaller than the *Surge*, barely half the size. I was told it was a Gulf Coast shrimper, not designed for the North Atlantic. Anderson had outriggers fitted port and starboard to provide stability in high seas.

As the *Valhalla* was being prepared for the journey, I gathered up what weapons I could. I decided to take any "junk" we had accumulated—shotguns, bolt actions, etc. I had acquired oddities from IRA sympathisers such as a Schmeisser MP40, a Russian PPSh-41 submachine gun with a 71-round drum, and a German StG-44 Sturmgewehr, all from the Second World War. Anything like that, I would throw on this load to get rid of it and test the route. Of course, I would take along some good rifles and ammunition, but the main shipment of quality equipment would wait for the *Surge* to sail.

The *Valhalla* was a "straight-in, no-kissing" job. The long-term plan with the *Surge* was to find a cargo we could take to a European port such as Rotterdam—a genuine cargo that would not only explain the trip but help fund our operation. With a trusted crew on board, it would offload weapons onto an Irish fishing trawler three or four times a year and then continue to Europe to deliver its legitimate consignment. We had no specific cargo identified as yet. I was no shipping magnate and a lot of this planning was over my head. It was a steep learning curve.

I knew the IRA could not expect Boston criminals to keep handing us money. Pat Nee was sincere and so was another guy in Charlestown who must remain nameless because his activities on our behalf were never made known to the authorities. Their hearts were in the right place and they took genuine risks for us, asking nothing in return. Whitey Bulger, on the other hand, would certainly expect something in return, but there was nothing we could do or would do for the guy. When that penny dropped, I wanted to be as far away from Southie as possible.

We would have to find other sources of income to bring things to the next level. Liam Ryan was able to get money from wealthy Irish and Irish Americans as long as they were given specific assurances that the money was going to fund the armed struggle and nowhere else. But that couldn't last forever. No one could be used as a bottomless pit for donations. Robbing banks in Ireland only provided so much and sometimes led to volunteers going to prison. I wasn't at the finance end of things, so I didn't know how to get the money we needed to win the struggle against the British.

I heard rumours that if Libya gave us weapons, they would also give us millions of oil dollars. We weren't allies of Gaddafi, but we had a joint enemy—the British. One million dollars in America would supply everything we needed for years to come. I also hadn't been told how much the *Surge* cost and I couldn't rule out having to pay Joe Murray back at a later date.

The rush job with the *Valhalla* meant we would have to make a direct run to meet an Irish fishing boat at the Porcupine Basin, 200 miles off the west coast of Ireland. It was a crude operation lacking finesse, but it should work as a one-off, provided everyone kept their mouths shut.

As we were preparing for the crossing, I went down to New York to buy some more guns. Liam Ryan said he had a young Tyrone lad who would drive me around for a few days. When the kid arrived, I nearly fell over. He was about nineteen years old and was wearing a "Bobby Sands Lives" T-shirt with a portrait of the hunger striker on the front. The back of his car sported a pro-IRA bumper sticker with a map of Ireland and the slogan "26 + 6 = 1." I looked at Liam and said, "You gotta be shittin' me." Liam was embarrassed. We sent the kid home.

While I was in New York, Liam introduced me to some IRA men who had fought in the Tan War and on the republican side of the Civil War. Their bitterness against Free Staters remained palpable. Fifty percent of the Free State army in the Irish Civil War was composed of Irishmen demobilised from the British Army—men who had never fired a shot in any cause but Britain's returned to wage war on men loyal to the Republic with weapons supplied by the British government. Some had even fought the IRA in the Tan War. As IRA veteran Tom Barry noted:

> Another thing that made our [anti-Treaty republican] position impossible was the build-up of the Free State Army from the Irish regiments of the British army . . . Now, some of these were probably decent men driven by hardship to join the British army. But others were violently anti-Irish and some had left Ireland in very unfavourable conditions; they were driven out because of their having done things against the Republican movement. We might well have been able to defeat the Free State until this lot came over, but after that it was impossible.

I stayed for a night in the apartment of one of these men, a distinguished gentleman who was in Clan na Gael, a republican support organisation founded in the States in the nineteenth century. He was in Croke Park in Dublin in November 1920 when the RIC and Tans opened fire on a crowd of football spectators, killing fourteen civilians. He knew Michael Collins and showed me a photograph of himself standing beside Collins, taken before the Treaty split. The old man was one of those fellows who didn't go bald and had not developed a middle-age spread. Except for his white hair, lined face and a slight stoop, he was unmistakable from the man he'd been sixty years before.

That evening, he told me an interesting story about the Tan War. He had an in-law in a large Leinster town who was a member of the IRA but had not seen action. His in-law claimed he had identified a pub frequented by British soldiers and RIC men who drank after closing hours when no civilians would be present. He said that if only he could get his hands on some proper weapons, he and his men could inflict substantial casualties on the enemy. After listening to this for some time, my friend cycled out to the town with a couple of Webley revolvers and two Mills bombs he had obtained from Collins. He handed them to his in-law. Nothing happened. There was one excuse after the other. When the Truce came, still nothing had happened. After the signing of the Anglo-Irish Treaty, his in-law, who had never fired a shot, became a captain in the Free State army and went on to become a prominent Fine Gael politician. When he passed away fifty years later, the local newspaper carried a banner headline declaring, "Tan War Hero Dies." Ireland was full of these bluffers.

Upon my return to Boston, we began preparing the arms for shipment to Ireland. One evening, I was in the basement of a South Boston house belonging to someone who knew Whitey Bulger and let us use it while he was away. I was drilling out serial numbers on some AR-15s and Colt Commandos. It was an easy operation as the numbers are located on the magazine well and the holes bored through it did not affect the weapon in any way. I usually had help from Pat Nee and others while performing this task, but on this occasion, I was working alone.

Later that evening Whitey and Steve Flemmi came down the steps into the dimly lit basement and stood watching me for a while. We engaged in small talk as I worked. Suddenly, I felt a wave of paranoia sweep over me. It crossed my mind that if Whitey wanted me out of his way, for whatever reason, now was the time to do it. I felt alone, cornered and defenceless. None of the guns in the basement were loaded.

As I drilled and chatted, I remember thinking I should have taken my Colt Python revolver and hidden it beside me underneath a jacket or a towel. At the first hint of aggression, I could have grabbed it. Then again, the six-inch barrel on the Python might have made it unwieldy at such close quarters. A snub nose would be better and could fit into my pocket. I quietly swore to acquire one and not let it out of my reach in future.

I was still sore about Whitey's pimp remark and his bullying of me and his girlfriend in her apartment. Not sore enough to shoot him over it—I'm not that precious—but angry that at some point he must have come to regard me, or my mission, with a degree of contempt. Otherwise, why would he have spoken like that? Was he jealous of my relationship with Pat Nee? Had he concerns about Pat and the Charlestown crew putting their heads together and coming up with plans that didn't include him? A scheming mind incessantly presumes everyone around him is scheming also.

Despite his apparent civility, something about the vibe in that basement spooked me. Had I been armed and had Whitey made a threatening gesture, I would have killed him without a moment's hesitation. When he left the basement with Steve, I breathed a deep sigh of relief. I vowed I would never again place myself in such a vulnerable position. The very fact I had these thoughts spoke volumes about where I believed my relationship with Whitey Bulger was inevitably going.

The weapons and accessories were gathered up and brought to various properties in the New England area, some of them owned by Joe Murray. Any remaining serial numbers that could be removed from weapons were drilled or scraped off. I put most of the rifles in special waterproof bags impregnated with chemicals to prevent corrosion.

It was at this point that I met Bob Anderson for the first time. He certainly knew his way around a fishing boat, having been trawling the North Atlantic for twenty-five years. Bob wasn't Irish and had no dog in the fight; he knew he'd be running guns to Ireland, but it was a business transaction. We never discussed politics. Had he been a blowhard or overly talkative, I might have worried, but Bob's calm, quiet demeanour and vast experience at sea gave me confidence that Joe Murray had picked the right man to captain our voyage.

John McIntyre was chattier and more excitable but had a pleasant manner and was a good worker. He showed initiative and didn't need to be micro-managed. He was enthusiastic at the thought of smuggling guns to Ireland and we engaged in some political discussions. I attempted to explain the situation from a republican perspective as John knew nothing about Ireland and had many misconceptions. He seemed to romanticise the struggle in a stage-Irish way. I knew he drank and frequented bars and I hoped he would keep quiet about our operation.

One thing I had noticed about the Boston gangsters was they all seemed to be of sober habits. Those who drank did so responsibly and I never saw any of them intoxicated. I also never saw drugs or any evidence that they used such substances. Indeed, I heard Whitey speak scathingly of drugs and drug dealing. He told me he kept hard drugs out of South Boston, a fact which, he implied, made him a hero in the eyes of many parents.

The night before our departure for Ireland, the guns were moved to the Gloucester dock that berthed the *Valhalla*.

She was tied up, her bow pointing towards the Atlantic. It took us about three hours to carry everything on board and stow it below deck. We didn't weigh the consignment, but later reports said it came to seven and a half tons of weapons, ammunition and accessories.

Three other men were coming on the trip with us. I didn't know any of them. They were there to help move the heavy cargo. None of them were sailors or fishermen. Bob Anderson and John McIntyre were the only two on board capable of running the boat and navigating her to the Porcupine Basin, where Bob had agreed a meeting time and place with the IRA.

Whitey Bulger, Steve Flemmi and their colleague Kevin Weeks performed overwatch. They sat in a car observing the dock and surrounding area with binoculars. They had a radio scanner monitoring police and Coast Guard frequencies. Whitey assured me he had reliable information that there was no FBI surveillance operation against the IRA in the New England area. If a local police car came along to investigate suspicious activity, he said he would ram them with his vehicle while we scattered.

When it came time to take my leave and board the *Valhalla*, I shook hands with Whitey, Steve and Kevin and thanked them for the help they had given us. Despite my suspicions about Whitey's agenda, I could not deny he had given valuable assistance or permitted others to do so. I didn't kid myself that he had any ideological or philosophical interest in the reestablishment of the Irish Republic, but help was help at a time when we didn't have many friends.

I also shook hands with Joe Murray, who cracked a joke I can't remember. Joe could be funny and was usually optimistic and upbeat. I liked him, but his access to wealth and resources tended to generate a tinge of arrogance in him, like many people who are rich and know it. Whatever motivated him to help us, it was not a burning desire to set Ireland free, but there was no point overanalysing it. The important thing was I had guns and was heading home.

Saying goodbye to Pat Nee was tougher. Without Pat, none of this would have happened. He was the driving force behind our Boston operation and the one who was most genuinely invested in our cause. We shared the Marine Corps experience and brotherhood. Whatever our differences and chosen paths in life, there was always that. I had spent most of my time living in his apartment, where he kept me, fed me and watched my back. We shook hands and gave each other an uncharacteristic hug.

I stepped on board the *Valhalla*. John McIntyre threw off the ropes tying us to the dock. As we slowly chugged away into the night, I gave a final wave to Whitey, Stevie, Kevin, Joe and Pat. We would never meet again.

9
RENDEZVOUS WITH
AN INFORMER

I MOVED TO the bow of the *Valhalla* and inhaled a deep breath
of sea air. The weather was mild with no rain and good visibility. Shore lights shimmered on the dark water in Gloucester
harbour. There was a gentle swell, but it wasn't bad. I had been
on boats a lot in the Marine Corps, so I wasn't afraid of the
water and didn't normally get seasick.

It occurred to me that this wasn't my first time sailing the
Atlantic. In 1959, at two years of age, I had travelled to Ireland
and back on the ocean liner SS *United States* with my mother,
Josephine, and infant sister, Ann. The *Valhalla* was a wee bit
smaller and a lot less comfortable.

An initial taste of what might lie ahead occurred when we
left the harbour mouth and ploughed into the first of the wild
Atlantic swells. They were moderate, but the boat shuddered
like a car going too fast over a speed bump. I braced myself
and stood for a while at the bow. The lights from the American east coast receded behind us as the ocean before us grew
blacker. I recalled John McIntyre voicing his concern at crossing this time of year on the *Surge*, a boat twice the size of the
Valhalla. I hoped we would make it.

In fourteen days or so, all going to plan, we should land the weapons and ammunition in Ireland and I could visit Sharon at last. I'd had no communication with her for months. She didn't know I was on my way home.

I had no idea where we would land the guns when we got to the other side of the Atlantic. The fishing boat coming to meet us in the Porcupine Basin could be from any port in Ireland. For all I knew, we could be landing in Donegal, Galway, Cork or Waterford. You name it. Wherever it was, it would be good to be back on home soil.

The whole *Valhalla* operation was a curveball I hadn't expected. I'd been bounced into it by someone in the IRA leadership. I didn't know who, but I was determined to find out when I got to Ireland. I deserved an explanation as to why a far larger operation had to be sidelined to pursue a diversion that, even if successful, would make no discernible difference to our military capabilities.

Despite this, however, I was pleased with our efforts. I had left Ireland with 9,000 pounds and a torn five-dollar note with instructions to build an arms network from scratch. I was returning with a quarter of a million dollars' worth of equipment and a boat and crew prepared to take it all the way. I had also acquired contacts and resources that would prove invaluable in the future.

I was relieved when Bob Anderson announced we had left American territorial waters. If the FBI had any intelligence on our operation, I knew they would never let us get this far without an arrest. For one thing, what if we sank? Furthermore, they certainly weren't going to hand the credit for the investigation and arrest to a foreign jurisdiction.

The first few days at sea were routine and uneventful. One

of the Boston men who came along could cook. He did his best to provide some tasty roast dinners, but most of the guys were queasy from the rolling waves and ate little. A couple of them were quite sick.

One night, off the coast of Canada, Bob Anderson spotted a large blip on the radar screen coming directly towards the *Valhalla*. It seemed to bear down on us with purpose. Bob didn't like the look of it and neither did I. We brought John McIntyre into the pilothouse to discuss our options. It could be something or it could be nothing.

Worst-case scenario, according to Bob, who had vast experience in these waters, was a Canadian naval vessel coming to board and inspect us. We may have raised a suspicion with the Canadian authorities for some reason or other.

We decided to move all the guns, ammo and equipment from the forward engine room to the main deck. If the blip came any closer than three miles, we would toss everything overboard. Moving tons of equipment up narrow ladders to the deck was gruelling labour in rolling seas. We were exhausted when we brought up the last box of ammunition. Bob and John threw a tarp over the haul. Bob then cut the engine and lit up the *Valhalla* like a Christmas tree. He said it would appear as if we were sword fishing.

We didn't have a visual sighting of the ship that concerned us. It was night-time and all we had to go on was a blip on the radar screen. We couldn't be sure it was the Canadian Navy, but we couldn't chance it wasn't. Shortly before dawn, the vessel, whatever it was, veered off in another direction. We waited a few hours and then moved our cargo back down to the engine room. Such are the joys of gun-running.

Around that time, we lost our autopilot. It allowed the steering wheel in the pilothouse to be set to a specific heading that could be maintained despite strong winds and currents, but with the autopilot out of action, someone had to be at the wheel at all times to keep us on course. It was mainly Bob, John and myself who took turns in four-hour shifts. The *Valhalla* was doing a steady ten knots per hour or approximately 225 nautical miles per day.

About halfway across the ocean, we had a day when the sea was like glass. I never saw calmer water, not even on a fishing pond. The wake from the *Valhalla* caused the only ripple in the utter tranquillity of the benign Atlantic. I had no idea I was experiencing the proverbial calm before the storm.

That night the winds began to build and the sea churned. Bob grew concerned. He told me that a hurricane he'd been monitoring in the Bahamas was coming up the Gulf Stream and heading in our direction. That's all I needed to hear.

I'm not a superstitious man, but I couldn't help thinking back to the night before we departed from Gloucester. Pat Nee and Joe Murray had taken me out for a meal in a fancy restaurant near Boston. I had steak and lobster. It doesn't get better than that in my book. Returning to Joe's Chevy Blazer, I climbed into the back and discovered my watch had slipped from my wrist. I thought it strange I hadn't noticed it falling off. It was a Seiko diver's watch I bought in Okinawa after I qualified at scuba school in the Philippines. We didn't have time to go back and look for it. I bought an inexpensive replacement the next morning.

That watch had been through thick and thin with me, from Marine Recon training in Asia and America to gun battles with the British Army in Ireland. It held real sentimental value. I joked to Pat that the watch may have abandoned me because it saw real danger ahead. Noting the unease on Bob's face as he talked about the approaching storm, I remembered my quip and shuddered.

Shortly afterwards, all hell broke loose. The hurricane seemed to be taking its residual violence out on us. For the rest of the day and all that night, our lives hung in the balance. The *Valhalla* wasn't designed for the battering it received. Enormous waves dwarfed the boat. Bob estimated them to be forty to fifty feet high. Ferocious winds, driving rain and crashing seas swept the deck, making any venture outside the pilothouse extremely hazardous. Bob told me it was the worst weather he had seen in twenty-five years fishing the North Atlantic.

The boat reeled violently from side to side, its stabilising outriggers almost touching the surface with each roll. I thought they would go under on several occasions and we would be flipped completely upside down. John and I went out to the main deck at the urging of Bob to check on something. I cannot remember the reason, but, as we stood less than two feet apart, a chain from the starboard outrigger ripped a steel cleat violently from its mooring. The cleat flew between our heads, missing us by inches. Had it hit one of us, it would have meant certain decapitation.

We took turns on the wheel, attempting to keep the *Valhalla* on course. When my turn came, I struggled to maintain the heading Bob had given me. Walls of cold dark water made endless attempts to swamp us. The ferocity of the storm and the unrelenting terror of being plunged to the bottom of the Atlantic frayed all our nerves. It was the middle of the night when my watch ended and I handed the wheel to Bob. That, it would turn out, saved our lives.

I retired to my bunk and lay there out of the way. The other men were doing the same. There was nothing else for it. As we rocked wildly from side to side, sleep was impossible. I wondered if my family or Sharon would ever learn what became of me when the Atlantic finally swallowed us.

About twenty minutes after handing the wheel to Bob, an enormous wave landed an almost knockout blow to the boat. There was the sound of a massive crash and I was thrown forward violently. It felt like a car collision. I stumbled from my berth to a chilling sight.

Four of *Valhalla*'s seven tempered glass windows had been blown in. Bob was on his knees with blood gushing from a head wound caused by broken glass. He was trying desperately to hold on to the wheel while John rendered him assistance. Water had poured into the pilothouse and down into the forward engine room, causing a short circuit and starting a fire. Smoke poured up from the engine room where the guns and ammunition were stored. Seawater sloshed around my ankles. I knew at that moment we were doomed.

I rushed over to Bob and John. There was blood everywhere. Head wounds can sometimes look worse than they are and I hoped this was the case, otherwise Bob would be the first of us to die that night. To my immense relief, however, Bob was lucid and able to function. John did his best to clean and dress Bob's wounds while I kept my hands on the wheel, trying to steer us into the waves so we didn't get broadsided.

There was so much damage to the boat and the storm was so fierce and persistent I could not conceive of us evading catastrophe for much longer. I asked Bob if we should put on the survival suits we had brought along.

"There's no point!" he gasped painfully. "We're in the middle of the ocean. We have no communications. Nobody knows we're here. Go ahead and put it on if you want to, but it'll take you eight hours longer to die." None of us put them on.

With Bob's bleeding stabilised and my hands on the wheel, I asked John to go below deck and put out the fire. All we needed now was for the ammunition to start cooking off. He did so successfully.

If anyone but Bob had been on the wheel when that wave hit, we'd have gone straight to the bottom. No one else would have known what to do. Bob thought the wave looked seventy feet high, but it was probably more like fifty. The *Valhalla* slid down the side of it, twisting out of control. When the windows imploded, showering him with glass and debris, he sank to his knees but managed to cling to the wheel through his shock and injuries. He steered the boat out of its spin, saving us all—at least for the moment. I knew with the windows gone, another such wave would certainly finish us off. It was as helpless and hopeless a situation as it gets.

Gradually, the storm abated. Our nerves were shattered and we were exhausted. At the first opportunity, we carried out a damage assessment. On the military principle that "two is one and one is none," we had doubled up on everything before leaving Gloucester, but our two VHF radios and both LORAN navigation instruments had been put out of commission by seawater. It would be impossible to make our rendezvous with the Irish fishing boat unless this was resolved.

After two days of drying out, one radio and one LORAN system returned to life. John did invaluable work in repairing the damage, including securing plywood where the windows had been, and he played a crucial role in making the *Valhalla* seaworthy enough for us to proceed with our mission. We could scarcely see out but sailed onward.

There was little further drama as we approached the Porcupine Basin. We were glad to be alive, but the poor *Valhalla* still had to make it back to America. I was lucky—I would transfer to the Irish fishing vessel once we hooked up.

I had no idea what fishing boat was coming to meet us or who would be on it. Pat Nee and Bob Anderson had flown to Ireland previously to meet the Irish skipper to agree on a longitude and latitude. I had not been involved in these discussions because I was never supposed to be on any boat in the first place. I didn't know the location because, at the time, I didn't need to know. Bob was our captain and navigator; as long as *he* knew where we were going, I was happy.

Reaching our destination on the fourteenth day at sea, we encountered another problem. We could observe on the radar screen that there were several fishing boats in the area. Which one was ours? It wouldn't do to approach the wrong crew and ask if they could take guns on board.

Bob and I discussed this for a while. He handed me the radio mic and suggested I say something to let the right boat know we were here. He said his accent would stand out as highly unusual in this area. I told him my accent didn't sound that Irish either, especially after being back in America for months, and I wasn't sure what to say.

While I was attempting to think things through, Bob suddenly grabbed the mic and, to my horror, broadcast, "Top O' the Morning, me Buckoo!"

"Bob," I exclaimed, "for fuck sake! Nobody talks like that in Ireland!"

"They don't?"

"No, they don't." I was afraid his silly but innocent transmission would draw unwelcome attention. There was no response from any of the other boats.

Suddenly, a plane seemed to come from nowhere. I was on the main deck and ducked into the pilothouse. As it flew directly over us at an altitude of less than a hundred feet, I could see that it was an RAF Nimrod maritime reconnaissance aircraft. I had been trained in the US Marines to recognise a wide variety of North Atlantic Treaty Organization (NATO) and Warsaw Pact weapons, tanks, artillery and planes. I was in no doubt what it was. This couldn't be good.

We had a quick look at the radar screen and could see no ship bearing down on us in the manner of a naval vessel coming to intercept us. We didn't panic. I knew that the RAF patrolled these waters for Soviet spy ships. We couldn't just toss our cargo overboard because of a single pass from a Nimrod, but I was understandably apprehensive. On the other hand, I wondered if they would have buzzed us like that if they were on to us. We weren't the only boat in the area. We decided to continue with our mission and see what developed.

In the meantime, Bob chastised John for running onto the main deck and looking up at the plane with his mouth open. "If we're under suspicion and that thing was taking pictures, your mug will be with the FBI by now!" John could only shrug and grin sheepishly.

I wasn't in the pilothouse when Bob and the skipper of the Irish boat made radio contact, so I can't confirm how they positively identified each other. We made for their location and pulled alongside. The crew from the Irish fishing trawler lined the gunwale of their boat. I didn't recognise any of them. We maintained radio silence from that point. Shouted discussions between the two skippers became our sole means of communication.

A force six wind had blown up. The seas were now heaving, making it impossible to tie the boats together and transfer the weapons from our deck to theirs. We tried a few times, but the vessels banged violently against each other, cracking timbers on the Irish boat. It was too hazardous to continue with the attempt.

John ended up taking everything across in a small rowing boat or "punt" belonging to the Irish vessel, which I later learned was called the *Marita Ann*. Its skipper was Mike Browne. Mike and Bob expertly steered their respective fishing boats on a heading into the wind without banging together while John made more than a dozen trips over eight hours. The punt was pulled back and forth between the *Valhalla* and the *Marita Ann* by nylon ropes. It was dangerous, exhausting work and John, in particular, performed splendidly.

After the last punt full of guns and ammunition was transferred, the crew of the *Marita Ann* handed John food and supplies for the *Valhalla*'s return voyage. John brought them over and then I boarded the punt for my transfer to the Irish boat which would take me home. Before leaving, I shook hands with the Americans and thanked them for their service. I hoped they would make it home in one piece.

As I shook John McIntyre's hand, little did either of us know that he would be dead within weeks. I have no first-hand knowledge of what became of John, but it is my understanding that he was arrested for drunk-driving shortly after arriving back in Boston and blurted out his involvement with the arms operation. He also spoke of criminal activity that had nothing to do with the IRA and which we knew nothing about. I don't think John had a problem smuggling guns to Ireland, but he was shit-scared of Whitey Bulger and wanted to escape from his clutches and sphere of influence. He may have agreed to cooperate with the police at that point.

With Bulger's contacts in law enforcement, Whitey would have learned of McIntyre's statement almost as soon as the words were out of his mouth. John was lured to a house in South Boston where he was interrogated for a while in the kitchen. He was then brought down to the basement. When I later read about that, I wondered if it was the same basement where I got the evil vibes from Whitey while I was removing serial numbers from weapons. John was brutally tortured and murdered by Whitey and Steve Flemmi. He was half-strangled with a rope, but it was too thick to finish the job, so Whitey asked John if he'd prefer a bullet in the head. "Yes, please," was McIntyre's pathetic reply. Whitey shot him in the back of the skull and several more times in the face. Stevie pulled his teeth out with a pair of pliers and pulverised them to avoid identification. There was no DNA profiling back then. John's body would not be discovered for sixteen years.

Once I was on board the *Marita Ann*, I helped the Irish crew stow the cargo below deck. When that job was done, I had almost reached the limit of my endurance. I had been two weeks at sea and survived a hurricane. I'd had little sleep and irregular meals. I was shattered. I asked one of the crewmen where we were going to land in Ireland. "You'll see when we get there," he replied.

I didn't care. I just wanted to deliver the arms safely and visit Sharon. I didn't ask any more questions. I ate a sandwich and retired to a bunk in the crew quarters, falling into a deep sleep.

I was woken by a crewman's hand roughly shaking my

shoulder. "Get up! We're being boarded!" It was in the early hours of Saturday, 29 September 1984. We were being arrested by the naval service of the Dublin government. They are part of the organisation that calls itself the Irish Defence Forces, but republicans referred to them as "Free Staters" because their foundational document was the Anglo-Irish Treaty which established the Free State in 1922, specifically Article 8 of that Treaty, in which Britain permitted the state to maintain a defence force proportional to its population.

IRA general orders forbade us from engaging in armed actions against Free State forces. They could shoot us, but we could not shoot back. On the rare occasions this happened, it was against orders. In this case, resistance would have been futile anyway as they had warships and we were in a wooden fishing boat. I thought back to the RAF Nimrod passing overhead and suspected the British were overseeing the entire operation. I knew that Irish Navy officers were trained at the Britannia Royal Naval College in Dartmouth and many were instinctively pro-British.

We were ordered by loudspeaker to move to the stern of the *Marita Ann* and we complied as we had little choice. A voice with a cut-glass accent called out, "Stop them from tawking." He was referring to us. At first, I thought he was a British officer but later realised his was an Irish middle-class "garrison" accent. It is sometimes called a "D4" accent for the affluent Dublin postcode in which it is often heard.

Zodiac rubber boats transferred a boarding party of gardaí and naval personnel to the *Marita Ann*. The gardaí refer to themselves as the national police force of Ireland, despite having no national jurisdiction. It is a strictly twenty-six-county force, intensely partitionist in its ethos.

The police and sailors were nervous. Two sailors fell into the water. There was consternation among the boarding parties as they tried to save them while simultaneously arresting us, but once we were tied up and placed on our bellies at the stern of the *Marita Ann*, they calmed down and began strutting like bantam roosters.

A sailor poked me viciously in the back of the neck with the muzzle of an FN rifle. "Don't move, punk!" I was in bare feet. He stood on my toes deliberately, leaning heavily into them to cause as much pain as possible. I said nothing and didn't flinch. I wouldn't give him the satisfaction. He jabbed me hard again with his rifle, a rifle that would never be pointed at the British Army or fired in the national defence. "Don't move, punk!" he repeated in a thick Munster accent. This imbecile was having his Dirty Harry moment and lapping it up. I was concerned he might fracture my spine or the gun would go off. My wrists were tied far too tightly by what I presumed to be leather shoelaces. I was losing circulation and the feeling in my hands.

We were brought one at a time to the hold near the boat's bow, where the weapons were stored. My head was shoved into the open hatch by a garda inspector who said, "What's down there, you bastard!" I did not reply. He again demanded an answer, followed by a hard slap to the back of my head. I made no reply and was dragged back to the stern with the other prisoners.

Martin Ferris, who I later learned was the IRA officer in charge of the Irish side of the operation, began singing "Take It Down from the Mast," a republican song from the Irish Civil War. I knew the words and joined in. The other crew members followed suit.

Take it down from the mast Irish traitors,
It's the flag we Republicans claim,
It can never belong to Free Staters,
For you brought on it nothing but shame.

"Stop them from tawking!" the voice boomed again over the loudspeaker. "Shut up! Shut the fuck up!" shouted gardaí and sailors.

You murdered our brave Liam and Rory,
You butchered young Richard and Joe,
Your hands with their blood are still gory,
Fulfilling the work of the foe.

I was lifted roughly by the back of my neck and frog-marched to the port gunwale of the *Marita Ann*. A cargo net had been draped over it and I was ordered to go down the net into a Zodiac below. Someone had to cut the laces tying my wrists for me to do this. I threw a leg over the side of the fishing boat but could not hold on to the net because my hands were completely numb. I tried to stick my elbows through the net to give me some purchase. A sailor reached up from the Zodiac and grabbed the belt on my jeans, pulling me down roughly so that I dropped about five feet, landing hard on my back. I was dazed and winded from the fall.

Another sailor in the Zodiac shoved the muzzle of a Carl Gustaf submachine gun into my face and began screaming, "Get on your back! Get on your back!" I was on my back, so I remained motionless. He was shaking like a leaf and acting half-demented. "Get on your back!" he shrieked again. I knew the Carl Gustaf, what the Americans call the Swedish K, fires from an open bolt and it wouldn't take much of a jolt to cause a negligent discharge. Finally, I spoke the only words I uttered during my arrest, "I'M ON MY FUCKING BACK!"

The sailor paused a moment for this to sink in. "Get on your belly! Get on your belly!"

I was transferred to a navy patrol ship along with one of the *Marita Ann* crew named Johnny McCarthy. We were taken to the sick bay. I was on the top bunk with Johnny below me. I was wearing only a T-shirt and jeans. I was drenched from the seawater and the air vents in the ceiling were blowing cold air directly onto me. I didn't want to shiver in front of these Free Staters, but it was impossible not to.

Two Special Branch detectives holding Uzi submachine guns guarded us while a sailor armed with a Carl Gustaf stood just outside the hatch. The sailors in my vicinity all seemed to have working-class Dublin accents. I overheard two of them talking.

"Dis is fookin' bedder dan catchin' Spanish fookin' trawlers."

"You're fookin' roight it is."

We weren't asked any questions. I wondered where we were going but was sure it was prison. I didn't know what had become of the other men on the *Marita Ann*. I presumed they were either on this boat or some other one.

I went over and over in my mind how we were caught. Who told on us? One thing I knew for sure—it couldn't have come from the American end. The Irish Navy had been waiting for us behind the Skellig rocks where radar from the *Marita Ann* could not detect them. Neither I nor anyone on my end knew we'd be passing the Skelligs.

I could hear the muffled sounds of a television in a room on the far side of a bulkhead behind me. It was obvious that it was some sort of recreation area and many of the ship's crew were in there waiting for the news. A while later, I could make out the time stamp of the main evening bulletin on RTÉ. Suddenly, the whole ship shook from the cheers, foot-stomping and clapping of the crew. Their boat had been mentioned in relation to our capture and they were ecstatic.

I remember thinking that British Crown Forces were regularly bringing tons of weapons into Ireland to enforce partition and arm loyalist death squads, yet these sailors would not have given that a second thought, much less have done anything about it. Nevertheless, the capture of a handful of arms to be used by the IRA to pursue our struggle for complete independence was seen as a glorious triumph.

Ironically, the day after our arrest, the Irish Navy provided the guard of honour at a ceremony in Ballyheigue, County Kerry, to unveil a statue to Roger Casement, a prominent Irish nationalist, who, during the 1916 Rising was arrested when he arrived in Ireland as part of a plan to land arms in the same area we were going to and for use against the same enemy in pursuit of the same political objective.

I later learned that the British played a major role in directing the operation against us, including the provision of air and submarine surveillance assets. British intelligence was able to inform their government of our capture before the Irish government knew of it.

We were brought to the naval base at Haulbowline in Cork harbour and taken individually in unmarked police cars to the Bridewell garda station in Cork city. Driving through the city centre in a light rain that Saturday evening, I could see couples going out for a drink or a meal. I knew it would be a very long time before I could join them.

10
PORTLAOISE PRISON

I WAS TAKEN into an interview suite in the Bridewell garda station in Cork for interrogation by the Irish Special Branch. Although certain members had a well-deserved reputation for brutality against republican prisoners, in our case they didn't feel the need to use physical coercion to extract a confession because we were caught red-handed. I didn't see any of the men I was arrested with but presumed they were somewhere in the building.

It was clear the police had no idea who I was or from where exactly I had come. The only information they seemed to have on me was their confident assurance I hadn't boarded the *Marita Ann* in Fenit.

They knew I had come from America but not from which port. They kept alluding to New York. "Some poor bastard in New York is going to get a bullet in the head for this," said one detective referring to the capture of the weapons. "If only you knew how close to home the information came from." He was hinting that we were informed on by an IRA man in Ireland. I dismissed his comment as a crude attempt at misdirection. He kept asking me to identify myself. I said nothing except to ask to see a solicitor. However, shortly after they fingerprinted me, a detective came into the interrogation suite with a smirk and said, "Marines, huh?" They had sent my prints to the FBI, who confirmed my identity.

Different detectives interrogated me, sometimes together as a team and sometimes individually. Some of them were involved in the notorious Kerry Babies Case in which an innocent woman was subjected to brutal treatment and forced into falsely confessing that she had murdered an infant. After a brief meeting with a solicitor, my stock reply to all questions was, "My solicitor's advice is to say nothing."

A detective launched into a bizarre rant about people from what he called "Northern Ireland." He told me that when the Troubles broke out, many nationalist refugees who fled south of the border came to Cork. He said they were given all kinds of help and benefits, and he seemed to begrudge the fact. What really got the detective riled up was his account of a drunk Belfast man who took a taxi from a city centre pub to the refugee camp. Alighting from the taxi, he told the driver, "Charge it to Jack." The implication was that Taoiseach Jack Lynch would foot the bill. "Charge it to Jack," the detective repeated with scorn. I got the impression he was particularly pleased about capturing the *Marita Ann* because he saw it as a little "fuck you" to Northern nationalists.

At one point, another detective stuck his head in the door and told me I might as well come clean because Martin Ferris had broken and told them everything. I laughed and the detective disappeared with a scowl.

Two Special Branch men came in for another session. They began with the good cop bad cop routine. A squat blond detective who reminded me of Barney Rubble from the Flintstones played the good guy. He would be my bosom buddy who only wanted what was best for me. The other cop, the bad guy, was rake thin and balding with deep facial crevices. I reckoned he had a whiskey-drinking head on him if ever I saw one. This fellow played nasty far too well to be wholesome. I stared at a point on the wall and tried to go to my happy place. I kept my mouth firmly shut.

Keeping my mouth shut meant not only refusing to give information on IRA activity—anything I said might incriminate me and, far worse, be passed to British intelligence—it also meant engaging in no conversation whatsoever, not even about sport or the weather. The Garda Special Branch was notorious in republican circles for "verballing," that is, swearing on oath that a prisoner made admissions he never made. A garda's word was taken as gospel against the word of a republican in a Dublin court. Verballing might involve inventing an admission of guilt or twisting a denial of guilt.

I knew of one republican sympathiser who was not a member of the IRA but was questioned on suspicion of robbing a bank. The man was genuinely not involved in the robbery and blurted out, "I know you think I did it, but I didn't do it!" The detectives swore on oath that he had said, "I know you know I did it, but you can't prove it!" He received a twelve-year sentence.

My refusal to say anything beyond repeating my solicitor's advice to say nothing was answered by Whiskey Head with the comment, "We're going to have you committed to Dundrum." Dundrum was the state's principal mental hospital. "You can't talk or respond to simple stimulus. Fuckin' nut case. We couldn't allow you back onto the street."

Barney Rubble placed a reassuring hand on my shoulder. "John's okay. He was used by some manipulating godfather who's sitting in a pub right now laughing at him. Those bastards have him too frightened to talk, but John will come clean as soon as he realises the only way he can help himself is by helping us."

Whiskey Head turned a folding metal chair around backward and straddled it. He shuffled it close to me and rubbed the back of his hand on my face. I recoiled from his touch. "A nice-looking fella like this must have a fine thing parked up somewhere." I didn't respond. "Unless he's queer. Are you an arse bandit, Johnny?"

"I'm sure he has a lovely girl waiting for him," interjected Barney Rubble. "As soon as he comes to his senses and cooperates, we'll have him back with her in no time."

Whiskey Head sniggered and moved his chair closer again to me. He reeked of stale sweat and tobacco. "No doubt one of your chums is already comforting her and throwing the gargle down her throat. His spunk won't be long after it. Think about that, Johnny boy. He'll fire a load into her as thick as donkey's dung." The detective leaned forward and leered with a revolting grin. "You're going to get fifteen years for this, you scumbag. Her hole will be well widened by the time you get out."

They knew nothing about me or my personal life, but I would have preferred a physical beating to having to sit and listen to their puerile abuse. Whiskey Head seemed particularly stimulated by plumbing the depths of vile speculation. Quite frankly, I thought there was something wrong with him.

Later, a senior detective came in alone and spoke to me. He wasn't abusive and didn't ask questions. He knew by this stage I wasn't going to cooperate. He was contemplative and philosophical about the situation. He told me that justice had a long arm, that I may have had a good run of it, but the law would always catch up in the end. He offered his opinion that I was probably a good fellow from a respectable family but somewhere along the way some evil bastard had got a hold of my brain. "You know, John," he said, "you're taking on a lot when you take on the state."

He was right about that. A state can buy loyalty. A guerrilla army cannot. A state can draw on almost inexhaustible resources because a state has a tax base and the legal apparatus to enforce compliance. The IRA had to depend upon people who would volunteer for a life of hardship, danger and sacrifice without pay—a career opportunity that didn't recommend itself. A state bestowed salaries and pensions. It paid the mortgage. It offered position and prospects for advancement. It could put a man in uniform and award him coveted insignia. It provided opportunities to accrue honours and decorations. The state could arm him and professionally train him. It could assure him any violence he used would be sanctified as the lawful use of force. A state furnished the visible manifestations of affluence, status and authority that many valued far more than what they thought prudent to perceive as nebulous concepts of political principle.

I was returned to the cell. A detective came in holding a document and informed me I was to be charged with possession of arms and ammunition with intent to endanger life or to enable others to endanger life. I did not respond.

After two days in the Cork Bridewell, we were brought in a large convoy of police and army vehicles to Dublin for arraignment and then transferred to Portlaoise Prison. IRA volunteers captured in the South of Ireland were tried under emergency legislation called the Offences Against the State Act. A special court set up under that act had three judges and no jury. While the narrative propagated by the state was that the absence of a jury was to prevent tampering and intimidation of jurors, the real reason was that some jurors might feel unduly sympathetic to Irishmen fighting for the freedom of their country.

I stepped through the main gate of Portlaoise Prison on the night of 1 October 1984. I was handcuffed to a prison officer or "screw." Thick fog blanketed the ground. The eerie glow of diffused light from the prison security lamps gave the scene a surreal quality.

After processing, I was brought to a decrepit cell in what I later learned was "E-Wing," where IRA prisoners were kept. The filthy green paint and peeling plaster would have made a slum landlord wince. The cell contained a small rickety table, a wooden stool with no back, a steel bunk with dusty woollen blankets and a plastic piss pot in the corner. I reckoned it was a temporary holding cell where I'd be kept until morning. I would spend the next ten years in it.

The first man into my cell when the door opened at 8:30 the following morning was Jim Lynagh. I had met Jim on the outside several times, so I was happy to see someone I knew and liked. Jim was the IRA intelligence officer in the prison. He had to debrief me about what the police said to me and if I said anything back to them.

The IRA was keen to find out how our operation was betrayed. I knew they would assume the leak had come from the American end. I was told before I left for the States that only a handful of men knew about the operation in Ireland so that if we were caught, it would be my fault for trusting the wrong people. The trouble with that theory was explaining how the Irish Navy knew we were on our way to Kenmare Bay. I know I didn't tell them.

The Dublin government and their echo chamber in the media made a big deal about capturing the *Marita Ann*. They were beside themselves, boasting of their "crippling blow to the IRA." That was nonsense. The material on the *Marita Ann* would have made no difference to the IRA campaign one way or another. The real loss wasn't mentioned because it wasn't obvious to them—that was losing our network and the contacts which could have provided the material that would have been a game-changer. This included the boat that was to transport serious armaments from the Libyan government, although the IRA overcame that setback as it did others.

Four shiploads of weapons would reach Ireland from Libya in 1985 and 1986. The consignments included large quantities of AKM assault rifles, 12.7-millimetre DShK heavy machine guns, 7.62-millimetre FN MAG medium machine guns, RPG-7 anti-tank rockets, hand grenades, flame throwers, man-portable SAM-7 surface to air missiles, millions of rounds of ammunition and tons of Semtex plastic explosive. French authorities intercepted a fifth shipment in November 1987. Its cargo contained 106-millimetre recoilless rifles and 81-millimetre mortars, none of which had been on previous deliveries, so the movement never got its hands on these items. Despite this, the IRA had assembled a massive arsenal that made the loss of the *Marita Ann* irrelevant.

Some of the reports about the *Marita Ann* were laughable. One of the lads in prison asked me why we were smuggling toothbrushes to Ireland. He showed me a newspaper article that said we were bringing in green military toothbrushes for IRA men on the run. I had purchased a large quantity of rifle cleaning kits and each included a chamber cleaning brush that resembled a toothbrush. Other reports claimed we had hand grenades on board. A garda who had boarded the *Marita Ann*, gave a breathless account describing his shock at watching a grenade roll at his feet. One senior Fianna Fáil politician luridly speculated whether the IRA intended to toss these grenades into shops and pubs.

We didn't have grenades. I had purchased a single paperweight for five dollars in the shape of an old pineapple grenade. It was empty, inert and harmless. I thought our engineers might be interested in making a mould of it for future reference. The garda may have been sniffing for a medal or compensation for post-traumatic stress. One thing that struck me about many of Dublin's security forces was that when they were not defending the state, they were suing it.

I wrote to Sharon and organised a visit with her. I hadn't seen her or spoken to her in months. On the appointed day, we were separated by a long bench about three feet wide with a chicken-wire barrier on either side of it. A prison officer sat between the wire with a notepad and pen waiting to note down everything we said. We had no chance to hug or touch each other. The visit was painful and poignant.

Sharon told me the first she knew of my arrest was watching the evening news and seeing me in handcuffs taken off the navy ship and put into a garda car. She went to the toilet and threw up. It was difficult for us to talk in front of the screw and intimacy was impossible. Afterwards, a republican prisoner approached me and enquired about my first visit.

"How'd it go?" he asked with genuine concern.

"Nightmare," I replied.

"Oh? Why was that?"

"The second I walked into the visiting box, it started. Fuckin' hysterics. Wailing and gnashing of teeth. 'Why did this have to happen? I didn't put in for this! I can't take this! I won't take this! How do you expect me to cope?' A full hour of snivels and snotters. It was a humiliating display. And in front of the screw too, which made it all the worse."

"My God," he said, taken aback. "What happened then?"

"Then *she* started crying!"

The prisoner laughed. "You bollocks! You had me going there!"

But it was no laughing matter. While the IRA investigated the leak, our trial went ahead. In December 1984, three of us were sentenced to ten years in prison. Two of the crew, Johnny McCarthy and Gavin Mortimer, were acquitted. Martin Ferris and I made unsworn statements in the dock that the lads did not know about the operation until already at sea and were coerced into helping the IRA. The skipper, Mike Browne, joined us in Portlaoise.

The following year, in November 1985, I took part in an escape attempt with eleven other prisoners. Despite having closed visits and no access to the outside world, we produced fake prison officer uniforms, keys to thirteen of the fourteen gates we had to negotiate and a quantity of explosives, and we had two pistols smuggled into the prison. The escape came within a hair's breadth of success, but the explosive charge placed on the main gate, the only gate for which we didn't have a key, blew the latch deeper into the steel door, almost welding it shut. We received three months in solitary confinement and three extra years in prison for the attempt.

It was eventually discovered that Sean O'Callaghan, a senior member of the IRA's Southern Command, was a garda informant. He also worked for the British Security Service MI5. It was O'Callaghan, the man in charge of the shore party tasked with spiriting away the weapons, who had betrayed the *Marita Ann* operation. I believe he wasn't the only informer on the Irish end, but he got all the credit.

O'Callaghan would go on to inform on me a second time. In October 1984, Martin Ferris and I were supposed to be brought to the High Court in Dublin for a bail hearing. We hadn't a hope of getting bail, but the legal process still had to be observed. However, it was hoped that this trip would give us an opportunity to escape. The plan was that the IRA would tape a key under the rim of a toilet seat in one of the court bathrooms. Ferris would ask to use the toilet. Normal procedure was that a prisoner would have his handcuffs removed while prison officers guarded the toilet door. I would be in the toilet area waiting for him to finish, but I would still be handcuffed to a prison officer. Ferris would remove the key from the toilet rim, wash his hands at the sink and move to the towel dispenser where a small semi-automatic pistol had been secreted. Using the key, he would open the dispenser and remove the pistol. He would then force the screws to release my handcuffs. It was decided that Ferris would be the one to use the pistol because I was an unknown quantity to the screws. The prison officers might react more favourably to a man they knew had a long history of IRA involvement. They might believe Ferris would shoot them if he was forced to do so, whereas they had no knowledge of my operational background or experience. In fact, Martin Ferris would not have shot them as it was against IRA orders to attack members of the Irish security forces, but we hoped they would not be willing to bet their lives on that once a pistol was shoved in their faces. Armed IRA volunteers in and around the Four Courts would back us up and spirit us away on motorcycles.

The night before the bail hearing, our shoes were taken to the main gate to be X-rayed and examined for contraband such as weapons, explosives or messages. This was standard operating procedure. Only one other man in Portlaoise Prison knew of the escape plan and shook hands with us before lock-up, wishing us all the best on the operation.

I had a sleepless night anticipating the day ahead, hoping our escape would be successful and we wouldn't be shot dead by armed gardaí or the army escort. I became concerned when the time to open my cell for the trip to court passed. In the end, neither of us were taken to court and the unsuccessful bail hearing was held in our absence. That had not happened before. Sean O'Callaghan had been in charge of the escape operation.

I never met O'Callaghan, but after he was outed as an informer, I was told by several people close to him that he ticked a lot of boxes as a potential liability. Egotistical, a heavy drinker, a gambler and a womaniser, he had previously been investigated for misappropriating IRA funds. "The next thing is you'll accuse me of being a tout," was his defensive reply to enquiries.

He was intelligent and articulate. A large part of his value to the enemy came from the narrative spun for him by MI5, which he eagerly delivered to the media and anyone who would listen: that he was sickened by the sectarian terrorism of the Provos and longed to make amends to the Irish people for his republican past by sabotaging and disrupting the evil men and women of the IRA. Certain elements within Dublin's political, security and propaganda establishment hoped to spin this pathological liar into an Irish hero.

O'Callaghan's professed contrition about violence did not deter him from working for the British intelligence services who organised the Dublin and Monaghan bombings, armed and directed loyalist death squads against the nationalist community in the Six Counties, carried out countless black operations in his own country and plotted subversion throughout Ireland. Thirty-three years later, when he suffered a heart attack in a swimming pool in Jamaica, I thought of the poetic justice in the traitor who metaphorically sank the *Marita Ann* operation ending his life as a drowned rat.

Prison is a regimented and monotonous blur. Each day, month and year melds so seamlessly into the next it is difficult to remember what happened when. There are no good times in prison, but there are good memories—the comradeship, the loyalty, a shared sense of purpose. The Christmas concerts were usually quite good, with the better singers belting out their party pieces. One rarely heard a rebel song. In all my time in Portlaoise Prison, the only song with political content I remember being performed was an excellent rendition of the Spanish republican ballad "Viva la Quinta Brigada," sung by a Dublin lad accompanied by an acoustic guitar. When it came to music, the cassette tapes loaned, borrowed and bartered among the prisoners included Queen, Bruce Springsteen, Sam Cooke, Meatloaf and a range of the other '60s, '70s, and '80s contemporary music that resonated with young men everywhere.

Practical jokes were a constant hazard and those who practised them a little too enthusiastically were known as jockeys, because they were accused of trying to do their time on other men's backs. They were usually done in good humour and without cruelty, but some of the more strident practitioners had to be reined in from time to time. Every man had his cross to bear and a bad visit or the breakup of a relationship with a girlfriend or wife could leave a prisoner with little patience for the court jester.

The prison officers or "screws" were given nicknames based on some personal characteristic or incident: Sweet Pea, Fast Eddy, Olive Oil, Creepin' Jesus, Turf Head, Smiler and Single Schilling, who was awarded that moniker because he told an ordinary criminal brought down from Mountjoy to do prison maintenance that he was okay, "but for a single schilling I'd gas all those Provos."

An unexpected outcome of being in prison was that I learned far more about the inner workings of the IRA than I ever knew as a member of an ASU fighting the war in the North. In prison, a mix of volunteers from every command area and every army department were corralled into a tiny space—Belfast Brigade, Derry, East Tyrone, South Armagh, Southern Command, England teams, training officers, explosives engineers, intelligence personnel and armed fundraisers, as those caught robbing banks on behalf of the movement were called.

Prisoners were constantly warned about loose talk, but, after years of close confinement, it was impossible not to hear things and get a real sense of what the IRA was all about. It was an impressive organisation with an almost global reach. It could acquire guns and war material in North and South America and the Middle East. It could attack British bases on the European mainland and bomb targets in England. The full resources of the British and Irish states were ranged against it and yet, despite devastating setbacks, it would always bounce back, lethal and resilient. The IRA sprang from a deep tradition of national resistance that would never be eradicated while the British government claimed jurisdiction in Ireland.

Its greatest asset was an historic sense of mission that all the British and Free State propaganda on earth could not diminish. Its greatest threat was the enemy within—the informer, the agent and that insidious crumbling resolve, unspoken and hidden from view, that longed for a softer, safer life and might one day settle for less than the Republic.

I had great conversations with Jim Lynagh. He knew how disappointed I was to be sent to America instead of to his unit. "McGuinness wanted rid of you," he once said to me. I thought he was joking, so I shrugged it off. I now regret not asking him what he meant by that.

Jim and I were entirely on the same wavelength when it came to enhancing our professional development and upping our game. Before his release in April 1986, we spent several hours every Sunday morning for six weeks discussing training and weapons. We would get a Mars bar each from the prison shop and a large plastic jug of tea and sit in his cell talking. Although one of the IRA's most dedicated and experienced volunteers, Jim had none of the conceit or arrogance of lesser men. He cheerfully admitted his ignorance of military matters but was keen to learn all he could from anyone he could.

I told Jim about Aimpoints, night vision, sound suppressors, the .50 calibre Barrett, Teflon rounds and a host of other accessories and equipment that would improve our operational effectiveness. He was extremely enthusiastic and repeatedly asked me to go over everything with him and where to get it, so he had it firmly committed to memory for his release from prison.

Jim was perceptive and astute. He didn't feel the awe many volunteers seemed to have for the IRA leadership. He put nobody on a pedestal. While organisationally loyal and respecting some of them as individuals, he didn't trust others. Jim's brother Colm, who was also a republican prisoner in Portlaoise Prison and my first Irish language teacher, told me that when he joined the IRA, Jim warned him that, in the long run, his biggest enemy would prove to be certain elements within the IRA leadership. I asked Colm what made his brother say that, but apparently Jim didn't elaborate.

I saw uncomfortable evidence of the cult status the Adams-McGuinness team would achieve when a Sinn Féin Ard-Fheis (National Conference) video was sent into the prison. The camera focused almost exclusively on Martin McGuinness and Gerry Adams as other delegates were speaking. On occasion it concentrated on their empty seats when they were absent from the platform, even if other delegates were speaking. In fairness to the two men, they didn't film or edit the video, but there was something North Korean about it. How this burgeoning personality cult would be used to undermine the ideological foundations of Irish republicanism would emerge so incrementally and surreptitiously that it would be on top of us before we knew what hit us.

Not everyone agreed with myself, Jim Lynagh and others that the IRA needed to reorganise in a more professional manner. We took part in numerous debates and discussions around these issues. Some volunteers were repelled by any suggestion that we were not the greatest thing since sliced bread. These men were true believers. They believed in our innate competence copper-fastened by the fact we were led by a galaxy of talent unparalleled in Irish history.

Dark murmurings by some that the IRA might have been infiltrated at the highest level were dismissed as treacherous by most volunteers. Although we knew that the CIA had infiltrated the KGB and the KGB had, in turn, recruited top people within the CIA, FBI, MI5 and MI6, the notion that the Brits might have infiltrated the IRA in any meaningful way was laughed out of court. Even to hint that it might be possible was deemed to be letting the team down, if not bordering on disloyalty.

Groupthink was an enormous weakness within the Provisional movement. It stymied critical thinking and evaluation. Under constant assault by the British and Irish states, republicans tended to turn inward and develop strategies for cohesion and uniformity. They were appalled by internal criticism—there was enough censure coming from our enemies. The belief that the IRA could not be infiltrated at a high level was typical of the delusion of invulnerability that such groupthink engendered. The aura of leadership mystique also accounted for the sneering reaction to suggestions from volunteers for military improvements, which led to a reluctance to mention such things. Many republicans sensed the prudence of keeping their mouths shut about issues that troubled them. The fact these fears were not voiced led to a spiral of silence. People who shared similar apprehensions heard no one else speak of them and began to presume they were alone in their beliefs and probably wrong. It produced an organisational culture in which "Yes Men" flourished.

I noticed that many volunteers never offered an opinion until they were sure which way the IRA leadership was leaning on a particular issue. They would then weigh in fully behind them. They would vote with the majority at every meeting regardless of the topic. Too many played it safe, politically and militarily. I didn't believe we'd ever beat the British by playing it safe.

I had a long and exasperating discussion in Portlaoise Prison with a senior republican who had a reputation for being the quintessential big man's man. He would follow the leadership line regardless of which direction the leadership was going. He had shown courage on military operations, so I respected him for that but felt frustrated that his loyalty lay exclusively with the messenger and not the message. He would not accept for a moment that anything needed to be improved in the IRA.

"We're not a conventional army," he would say, "that type of training wouldn't suit us. Don't you think if anything could be done to improve things, then our leadership would have done it? You're impressed by your time in the Marines, I understand that. But bear in mind we have our own highly trained people in place. Just because you haven't met them, don't think they're not there. It may surprise you to learn you don't know everything, John."

I found it difficult to maintain my composure. Time and time again, I was told about these military wizards within the movement. Yet, I had never met one or spoken to anyone who had. I wondered who these prodigies were and why they were keeping their genius to themselves. I had recently read a book about Britain's Special Air Service, which described the difficulties its founder, Lieutenant Colonel David Stirling, had in getting the special operations concept accepted by a British Army mired in convention and tradition. Stirling wrote that he'd had to contend with "layer upon layer of fossilised shit." Speaking to this obstinate leadership loyalist, I could understand how Stirling felt.

Jim Lynagh's thinking was never fossilised. He was keen to improve military training and effectiveness while maintaining a sound political and ideological basis for struggle. Jim did his own thinking. Nobody handed him his opinions on a plate. He was a soldier but no militarist. Politically he was to the fore in discussions, debate and education in prison.

Jim played a significant role in inspiring my interest in political science and philosophy. I began to read as much as I could about history and political and economic theories. I read Karl Marx and Adam Smith, not just summaries but their entire volumes. I studied Friedrich Hayek, Che Guevara, Vladimir Lenin and Milton Friedman. I read Régis Debray and Thomas Jefferson along with Antonio Gramsci and Thomas Paine. I studied the works of philosophers such as Socrates, Plato, Schopenhauer, Voltaire, Hume, Hobbs, Locke, Spinoza, Kierkegaard, Mill and others. I read widely among theorists and philosophers who often took opposing positions, so as not to confirm any overt or subconscious bias on my part but to obtain as eclectic and rounded a view as possible.

I was captivated by the Enlightenment, that inspirational beacon of intellectual radiance that shone its light upon the murky recesses of a medieval mindset that fostered feudalism and monarchy and had entrenched superstition. Discarding the religious indoctrination of my youth, I became a firm believer in Voltaire's maxim that the first priest was the first rogue who met the first fool.

I admired the Protestant reformation, which broke the institutional hold of the Roman Catholic paradigm of hierarchy and blind obedience that, for centuries, had nurtured the dark ages. Without the Protestant reformation, ideas such as the right to an individual conscience could not have gained ground. Without that idea, concepts such as liberty, equality, democracy and republicanism would never have flourished. Irish Presbyterians formed the backbone of the American Revolution and the United Irishmen. Irish Anglicans produced Wolfe Tone, Robert Emmett, Thomas Davis and countless other patriots. Protestantism in Ireland had frequently been an inclusive tradition that strove to unite our citizens, unlike unionism, an exclusive philosophy that thrives on division. The United Irishmen were founded in 1791 to oppose sectarianism. The Orange Order was formed in 1795 to oppose the United Irishmen.

Playing one section of the Irish people off the other remains a key British tactic as relevant today as it was in 1791 when Lord Westmorland declared: "The present frame of Irish government . . . is particularly well calculated for our purpose. That frame is a Protestant garrison . . . in possession of the land, magistracy and power of the country; holding that property under the tenure of British power and supremacy, and ready at every instant to crush the rising of the conquered."

I constantly studied in my cell because, politically and militarily, I wanted to be the best I could be so that, upon my release, I could rejoin the Irish freedom struggle in the certain knowledge that all it takes is all you've got.

Jim Lynagh was released from Portlaoise Prison in April 1986. The night before, we held a party for him. Cream cakes and minerals were bought from the prison shop and we had a sing-song. I'll never forget the last time I laid eyes on him. I shook his hand on what we called "the Three's," the prison's third landing (there were four levels or "landings" in Portlaoise). I wished him well and the best of luck. He told me to get the hell out of there and meet up with him on the outside. I promised I'd do my best. As I watched his blond head disappear down the stairs to the landing below, I wondered would I ever see him again.

I knew the enemy considered Jim a dangerous adversary. In a conventional army, he would have made an outstanding Special Forces officer. Brave and intelligent, he couldn't be frightened and he couldn't be bought off—a bad combination that didn't augur well for his longevity. Within a week of his release, he was attending the funeral of his comrade and fellow Monaghan Volunteer Seamus McElwain, who had been killed in a British Army ambush in County Fermanagh. Sadly, a year later, Jim Lynagh himself would be dead, killed in action along with seven East Tyrone Volunteers at Loughgall in County Armagh.

About three years into my sentence, Sharon and I finally got open visits. The prison officer was still in the visiting box with us, but at least we could have a quick hug and a kiss hello and goodbye. Sharon visited me regularly for six years, although, because of my time in America, it was closer to seven years since we had last been together. I would get a visit from her every three weeks lasting around ninety minutes. We wrote almost daily. No phone calls were permitted back then.

We called it a day around 1990. It was too much strain on both of us. At least I didn't get a "Dear John." She told me to my face on a visit that it was time to move on. I reluctantly had to agree. Besides, I knew I would rejoin the IRA when I got out in 1994 and could give her no guarantee on anything. She cried inconsolably as she left the visiting box for the final time. As I walked across the prison yard on my way back to the cell, I felt as though my breaking heart had been placed in a vice that was cruelly squeezing the last drops of happiness and hope from my life. We would never see each other again.

I never thought I could love anyone else, but that's a jail thing.

Entering prison is like going into hibernation, not precisely leaving the world but the world leaving you. It's sobering how quickly one becomes erased from relevance by all but close family and friends when removed from circulation, how soon out of sight becomes out of mind, like being dead but alive to watch.

Feelings and fashions move on, but prisoners had few frames of reference to observe them. You couldn't meet women, so it was impossible to explore new feelings or forget the old ones. Except for visitors, the only outside people one saw were prison officers who wore the same uniforms and haircuts, so changing styles were merely a rumour.

I was told the story of the Belfast lad who came into Portlaoise Prison in 1974. For some reason or other, he never had a visit. Upon his release in 1984, he was handed the musty street clothing from his property that he'd worn in a far fresher state the night he came in. As he walked away from the main gate to catch a bus to Dublin, he wondered why so many people were staring at him. "Surely," he thought, "a released prisoner can't be that exotic a specimen in this town." It was only later he realised that with his shoulder-length hair, tank top, parallel trousers and platform shoes, he looked like a Bay City Roller who hadn't received the memo that that ship had sailed.

The worst prison experience was strip searching. Prison officers would come into the cell to strip a prisoner's clothes off and attempt to bend him over to look up his backside. We bitterly resented and fiercely resisted these state-sponsored sexual assaults. In all the years of strip searching, not a single item, proscribed or otherwise, was found up a republican's anal passage. Strip searching was a deliberate ploy to help break and humiliate the republican movement by attacking its most vulnerable component—its unarmed and defenceless prisoners.

The efficacy of strip searching and the casual cruelty of closed visits on republican prisoners and their families was demonstrated by our escape attempt in November 1985. Despite these security measures, we appeared on the prison landings one Sunday morning with fake prison officer uniforms, pistols, ammunition and explosives, not to mention keys for most of the gates in Portlaoise Prison. I cannot say how we obtained these items except to confirm we didn't pull them out of our arses.

Prisoners would come and go. Good friends would be released and lads you hadn't seen in years would appear on one charge or another. One republican who came in on an arms charge reminded me of an incident in South Armagh that had taken place some years previously. I had gone to the Crossmaglen area for a meeting and, while there, was asked if I wanted to go on an operation. It was unusual for them to invite anyone from outside their area, so I jumped at the chance. I was handed a balaclava and placed in the passenger seat of a car. The driver was a senior IRA commander. He told me I would be dropped off in a field while he went and collected the weapons. I didn't ask questions. I trusted him and obeyed his instructions.

Speeding through a warren of minor roads, we passed several men who signalled us as we drove by. I was told they were lookouts. The border meanders haphazardly in this area and I had no way of knowing whether we were in the South or the North. The car pulled up beside a farm gate. The driver told me to go into the field and wait until he returned. I did so. He took off over a rise in the road and disappeared.

Moments later, a British Army Wessex helicopter banked so low over my head I could see the pilot's face. I now knew

I was in the North. I was sitting in a field in broad daylight and realised he must have spotted me. Removing the balaclava from my pocket, I hid it in a whin bush and jumped over the gate onto the road. I figured my best chance was to walk in the direction we had come from, which should take me back across the border. If stopped by Crown Forces, I would lay the American accent on thick and say I had gone for a stroll while visiting relatives in the South, that I didn't know I had wandered into "Northern Ireland" and had gone into the field for a piss. It was a long shot, but I couldn't sit there like a muppet and be arrested with a balaclava in my possession.

As I walked a few paces down the road, I saw a figure crawl out of a hedge on his hands and knees about fifty metres away. I presumed it was one of the lookouts who had taken cover when the chopper passed overhead. I ran a few steps towards him and waved a greeting. When he stood upright, I saw that he was a British soldier carrying an SLR rifle. I stopped dead in my tracks. The soldier looked at me in bewilderment. Locals in South Armagh didn't normally run towards the Brits waving and smiling.

We froze and stared at each other, having what I can only describe as a massive what-the-fuck moment. Before I had a chance to think, the IRA commander's car sped back over the hill. He had seen the chopper and returned for me, despite being badly wanted by the Brits. I'll never forget his courage and loyalty. I dove into the car. We drove off while I waited for our vehicle to be riddled with rifle fire, but we escaped without incident.

I got some slagging for that. Twenty years later, I'd still meet men who would tease me about the day I rolled out the welcome wagon for the British Army in South Armagh.

Private John Crawley in dress blues taken at Marine boot camp, San Diego, California, August 1975.

Lance Corporal John Crawley with 3rd Recon in Okinawa, Japan, 1976.

With 3rd Recon in Okinawa. Note the camouflaged jeep to my right with its mounted M60 machine gun.

The sign for the 3rd Reconnaissance Battalion at Okinawa, Japan.

The *Valhalla*, pictured after its seizure on 16 October 1984 on Boston's Northern Avenue waterfront. The US Customs Service seized the trawler at Pier 7 in the Boston Harbor.
Photo by George Rizer/The Boston Globe via Getty Images.

The *Marita Ann*. *Photo courtesy of RTÉ Stills Library.*

A view of confiscated IRA weapons seized during the "Marita Ann" arms haul. *Photo courtesy of RTÉ Stills Library.*

Seized weapons from the *Valhalla-Marita Ann* gun running operation on display at the federal building at North Station in Boston during a joint press conference held by several federal law enforcement agencies on 30 June 1987. Our shipment contained no hand grenades. The bundle of grenades in the picture have been planted there. I can't begin to imagine why—as if being caught with 7 tons of arms wasn't enough! Claims that the haul was worth $1.2 million were grossly exaggerated by at least 5 times. The money was donated by Americans. In fact, the whole operation cost the IRA only the £9,000 Irish pounds they originally gave me to set up the network. The million dollar blow to the IRA hyped up by security forces on both sides of the Atlantic was complete nonsense. *Photo courtesy of Getty Images.*

In Portlaoise Prison visiting box
around 1992. I'm wearing a brown leather jacket
given to me by Whitey Bulger.

Volunteer Jim Lynagh.
A friend and colleague
both inside and outside of
Portlaoise Prison. Killed
in action with 7 other
IRA volunteers while
on attachment to the
East Tyrone Brigade at
Loughgall, Co. Armagh,
8 May 1987. I believe Jim
had the qualities and the
calibre to become an IRA
leader of inspirational
significance had he lived.

Surveillance images taken of me and Eoin Morrow
by British intelligence in London, 1997.

Mug shot of me, London, 1997. *Photo courtesy of Alamy.*

An article from *The Sun* newspaper of 3 July 1997.

John Crawley and Donal Gannon at IRA
Parade commemorating 1916 Rising at Easter 1998
in Portlaoise Prison yard. We were recently
repatriated from England.

Gerry Adams (l) and Martin McGuinness in May, 1987 at the funeral for Patrick Kelly, one of eight IRA members killed in an attack on the Royal Ulster Constabulary base in Loughgall, County Armagh. *Photo courtesy of Alamy.*

Whitey Bulger (r) with Bulger's long-term girlfriend Teresa Stanley, and Patrick Nee.
Photo courtesy of Patrick Nee.

II
POLITICAL CONTEXT

MANY PEOPLE HAD been surprised by my arrest, not least my parents. It was impossible to explain how I had ended up as a republican prisoner, so I didn't try. I wasn't seeking to gain what they perceived as notoriety. If I'd had my way, I would have quietly accomplished my mission and never seen the inside of a prison cell. No one outside of a small circle of volunteers should ever have known I was a member of the IRA. An informer put an end to that aspiration.

A republican prisoner from Cork said he was talking to friends on a visit. They told him that many of the Irish naval personnel involved in our arrest on the *Marita Ann* were proudly boasting in local pubs that, "I was on that mission!" On the other hand, several sailors whispered that they were not told of the operation until they were well at sea and, had they known, they would have tipped us off.

We frequently received information, help and intelligence from the gardaí and members of the Irish Defence Forces. Despite this, IRA volunteers were sometimes arrested because the information wasn't passed on or the receiver didn't know who to approach with it.

After years of observation, I concluded that approximately

10 percent of Dublin's security forces were unreconstructed Free State bastards—committed partitionists who looked upon British troops in Ireland with bovine docility and saw Irishmen resisting them as their only enemy. They were indoctrinated with the view that the Anglo-Irish Treaty, which was forced upon the Irish people, was the will of the Irish people. They were programmed to treat any effort to reestablish the all-Ireland Republic as "subversive." Their ilk would sanctimoniously refer to the twenty-six-county state as "our Republic" or "our democracy," despite the parameters of the state being determined exclusively by a Tory-dominated cabinet committee that consulted nobody in Ireland except unionists. They ignored the fact that the "democratic mandate" for the Anglo-Irish Treaty was profoundly compromised by Britain's threat of "immediate and terrible war" if it was rejected, not to mention the inherent dishonesty in claiming a national mandate from an exclusively twenty-six-county electorate. It's a curious form of patriotism to claim you love Ireland so much you'd prefer to see two of them.

Roughly 80 percent of Dublin's security forces simply went with the flow. They would hate whomever they were paid to hate. I know senior IRA leaders who remonstrated with Garda Special Branch detectives about beatings and ill-treatment of republican prisoners and were told that if republicans ever came to power, they would do the same for us. About 10 percent were strongly sympathetic to the aims and objectives of Irish republicanism, so, on the whole, Dublin's security apparatus reflected the opinions of the population from which it sprang. The good guys, the bad guys and a lot of undecided guys.

The Irish, as a race, tend to be afraid of the police. They don't want to get in trouble or be seen to be in the wrong company. Yet, I found that people from all walks of life liked to be able to claim they helped the struggle, or volunteers engaged in the struggle, in some small way, even if only as a one-off event.

The British and the partitionist propagandists who shaped the dominant ideology of the southern state boasted that the IRA had no support from the people. There was truth in that. For one thing, the IRA didn't contest elections. However, in few cases was that a position informed by morality. Over-whelmingly, it was motivated by the sheer utility of saving one's skin or not jeopardising one's employment. On the other hand, neither was there active opposition from the Irish people—if that had been the case, the IRA could not have lasted six months.

A historically crafted ambiguity was subliminally negoti-ated by all sides, especially in border areas. As long as the IRA didn't make stupid mistakes and kill or wound innocent civilians, an acceptable level of passive support would allow the guerrillas to function. Few in the nationalist community, North or South, lost much sleep over British soldiers killed on Irish soil. This was something the Brits never quite grasped.

I heard from several high-ranking IRA commanders that they occasionally received messages from intermediaries acting on behalf of members of the RUC and the UDR who wished to inform the Provos that they had resigned from the police or army and sought an assurance they were no longer under threat.

Despite cherished propaganda that the IRA was attack-ing members of these organisations for sectarian reasons, the locally recruited soldiers and police officers were themselves aware they were being targeted for their British war service and not their religion. While the vast majority of these combatants were indeed Protestant, there were deep historical reasons for that. Revealingly, despite the sectarian motives attributed by our enemies to the republican movement, none of the supplicants who claimed they were no longer members of the Crown Forces claimed they were no longer Protestant.

A dubious advantage of sitting in prison was being able to read the newspapers and listen to all the broadcast news that one wouldn't have had time to digest on the outside. The incessant counter-republican propaganda from the South's partitionist media would fry your brain, especially from the Irish Independent group of newspapers and the heavily censored state-controlled broadcaster Raidió Teilifís Éireann (RTÉ), which republicans called Raidió Teilifís England. The Six Counties was always referred to by its British designation of Northern Ireland. Crown Forces were security forces. IRA volunteers were terrorists. IRA officers were godfathers. ASUs were gangs. The British Army and RUC shot people, but the IRA murdered them.

Of course, the IRA carried out operations from time to time that shamed and embarrassed us all. Innocent civilians would unintentionally be killed. As inexcusable as that is, it was never deliberate. There was never an intention to inflict casualties on anyone but British military and police forces and their collaborators.

The British government, on the other hand, secretly sanctioned a deliberate policy of killing innocent civilians. Over three days in August 1971, the 1st Battalion of the Parachute Regiment knowingly and methodically shot down eleven innocent civilians, including a mother of eight and a Catholic priest. In January 1972, the same battalion murdered fourteen peaceful protesters in Derry in what became known as Bloody Sunday.

The strategy was aimed at terrorising the nationalist population into submission. Senior British Army officers momentarily forgot they were no longer in Aden, Kenya or Malaya. The public nature of the killings in a Western European country backfired spectacularly, bringing odium upon London from around the world. Protestors in Dublin burned down the British embassy.

British military intelligence then turned to unionist paramilitaries as proxy killers for the UK government. From that point on, they would arm and direct loyalist death squads to do their dirty work for them. When the British Army's FRU recruited loyalist agents, it was primarily to form them into "pseudo-gangs" to attack nationalist and republican targets. Deniability is a major consideration in black operations. The British became firm believers in Sun Tzu's dictum, "Always kill with a borrowed knife."

The Czechoslovakian Vz58 assault rifle had been imported in large numbers from South Africa by British intelligence in 1987 for use by loyalists. It fires the same ammunition as the AK-47. Loyalist paramilitaries received RPG-7s, RGD-5 Soviet hand grenades and Browning pistols in the same shipment. Warsaw Pact weapons were chosen to enhance deniability for the British state.

The FRU and RUC Special Branch supplied loyalist death squads with photomontages and other intelligence documents to assist in these killings. They further facilitated them by ensuring there were no roadblocks or security checks in the vicinity of their escape routes. Some killings were targeted and specific, while others were quite random to instil terror in the nationalist community, who, it was hoped, would turn against the IRA and demand they end their campaign.

Senior British Army officers involved in Bloody Sunday and other atrocities were subsequently awarded medals and knighthoods by their government. It is inconceivable that the IRA Army Council would have rewarded a volunteer involved in killing civilians. Yet, according to London and Dublin, *we* were the terrorists.

But why does Britain continue to interfere in our internal affairs and exploit our differences and divisions? First and foremost is the strategic imperative of maintaining the political and territorial integrity of the United Kingdom. How could Britain reassure citizens and subjects in places as diverse as Gibraltar or the Falkland Islands if it withdrew from a country on its doorstep and was perceived to abandon Ulster unionists? Furthermore, prestige is a significant factor in international relations. It is as relevant today as when Unionist leader Sir Edward Carson made the point in 1921:

> If you tell your Empire in India, in Egypt, and all over the world that you have not got the men, the money, the pluck, the inclination and the backing to restore order in a country within twenty miles of your own shore, you may as well begin to abandon the attempt to make British rule prevail throughout the empire at all.

There are also important geographical and strategic factors. Ireland will always be Britain's back door. Northern Ireland is part of NATO while Southern Ireland is not. The North affords rapid access to areas of the North Atlantic vital to British defence interests, particularly the GIUK gap, a naval choke point between Greenland, Iceland and the United Kingdom. Russian ships and submarines must navigate this gap to reach the North Atlantic.

A crucial consideration is that Britain's strategic nuclear deterrent, consisting of Trident ballistic missiles on Vanguard-class submarines, is based at Faslane in Scotland. They have to pass through the narrow North Channel between Scotland and Northern Ireland when leaving or returning to base. Under no circumstances would a government independent of the United Kingdom be allowed unfettered control of that channel's western flank if it could be avoided. Furthermore, in the event of Scotland voting for independence, the British may require ports in Derry or Belfast Lough to dock their nuclear fleet. Jeffrey Donaldson, leader of the Democratic Unionist Party, has already offered Northern Irish ports to base Britain's nuclear missiles. It would take a peace process directed by Britain to end with Ireland becoming a nuclear target.

While in prison, I completed an Open University degree in political science. I was a firm believer in republicans becoming involved in politics throughout Ireland. I believed building political strength was the key to making the case for the Republic. I don't mean simply electoral strength, which is fickle and can disappear like snow off a rope. I mean the real political strength that comes when the vast majority of the Irish people demand the Republic and are determined to support and defend the constitutional model it represents.

The armed struggle could not remain a spectator sport with a handful of volunteers taking all the risks and our support base cheering us from the sidelines while voting for non-republicans, as had happened in the early 1970s when republicans who supported the IRA had no option but to vote for the SDLP. Even if we had the strength to win militarily, which we never would, it would be pointless if we were to inherit a sullen or even hostile population.

We were fighting a war in which the battle of narratives was centre stage: the republican narrative that we were resisting the British occupation to restore the national Republic proclaimed in 1916; the British narrative that they were only here to prevent the Irish from killing each other; the Irish government's narrative that the notion Ireland hasn't achieved complete independence is a subversive delusion. Seizing the narrative is why the enemy places such emphasis on cultivating journalists and academics.

From the mid-nineteenth century to the present-day, Britain has created various "counter-republics" to prevent the concept of an Irish Republic from gaining traction. Over the years, it has appeared in various guises—Home Rule, the Free State and now the "New Agreed Ireland" or the "Shared Island" proposed by the Good Friday Agreement. The shared history narrative implies the existence of two legitimate and equal sources of constitutional sovereignty between the Irish people and the British Crown, a muddled belief that the conquest and colonisation of Ireland shares reciprocal legitimacy with its struggle for independence.

A respect for diversity is duplicitously conflated with an embrace of constitutional division. Melding a progressive political outlook with national sabotage is a formula Britain relentlessly pursues via a warren of influencers in Ireland. Its purpose is to cloak continuing British interference in our country beneath a mantle of moral authority and the veneer of democratic legitimacy. All counter-republics in the Irish context have aspects in common, but ambiguous citizenship and compromised sovereignty are key components.

Although most Englishmen are quite ignorant about Irish history and politics, there is a core group of British diplomats and intelligence officers who understand the Irish and Irish political culture very well. Ireland is not the cesspit of terrorism and rebellion many Englishmen presume. While less than 2,000 Irishmen turned out for the Easter Rising, more than 200,000 others fought for the British in the Great War. Another 9,000 Irishmen served in the RIC (80 percent of them Catholic).

During the 1916 Rising in County Galway, Irish National Volunteers loyal to Irish Parliamentary Party leader John Redmond and pledged to secure Home Rule mobilised to aid British forces. They helped direct Royal Naval gunfire from a warship on Galway Bay against suspected rebel concentrations around Athenry. They also carried out joint patrols with the British Army and RIC. From a British point of view, despite the prejudice of many of their countrymen, there was always far more to work with in Ireland that was good for Britain than was bad. The vast majority of Irish people never resisted the British occupation of Ireland but sought to prosper within it.

Perhaps the most significant factor in Britain's favour is that most Irish people are nationalists or separatists, not republicans. They have never demanded freedom in the sense that a republican understands it. They have never taken a non-negotiable position that Irish constitutional sovereignty be vested exclusively within an all-Ireland parliament. Genuine republicanism is rare in Ireland. Many associate it with militant nationalism or a willingness to engage in armed struggle, not as the political philosophy of liberty.

I knew that people would never vote for republicans in large numbers while we were engaged in armed struggle, because war involves hardship and sacrifice. People won't vote for hardship and sacrifice. The enemy knows this and plays on it relentlessly. However, I didn't volunteer for IRA active service with an eye to mobilising an electoral base so that I could one day enjoy a political career. I didn't risk my life and sacrifice my liberty to put Sinn Féin into any office at any price but to play my part in helping to end British rule and reinstate the Republic. Like most volunteers, I wanted to free Ireland, not run it. Political struggle is essential to convincing the Irish people of the imperative of achieving complete independence. Armed struggle was required to convince the British of it.

Of course, the unionist minority in Ireland would never vote for the Republic. No planter political culture nurtured in any colonial system on earth has voluntarily relinquished its contrived hegemony. Republican concepts of equality and fraternity are daggers at the heart of the sectarian supremacy upon which unionists base their core beliefs.

Unionists claim that when republicans say we were fighting to end the British presence, it was really about getting rid of them, that *they* are the British presence in Ireland. Irish unionists are pro-British, but republicans do not accept they are the British presence. Few unionists were born in Britain, they do not live in Britain and many have never visited Britain. If qualifying for British citizenship while residing in Ireland defines the British presence, then by that logic, the entire Irish population prior to the Free State leaving the Commonwealth in 1949 could be said to have been the British presence.

Furthermore, many unionists consider their British identity to be strictly conditional. The Orange Order was set up in

1795 to support "the King and his heirs so long as he or they support the Protestant Ascendancy."

The term "British" is a political construct, not an ethnic one. When Irish republicans speak about removing the British presence, we mean the United Kingdom's claim to sovereignty in Ireland and the military and civil apparatus that makes that possible. Republicans believe Ireland belongs to all who live in it. None of it belongs to Britain.

In 1993 we first heard of the Hume-Adams dialogue. These were discussions between Gerry Adams, the President of Sinn Féin, and John Hume, the leader of the SDLP. The republican prisoners in Portlaoise had no idea what the talks were about beyond a vague notion they were an attempt to explore whether a pan-nationalist front consisting of Sinn Féin, the SDLP and the Irish government could be forged to convince the British government to withdraw from Ireland. This would end the necessity for armed struggle. I was asked my opinion on the talks by a senior republican. I replied, "As long as Hume comes away with Gerry's analysis and Gerry doesn't come away with Hume's."

I was being facetious. I knew that Adams coming away with Hume's perspective could never happen. Adams was the public face and acknowledged leader of Irish republicanism. His job was to make a case for the thirty-two-county Irish Republic and to defend it from all enemies, foreign and domestic. I had no reason to doubt he would do so.

Of the many leadership traits, I believe trust is the most important. It cuts to the heart of everything. General Dwight D. Eisenhower said, "The supreme quality of leadership is integrity. Without it, no real success is possible . . ." Trust in the leadership meant more than trusting them to keep secrets.

It meant trusting them to be militarily and politically competent, trusting them to have no personal agenda that could cloud their judgement, trusting they prioritised winning the struggle over surviving the struggle. And most important of all, it meant believing that they could be trusted to preserve and defend republican principles—principles that would never be bartered, distilled or diluted by British lures to entice and ensnare us into their system. We trusted Gerry Adams and Sinn Féin's chief negotiator, Martin McGuinness, to have the courage and integrity to remember who we were and what we represented.

John Hume was the leader of loyal nationalism in the Six Counties. He recognised the constitutional legitimacy of Northern Ireland and the lawful authority of Her Majesty's Constabulary in the RUC. He never clarified at what point in history Britain gained democratic title in Ireland, when, precisely, the Brits achieved political and legal legitimacy over whatever section of the Irish people they could control, their laws elevated to a moral imperative and the British soldiers and constables enforcing those laws invested with a sole monopoly on the lawful use of force.

Hume paid lip service to Irish unity, but his raison d'être was to achieve reforms he believed would end the Troubles by allowing nationalists to become stakeholders within a devolved British administration. Irish republicans believed Hume's political analysis was based on a number of flawed assumptions and strategic miscalculations.

The first of these miscalculations was that the British government was neutral between nationalism and unionism. Related to this was Hume's theory that the British had no strategic interest in remaining in Ireland, as if London considered the maintenance of the political and territorial integrity of the United Kingdom to be little more than a notional preference.

Hume knew the Provisional leadership needed a declaration along these lines to sell the notion to their grass roots that the Brits had a change of heart and were looking for a way out. Britain's Secretary of State for Northern Ireland Peter Brooke duly obliged in November 1990 with a slippery statement declaring that the British government has "no selfish strategic or economic interest in remaining in Northern Ireland." The Brits were simply stating their strategic interests there weren't selfish.

In the British and original version of the statement, there is no comma after the word "selfish." In many Irish versions the comma is added, changing the tone and context. Nationalists leapt on this as a declaration of intent by Britain to reconsider its position in Ireland. With the issuing of this statement, John Hume believed he had won the argument. The Provos believed they had won the war.

Hume's second miscalculation was that the British government had no problem in principle with a united Ireland. This, at least, was partly true. England ran a united Ireland for centuries—one that brought subjugation, plantation and starvation; a polity that delivered all-Ireland institutions such as the workhouses and all-Ireland police services such as the RIC and the Black and Tans. A united Ireland could still theoretically work for the British government provided Ireland was reunited on its terms.

The third flawed assumption was that Irish unionists are the British presence in Ireland, a point already covered.

Fourth was the assumption that we must embrace the British tradition in Ireland as an integral part of our national fabric. A tradition is an idea, an attitude or a trait that holds a unique or symbolic significance in the evolution of one's national character. Britishness in Ireland did not evolve as a national tradition. It was imposed by a foreign country in an act of conquest and colonisation. The republican hope that divisions Britain fostered between Planter and Gael could be replaced by a national civic identity is symbolised in the green, white and orange of the Irish tricolour.

Contrary to what John Hume and others tried to contend, the tricolour does not represent an "agreed Ireland" where the two traditions agree to disagree in peace and harmony about the constitutional source of Irish sovereignty and the legitimacy and extent of British influence in constraining Irish democracy. The republican prisoners in Portlaoise Prison remained confident in our struggle, our analysis and our certainty that Gerry Adams would run rings around John Hume.

Hume's ideas, none of which were original, were vigorously promoted by London and Dublin because they let both governments off the hook. He let Britain off the hook because he agreed, or was perceived to agree, with London's analysis of the nature of the conflict. He pushed the line that Ireland contained two traditions that would continue to be policed apart until they came together and agreed to an internal settlement on British terms. The problem with Ireland is the Irish—it is the Irish who are divided not the British who divide them. Were it not for this intrinsic fault in the Irish political character, Britain would not stand in the way of eventual unity.

Hume ignored the fact that structural and institutional divisions designed to keep Ireland politically weak and vulnerable to British manipulation have been an English strategy since the Tudor conquest. As far back as the 1580s, Queen Elizabeth I's counsellors were advising her on the Irish, writing:

> Should we exert ourselves in reducing Ireland to order and civility, it might soon acquire power, consequence and riches. The inhabitants will be thus alienated from England; they will cast themselves into the arms of some foreign power, or erect themselves into an independent state. Let us rather connive at their disorder, for a weak and disordered people can never attempt to detach themselves from the Crown of England.

John Hume sought what the British government had been seeking since the First Home Rule Bill in 1886: to reconcile Irish nationalism with British sovereignty.

Dublin strongly supported Hume because they hoped to pacify the North and stabilise the status quo. Despite assurances that the Anglo-Irish Treaty would be used as a stepping stone to achieve complete freedom, Dublin's political elite viewed partition as an essential mechanism of its independence. As one of the highest-paid political classes in Europe, it didn't want a million and a half Irish citizens from the Six Counties upsetting its cosy cartel or thrusting their snouts into the Southern trough. Hume's call to embrace division for the sake of peace, as opposed to ending division for the sake of peace, was music to Dublin's ears—a far cry from Abraham Lincoln's republican resolve that a house divided against itself cannot stand.

The Downing Street Declaration, agreed between British Prime Minister John Major and Irish Taoiseach Albert

Reynolds in December 1993, referenced the Unionist veto eight times in its twelve points. Incredibly, it flagged up the destabilising effect not of partition but the Irish government's claim to all of Ireland in Articles 2 and 3 of its Constitution. Nowhere in the Downing Street Declaration was the Irish nationalist or republican community mentioned by name. Instead of a pan-nationalist front to end the Union, we had a pan-London-Dublin front to end republicanism.

In March 1994, I was given a day's parole to attend a meeting at University College Dublin (UCD) to enquire about doing a master's degree in political philosophy upon my release, which was due the following September. While there, I met visiting professors from America and Canada. When they asked me for my opinion on the upcoming IRA ceasefire announcement, I smugly replied they must be mistaken. The IRA was repeatedly on record as vowing there would never be a ceasefire until the British government made a declaration of intent to withdraw from Ireland. The academics told me the political department of UCD was doing research for the Irish government pursuant to talks that would follow the ceasefire. Reporting this conversation to my fellow prisoners in Portlaoise, we laughed at the gullibility of the professors. We would soon discover who were the gullible ones.

I was released from Portlaoise Prison on Saturday, 10 September 1994, only days after the IRA ceasefire on 31 August. My release had nothing to do with the truce. I served every day of my sentence.

12
SWEET FREEDOM

THE OC REPUBLICAN prisoners in Portlaoise Prison stood rigidly to attention at the northern end of the uppermost landing of "E-Wing," the prison block which housed all the IRA men imprisoned by the Dublin government. His adjutant, or second in command, stood beside him. The remaining volunteers waited patiently at the parade rest in front of their cells. Prison officers on each landing hung back quietly, some respectfully, others sullenly, waiting for the ritual to play itself out before they could scoot down the landings to lock the cell doors for the night and head off up the town for a pint.

"Parad!" The OC called out the preparatory command in Irish as each volunteer stiffened, waiting for the command of execution.

"Parad! Aire!" The order to come to attention resonated loudly throughout the stone corridors.

"Tomorrow morning, John Crawley leaves this place. On behalf of the unit, we'd all like to wish him the best of luck. Parad! Scuipigi!"

With the final order in Irish to fall out, a massive cheer shook the building. A sustained burst of applause from the prisoners echoed around the wing as four of my friends lifted me shoulder high and carried me to the deep sinks at the end of the landing where I was unceremoniously dunked while other comrades threw basins of water on me and each other.

After a brief burst of horseplay and banter, I walked slowly back to my cell in drenched clothing. I shook hands and accepted best wishes from as many of the men as I could reach in the few short minutes before lock-up. Stopping outside of my cell, I could hear heavy steel doors at the far end of the wing being slammed shut as a surge of blue uniforms swept up the landing. Turning for a last wave at my friends, I heard what I'd heard over 3,000 times over the past ten years and hoped I'd never hear again, a Free State screw locking me into a cell for the night.

Many lads continued to cheer, whistle and catcall out of the spyhole in the centre of their doors.

"Good luck, John!"

"*Tóg go bog é a chara!*"

"Keep yer nut down out there!"

"Keep 'er lit, John!

I stood with my ear to the door listening to the farewells. A few moments later and you could have heard a pin drop. Then another ritual played itself out. One of the Belfast lads placed a tape cassette flush against the spyhole of his door and played "Back Home Again"—not the John Denver original but the Dickie Rock version. He'd played it for every man leaving the prison for years past. I often wondered whether my turn would ever come. I listened with mixed emotions as the music echoed throughout the prison block. Having waited so long for this moment, I felt surprisingly ambivalent. I was elated at the thought of being released in the morning. Yet, I felt guilty leaving so many friends behind, some with families, serving long sentences—they may never hear this played for them.

I couldn't help but think of Sharon. Hearing this song during the first few years of my sentence gave me butterflies at the thought of what it would be like if it were only me getting out the following morning, meeting Sharon at the gate and picking up where we had left off. But that happy ending was no longer waiting for me.

Ten years after my first disorientating night in this prison cell, I awoke to the jangling of keys in a steel lock and the opening of a door. It took less than a heartbeat for the realisation to sink in that my legendary release date had arrived. The prison officer glanced at me but said nothing. He walked off, leaving the door open. I stared for a moment at the resulting gap. It was a novelty I had longed to behold. I leapt from the metal bunk, feeling surprisingly fresh and alert. I had anticipated remaining sleepless with excitement the night before my release but reading until dawn the previous evenings and increasing my exercise had tired me enough for me to slumber soundly. I was usually awake long before the cells were unlocked at 8:30 a.m. and was surprised I had remained oblivious until this early call at half-past seven.

Grabbing a towel and a bar of soap, I slipped into a tracksuit and a pair of flip-flops and slapped my way down the Four's landing to the showers. Passing the locked cells of fellow prisoners, my elation receded and I felt an intense pang of longing and regret—longing for the release of my comrades and regret at leaving behind so many friends. The IRA staff in the prison had an agreement with the authorities that a released prisoner would be off the landings before the rest of the cells were opened, so I knew I couldn't dawdle, not that I was inclined to. Taking what I hoped would be my last prison shower, I padded back to my cell, passing the hot plate at the top of the landing where the state had thoughtfully provided me with a bowl of cornflakes and bread for the toaster. I hadn't a notion of touching it. I was far too excited and looking forward to a proper breakfast on the outside.

I threw off the tracksuit and dressed in my street clothing. I gathered my last few belongings from the cell and placed them into a small plastic bag. The bulk of my possessions had been sent out a week previously. They were collected by a friend who took them to a house in Dublin where I could pick them up later. I had also given away a lot of my bits and pieces in the preceding days. I gave my radio cassette player to a lad who only had a cheap radio that couldn't play tapes. I also gave away some clothing, as well as my prized possession, a glass jar that had once contained strawberry jam. Glass jars had been confiscated and prohibited long before. Still, for some reason, my jar was never taken during the many cell searches. Two years prior to my release, an IRA prisoner from Dublin called Billy Shannon had asked if he could have the jar when I got out. It was invaluable for whipping cream at Christmas to make homemade trifles in the plastic prison-issue washing-up bowls. Cream purchased from the prisoner's funds would be poured into the jar and shaken until it thickened. When I handed the jar over, Billy was ecstatic. He thanked me half a dozen times. Finally, I burst out laughing.

"What's so funny?" asked Billy.

"Can you imagine anyone on the outside being so happy about an empty jar?"

Billy saw the absurdity and laughed too. "I suppose, but for fuck sake, I've waited years on it."

I tied on a pair of cheap, prison-issue runners. My shoes had been taken by prison officers two days before my release to be X-rayed and checked for any hidden "comms" or messages in the soles or heels. It was an attempt by the state to prevent messages and reports from being sent from the prisoners to the IRA but was, in effect, a useless procedure that made no impact on the ingenuity of republicans in maintaining contact with their comrades on the outside.

I took a last look around the cell to ensure I hadn't forgotten anything, then headed for the door. When I reached it, I turned and stood for a moment. I hoped I would never again see this place.

I presented myself at the Four's landing gate that led downstairs to the ground floor or "Base." A prison officer met me there and placed a pair of heavy Victorian-era handcuffs on me. The screw was a harmless creature from County Mayo who had never abused prisoners or given them cause for complaint.

"We can't have you escaping now," he grinned.

"Oh, I could still make a break for it," I countered, trying not to sound giddy.

As we descended the iron steps to the ground floor of the building, I looked down the foreboding corridors of stone and steel as we passed each landing. The Four's, the Three's, the Two's and the Base. They appeared as menacing leaving as they had arriving. Endless pain, heartache and desperation occupied those cells. So, too, inspiration, resolve and commitment. Volunteers had left them with relief to reenter civilian life, never to be heard of again. Others had gone to be killed on active service or reimprisoned in Ireland, England or on the continent. I had no doubt I would rejoin the resistance. I fleetingly wondered where my path would lead. But this was not the day to dwell on it.

The prison officer, with myself in tow, arrived at the final gate on the Base and we were shunted through. We reached a series of canal locks, which we passed through, before finally stepping outside E-wing to walk across to a further series of control points at the main gate. I looked back towards the top of the cell block, at the Irish soldiers who guarded the prison. For years I had listened to their footsteps as they paced the roof above me. A couple of soldiers gazed down at the prison officer and me crossing the yard to the main gate. They looked bored and unmotivated.

Upon reaching an administration room, I was released from the handcuffs. As the Mayo screw turned to walk away, he quipped, "You should thank us, young Crawley. Sure, we reared you." I grinned weakly but said nothing. My head was spinning with the thought and anticipation of my first steps to freedom.

I was handed the small amount of money remaining in my prison account. When money was sent to a prisoner by friends or family, it would go into his "account." If he ordered anything from the prison shop, it would be deducted from this account. The prisoner never handled real money. Anything left in his account upon release was given to him as cash. I hadn't seen any in years. The coins felt heavy in my pocket.

I was handed the watch from my "property." It had been taken off me the night I arrived. Prisoners weren't allowed to wear watches. I wound it and asked a prison officer for the correct time. It felt strange and foreign on my wrist. I kept looking at it every few seconds. I was then handed a padded Valentine's Day card that Sharon had sent my second year there. Padded cards were not allowed into Portlaoise Prison because hidden messages could be concealed within the padding. I hadn't been told about the card at the time. It had been sent straight to my property. I was surprised to see it. Opening it, I read the words from Sharon, which told me how much she loved me and how easy it was to wait for a man so worth waiting for. My mouth went dry. I folded the card and placed it in the small plastic bag I was carrying.

The last thing I was given was a prison travel chit that would provide me with a one-way train journey to Heuston Station in Dublin. Prisoners had a choice of bus or train. About 8:30 that morning I was led to the final gate, which was opened by a sleepy-looking prison officer who neither looked at me nor spoke. I stepped out onto the public footpath, free for the first time in ten years.

Nobody met me at the gate. I made sure of that. A number of my family and friends had wanted to come to greet me, but I had told them not to. I had been advised to do so by a republican prisoner who was in for the second time. He told me the first time he was released he was met by a gaggle of people who drove him off in a five-car convoy honking their horns and cheering. They meant well but kept asking him every two seconds, "How does it feel to be out?" After years alone in a cell, he couldn't cope with the crowd and the questions. "Walk out alone," he told me. "Savour every minute of it. Keep the moment for yourself. You'll have the rest of your life to tie in with people when you get home."

Sauntering up the Dublin road towards Portlaoise train station, I passed a small corner shop. I went in to buy *The Irish Times* and an ice cream cone. The shopkeeper would have known I was a released prisoner but betrayed no interest. He saw guys like me every other day. I fumbled with the money and paid the man. I continued to follow the signs to the train station. The ice cream was delicious. Simply having the freedom to buy one meant the world.

The day was sunny and warm, with tufts of clouds hanging soft and gentle above me. The streets were quiet, with few pedestrians. I couldn't help gawking at family pets loitering in some of the yards. I hadn't laid eyes on a dog or a cat in years. Glancing at my watch for the umpteenth time, I kept thinking about the lads I had left behind and what they would be doing at this moment.

Reaching the ticket window at the train station, I slid my travel chit through the aperture. The ticket master was an older, gruff-looking man in a blue uniform similar to what the screws wore. I smiled and half expected some comment or acknowledgement. "Nice to be out," or maybe, "Good luck on your journey home." Or perhaps a return smile. But the grumpy civil servant simply stamped the ticket and shoved it back with an ignorant scowl. I turned on my heels, realising that not everyone would share in my happiness this day. "Blueshirt bastard!" I surmised and put him out of my mind.

Crossing over a pedestrian bridge to the far side of the station to reach the platform for the Dublin train, I mingled with a small group of people waiting for the same. I was anonymous now. Nothing more to indicate I was a released prisoner. A sharp and perceptive observer may have discerned a slimmer and more athletic passenger than most, with eager and alert eyes. But no one noticed or cared.

A sparrow hawk alighted on the branch of a tree less than ten metres from the platform. I stared in amazement. It was a beautiful bird. I was surprised it came so close and sat so serenely without a flicker of alarm. Moments later, the noise of the approaching train caused it to fly off.

I boarded a packed carriage and stood near the exit door as there were no available seats. I thought the passengers looked pale and overweight. Coming from a prison full of young men who exercised daily and had no access to alcohol or unhealthy diets, it was little surprise I came to that conclusion. I was still on a high but had plenty of time to think and reflect on the hour-long journey into Dublin.

As the train sped towards the city, I looked forward to contacting IRA comrades I hadn't seen in years. I wanted to catch up on news and events and hear from the boys at the cutting edge of the struggle. I wondered if Sharon would remember this was my release date. Would she regret not waiting now that what once appeared so impossibly distant had finally arrived with as much hope and promise as the previous years had been full of sadness and despair? Probably not. I knew it was a selfish thought. I was going to rejoin the armed struggle with God knows what outcome. I would have done so even if Sharon had been waiting for me. This wasn't a life for relationships.

The train pulled into Heuston. I alighted, heading for the main concourse and exit. I looked forward to finding a place to eat my first breakfast in freedom. As I stood for a moment looking at the swarms of people dashing hither and thither, I felt a fleeting pang of anxiety. The hustle and bustle of the station almost overwhelmed me. Taking a few deep breaths, I grasped my small bag of belongings, shoved *The Irish Times* under my arm and melted into the crowd.

13
REACTIVATION

UPON MY RELEASE from prison, I immediately reported back to the IRA and volunteered for active service. I was advised to take a break for a while. I hadn't much choice as a ceasefire had been declared ten days earlier.

Despite this, I attended IRA meetings to reconnect with the republican movement and get a sense of what was going on with the "sos" (pronounced "suss"). "Sos cogaidh" means "truce" in the Irish language. There was a lot of confusion about political developments and many were asking if we were fooling the Brits or if the Brits were fooling us.

Credible alternatives to armed struggle must always be explored. A ceasefire, however, is a risky departure and should only be called from a position of strength. Otherwise, the enemy will use the opportunity to seize the initiative in future engagements, be they military or political.

There were hard lessons from the truce that followed the Tan War and the IRA ceasefire of 1975–6. I could only hope those lessons would be heeded. Volunteers get slack and let their guard down. Complacency can acquire a foothold. Excessive sacrifice, prolonged pressure and hunger for normality can, in time, lure guerrilla fighters towards the less dangerous and more lucrative paths of least resistance. Some, who proved brave in the past, want to believe there is a safe and easy road to achieve their objectives in the present. In time, the easy route may become an end in itself and though the road may eventually prove to be going in the wrong direction, they cannot find it within themselves to change course and find it easier instead to change goals. Others will eventually believe any lie that comes wrapped in a British pound note.

The British government has a remarkable capacity to channel Irish political trajectories in a particular direction, harness Irish leaderships to drive the strategy and make the Irish believe it was their own idea. James Connolly wrote, "Ruling by fooling is a great British art. With great Irish fools to practice on."

Few, including myself, initially doubted that we had the upper hand. The massive arsenal we had acquired from Libya lent enormous weight to that assumption. The leadership team responsible for obtaining those weapons and smuggling them into Ireland under the watchful eye of the British government did a remarkable job. With input from some very capable figures from South Armagh, the Quartermaster Department and other trusted volunteers, the IRA now had the logistical capacity to wage an enhanced war of national liberation with a genuine prospect of success. If a certain clique within the leadership secretly nourished a different agenda, it was not the fault of those volunteers who provided us with the means to fight on.

In addition, the IRA could produce an almost unlimited tonnage of improvised explosives, some of which had been delivered to the heart of London's business and financial district. The IRA was manufacturing heavy mortars and shoulder-launched armour-piercing projectiles. We didn't appear to be in a position of weakness. This perception gave the leadership team of Gerry Adams and Martin McGuinness enormous leeway in making some disconcerting constitutional contortions.

IRA leadership figures would frequently state the obvious that we could not militarily defeat the British Army. In my opinion, and that of many others, we didn't have to. We could militarily defeat the police. The key to IRA success in the South during the Tan War was neutralising the RIC. No police force could absorb the punishment we could inflict if our will matched our weaponry. Defeat British policing and we would defeat Ulsterisation, criminalisation and normalisation, thereby demolishing the holy trinity of the British counterinsurgency strategy in Ireland. If the Brits can't police us, they can't govern us.

After Jim Lynagh was killed in action, many reports claimed he operated a "Maoist" strategy to create liberated zones by demolishing RUC barracks in rural areas. I don't know where this narrative emanates from, but this was an IRA tactic that predated Chairman Mao. During the Tan War, the IRA attacked RIC barracks throughout Ireland and, by June 1920, 456 RIC barracks had been evacuated and forty were damaged or destroyed.

In the modern campaign, the South Armagh IRA demonstrated what could be done by a handful of courageous and highly motivated patriots unburdened by informers contaminating their ranks. They defeated British policing in their area and contained the British Army. Crown Forces in Crossmaglen hunkered down in a warren of bunkers and tunnels protected by tons of steel and reinforced concrete. A police constable could not stick his nose outside that barracks without a patrol of British soldiers to guard him, and those soldiers, in turn, needed more patrols and air assets to protect themselves.

The South Armagh IRA was ruthless in culling the movement of informers. One of their volunteers told me, "You know you're in trouble when you see the blue baling twine!"—a reference to the fact suspects were trussed in the cord used to bale hay. It was a prelude to being awarded an "OBE," a pun on England's "Order of the British Empire"—signifying "One Behind the Ear" to republicans.

Contrary to lurid media propaganda, the IRA did not torture suspected informers. It would have been completely counterproductive. The IRA needed to find out what the Brits actually knew and not what some tortured wreck would invent to stop the pain. Furthermore, no IRA volunteer would feel safe or confident in the organisation if they believed they could be arbitrarily arrested and tortured on some paranoid whim.

To prevent mishandling of suspected informants, they were not interrogated in their areas or by volunteers from their units. Were that the case, men might indeed be tempted to beat a prisoner they believed had betrayed them personally or had set up comrades for death.

Most suspects went through a tried and tested procedure. The South Armagh IRA was impersonal and thorough. An investigation could last hours or more than a month depending on the evidence. Some informants broke like a plate and admitted everything immediately. Others might hold out for days until the investigation gradually widened enough cracks in their alibi for the informer to fall through. Investigations could last weeks while the information provided by the suspect was dissected, checked and rechecked.

Executions of those found guilty of treason by an IRA court martial could only be carried out by order of the Army Council. The standard procedure was for a taped confession to be played to the army leadership of the volunteer admitting his activities on behalf of the enemy. Only then would the Council order the death sentence. While news of a hooded and trussed body being left on the border made national headlines, one never heard of the many suspected informers found not guilty and released. An IRA volunteer could only be executed if they admitted their guilt. Some guilty suspects managed to hold out without breaking and had to be released. They might be expelled from the IRA on suspicion of being an agent, but they couldn't be shot unless they owned up to it. Others, of course, were genuinely innocent and released with a profound apology not always graciously accepted.

The gravest threat was the deeply embedded British agent of influence. In the words of Sir John Cecil Masterman OBE, who chaired a British intelligence committee running double agents in the Second World War, "On balance it appears that the best agents for deception on a high level are long-distance agents, who have been carefully built up, and who have served a long apprenticeship before any major deception is attempted through them." Britain's intelligence services are firm believers in Vladimir Lenin's observation that, "The best way to control the opposition is to lead it ourselves."

There is a widely believed narrative that, since the late 1970s, the IRA operated a tight cell system in which members of one ASU would not know members of another. Yet, in 1982, information from the Derry IRA informer Raymond

Gilmour led to the arrests of around 100 republicans, of whom thirty-five were charged with "terrorist" offences. Belfast informer Christopher Black put thirty-eight men in the dock, of whom twenty-two were convicted. We would later learn that the chief of the IRA Security Department, Freddie Scappaticci, was himself a British agent codenamed "Stakeknife."

In reality, the "cell system" was effectively neutralised by tight hierarchal and centralised control from the top. Operations had to be cleared with Northern Command. The ostensible reason was to ensure acceptable political consequences for any military action and the need for coordination between adjacent units in case an ASU drove into an enemy cordon hunting down a separate IRA unit that had pulled off an operation they knew nothing about. Notifying Northern Command meant that people not directly involved in the action were in the know. The danger was that if the Brits infiltrated Northern Command, they would better be able to kill or capture IRA volunteers.

The South Armagh IRA also gave substantial input to the Engineering Department in its development of a wide range of improvised weapons. I became concerned when told by a member of the Army Council that before long all a volunteer would need to know would be how to push a button. He believed that was a good thing. Push a button? He was advocating deskilling the IRA precisely when we needed to be upskilling. He was happy to train killers, but we needed to train soldiers—or at least a core group of commandos with the military acumen and competence to do the heavy lifting, volunteers who would be trained tactically to strike strategically. I believed this was critical for our success, although there'd still be plenty of work for the button pushers.

The IRA could never consistently engage the British on military terms, but the right people in the right place at the right time would have far-reaching effects. Provided we preserved our security and the element of surprise, we could achieve relative superiority over British Crown Forces at carefully selected times and places.

An example of what could be done occurred at the Derryard British Army checkpoint near Roslea, County Fermanagh, in December 1989. An IRA unit hidden in the back of an armoured Bedford dump truck drove straight into the checkpoint and opened up with two belt-fed 7.62-millimetre FN MAG general-purpose machine guns, Kalashnikov assault rifles, hand grenades, RPG-7s and a flame thrower. Two British soldiers were killed and two wounded. Only the failure of a van bomb to explode after the IRA withdrew prevented a dozen more British soldiers from being killed. The raiding party consisted of volunteers from South Armagh, North Monaghan, Fermanagh and East Tyrone. One of them was former Crumlin Road Prison escapee Pete Ryan, Liam's cousin. Pete would be killed in action eighteen months later. A senior British Army officer commented, "They are murdering bastards but they are not cowards. This team actually pressed home a ground attack right into the heart of the compound. That takes guts when there are people firing back."

Notwithstanding the availability of hitherto unimaginable firepower used in the Derryard assault, no further commando raids took place. In fact, despite the acquisition of this unprecedented arsenal, British military and police casualties decreased every year between 1989 and the ceasefire in 1994.

My initial optimism about IRA capabilities began to wane as I spoke to more people. I met no one who said the procurement of high-grade military weapons was being matched by enhanced military training or any substantial reorganisation. I began to wonder if the IRA was being surreptitiously run into the ground.

In early 1995 I was introduced to Patrick O'Callaghan from Crossmaglen. Patrick was the operations officer for Northern Command. A dynamic and daring resistance fighter who habitually led from the front, he played a significant role in making South Armagh a formidable bastion of resistance to British rule. His brother Seán was a key contributor in the development of improvised mortars and explosives.

Although I was never on a military operation with Patrick, I heard enough from men who were in action with him to know he was an outstanding volunteer. He was dedicated, brave, calm, grounded and possessed that formidable physical and moral fortitude one sensed in the presence of volunteers like Jim Lynagh. Men like these personified Napoleon's observation that, "Courage cannot be counterfeited. It is one virtue that escapes hypocrisy."

Patrick asked me if I would agree to become the director of training for Northern Command. He told me he was basing that decision on reports from volunteers who knew me in prison and believed I was the right man for the job. However, I told him I didn't want a staff position. I wanted to operate with an ASU but said I would help anyone appointed to the job. He said he'd think about it and get back to me.

About two weeks later, I met Patrick again. He told me a member of the Army Council refused to endorse me for the post. He didn't reveal who had given me the thumbs down but said it wasn't personal; the IRA already had a director of training at General Headquarters and didn't want to replicate the position. I thought that a bit odd considering many IRA departments were replicated between these bodies. I didn't mind, but, reading between the lines, I sensed something was going on between personalities in general headquarters (GHQ) and Northern Command that was way over my head.

One of the more despicable cop-out comments I heard from some IRA leadership figures when it was put to them that we needed to increase our operational effectiveness and tempo was, "There's plenty of gear there, and nobody is stopping you from using it." Imagine a football manager throwing balls, boots and jerseys onto the pitch and telling the team before the match, "I'll neither train you nor lead you, but I've supplied the equipment, so if we lose, it's your fault!"

These comments came chiefly from senior and middle-ranking men who lacked technical proficiency and tactical competence but had achieved rank and status by toeing the line, whatever the line. They usually held managerial positions in the army as opposed to combat roles. One, in particular, reminded me of a description of Henry Kissinger given by an American State Department official: "Devious with his peers, domineering with his subordinates, obsequious to his superiors." Or, to quote another American, Steven Wright: "Eagles may soar, but weasels don't get sucked into jet engines."

Of course, there were members of the IRA leadership who had led from the front at great personal risk to life and liberty. Although I would come to question the political judgement of some of these men, I never doubted they had demonstrated courage in the past.

Courage and commitment, however, are perishable commodities. One of the more challenging aspects of being an Irish republican is that a republican has to be brave all the time—brave enough to believe the truth and sometimes act on it, despite all the pressure, threats and inducements to do otherwise. That truth was spoken by James Connolly at his court martial in 1916 when he said, "The British Government has no right in Ireland, never had any right in Ireland, and never can have any right in Ireland . . ." British policy is to ensure that remaining faithful to that truth incurs a cost few Irishmen will consistently pay.

One of my best friends from Portlaoise Prison, Declan Dalton from Ballyfermot in Dublin, was tied in with the Engineering Department. Shortly after my release from prison in 1994, we discussed operations "over the water" as we called active service in England. It was a general conversation. I had no particular interest in operating in England as I was focused on helping others to improve things at home. Moreover, the ceasefire was ongoing, although no IRA volunteer I spoke to was sure how long it would last or if it would become a permanent feature of the political landscape. We knew we'd have to remain on our toes for the foreseeable future.

The ceasefire lasted seventeen months and ended on 9 February 1996 when the IRA detonated a massive truck bomb at Canary Wharf in London. Despite a ninety-minute telephone warning, two people were killed. The IRA later claimed they ended the ceasefire because the British were dragging their feet on negotiations and had introduced a demand that full IRA disarmament take place before peace talks could begin.

The IRA's history of attacks in Britain were erratic and operations there were rarely strategic in scope. There was a prevailing attitude that "one bomb is England is worth a hundred in Ireland." This was interpreted by many as "any bomb in England is worth a hundred in Ireland," which sometimes led to things being done for the sake of doing something. This would have disastrous consequences at Warrington.

One of their more targeted attacks was carried out in October 1984, when an attempt was made to kill British Prime Minister Margaret Thatcher in a bomb attack at the Tory Party Conference at the Grand Hotel in Brighton. Thatcher was considered Public Enemy Number One due to her callous handling of the hunger strikes and her government's "shoot to kill" policy against IRA volunteers and their support base. She escaped the blast, but five people connected with the Conservative Party were killed and thirty-four injured.

In the mid-1980s, the England Department was infiltrated by the informer Sean O'Callaghan. When O'Callaghan's perfidy was exposed, it was decided to form three separate departments to provide redundancy in the event of another infiltration by informers working for MI5 or the gardaí: one run by Southern Command, one by Northern Command and another by General Headquarters.

A new, more strategically focused campaign was initiated with an audacious attack on 7 February 1991, when a battery of three Mark-10 improvised mortars was fired from the back of a van at the British Prime Minister's residence at 10 Downing Street in London. Each mortar contained twenty kilograms of Semtex plastic explosive and one detonated in the back garden of Number 10, only thirty metres from where Prime Minister John Major was meeting with his ministers. Had it hit the building, it would have wiped out the British cabinet.

On 10 April 1992, a ton of improvised explosives was detonated in front of London's Baltic Exchange building in the heart of Britain's primary business and financial district known as the City of London. The device was placed in the back of a

Ford Transit van. It was the largest explosion in England since the Second World War. Despite a series of telephone warnings, three people were killed. As a result of this, key foreign investors began asking the British government whether they could safely do business in London. This risked irreparable damage to the British economy and the government vowed to place a "ring of steel" around the City of London. Permanent road barriers and checkpoints manned by armed police were set up on all entrances to this economically vital district, measuring barely a square mile. Over 1,500 surveillance cameras covered the entire area.

A year later, on 24 April 1993, the IRA planted a massive bomb hidden inside a Ford Iveco tipper truck at Bishopsgate, less than 200 metres from the Baltic Exchange bomb site. The IRA circumvented the "ring of steel" by taking advantage of the fact building vehicles were permitted to park on double yellow lines on Saturday mornings. Despite a series of telephone warnings to evacuate civilians, a news photographer who remained too close to the device was killed. Damage was estimated at over a billion pounds.

These two London blasts cost the British exchequer more than the 10,000 explosions in the North of Ireland over the whole course of the Troubles. The Bishopsgate bomb, in particular, caused consternation within British banking, insurance and financial circles. While the original blast could be seen as a one-off, the second blast dispelled any hope the IRA was not determined to hit the British government where it hurt, in their pockets.

This policy of pulverising the heart of England's financial district was not the result of the IRA Army Council sitting around a table, hammering out a grand strategy and ordering it to be implemented. Six of the seven men on the Council knew nothing of these attacks until they heard about them on the news. The Baltic Exchange and Bishopsgate bombings took place because a handful of volunteers in the GHQ England Department, with significant input from South Armagh, put the operations together on their own initiative.

Leadership devotees would later point to the success of the London attacks as proof positive that the IRA Army Council could not have been penetrated by British intelligence, thus giving them credit for keeping secrets they never held. Far from encouraging these attacks, I was told by an impeccable source that two members of the Army Council wanted them curtailed because, in the words of one, "It's hard talking to the British when we're bombing them."

Of course, no volunteer operating on the ground in England or anywhere else knew a thing about ongoing talks with the enemy. Nor did they know that these attacks and the Libyan arsenal, far from being used to help win the war, would be used as negotiating capital to end it on terms that would make the reestablishment of the Irish Republic virtually impossible.

The ad hoc nature of the IRA campaign and the absence of a coherent military strategy was flagged up only weeks before the Bishopsgate bomb, when two devices went off in litter bins in a busy shopping thoroughfare in Warrington, Cheshire, killing three-year-old Johnathan Ball and twelve-year-old Tim Parry. Warnings were given but proved to be inadequate. No one joined the IRA to kill children. There could be no discernible strategy behind placing Semtex in litter bins in a crowded shopping area on a busy Saturday morning beyond the "any bomb in England is worth a hundred in Ireland" mantra.

The gulf between the conception, planning and execution of the Downing Street mortars and the City of London attacks compared to the Warrington fiasco was clear. That is not to say IRA volunteers were rudderless. Many indeed had a strategy, but it didn't come from the leadership, and opinions on strategy could diverge between various departments and ASUs. There was no centralised plan to win the war.

In March 1994, Heathrow airport was attacked three times over five days by improvised mortars. Warnings were given and there were no casualties. The airport was closed for most of the five days causing severe disruption to this crucial transport hub. Again, this attack was carried out by IRA volunteers acting on their own initiative.

Winning the war did not mean driving the British Army into the Irish sea. It meant using the military instrument to shape the strategic environment in a way that ensured eventual negotiations would lead to the ending of Crown dominion in Ireland and the establishment of a truly national republic—a republic untainted by the residue of imperial conquest and oblivious to the differences carefully fostered by an alien government, which have divided the minority from the majority in the past.

Unfortunately, we didn't know what British intelligence knew and facilitated: that some members of the IRA leadership were more focused on surviving than winning the struggle. These figures were determined to convert the republican movement from a resistance organisation into a vehicle that would service their private political ambitions—ambitions that did not include a prison cell or the republican plot in Milltown cemetery. To achieve this, they were prepared to allow the British government, who were ultimately responsible for the war in Ireland, to define the very concept of peace.

My involvement with the England Department had its roots in a private plane journey I took in Chicago around 1983. The pilot was the son of an old friend of my father. He had no idea I was in the States on an IRA mission to acquire arms. He took me up twice, letting me have the controls in a Cessna single-engine prop and then a Beechcraft twin turboprop.

Following this, I obtained brochures for various flight schools. I was keen on bringing two or three volunteers over to America to take flying lessons. Having trained and trusted pilots would have several benefits for us. One would be the ability to fly weapons home from the European mainland, especially if we acquired a surface-to-air missile or other vital armaments.

I showed Martin McGuinness the brochures on a trip home to Ireland and he scoffed, "So what are you proposing to do now? Drop mix over London?" By "mix" he was referring to improvised explosives. He was openly mocking my suggestion. Months later, when captured on the *Marita Ann*, I thought how much prison time could have been avoided for three IRA volunteers if a small private plane had scouted us in. It would have spotted the Irish Navy behind the Skellig Rocks long before we entered Irish territorial waters. We may have had to ditch the weapons, but we would not have gone to prison for ten years.

While flying over Chicago, I noticed that US aeronautical charts showed the paths of electricity pylons. I asked the pilot the reason for this and he told me they could be used as a navigation feature if the pilot was lost or had compass trouble. It seemed obvious that wherever these pylons met on the map was a power station or substation.

Even though I had no particular interest in operating in England, I had what I thought was a good idea and was keen to pass it on in case it was useful to others. When I was released from Portlaoise Prison in 1994, I asked Declan Dalton to obtain flight charts for England. It took Declan a few weeks, but he did so. I confirmed that they, too, showed the paths of electricity pylons. I suggested that there was the potential to do something strategic across the water, but I had no experience over there and it would take someone with knowledge, guts and real capability to put it together. Declan told me he knew just the man.

Shortly afterwards, Declan introduced me to an astute and highly motivated IRA operative from Dublin called Donal Gannon. Donal, a former bank employee, came from a middle-class family in South Dublin and, like me, he had no republican background. He had been studying for a commerce degree but his republican activism led him to qualify as an electronics technician and a trained marine radio operator where, among other things, he learned Morse code. Knowledge of electronics and radio frequencies are invaluable skills for an IRA operative. I would come to appreciate Donal's attention to detail and his zero tolerance for fools.

The idea for putting out the lights in England was not a new one. The IRA "S" plan ("S" for sabotage) was conceived in the late 1930s to knock out critical elements of England's civil and public infrastructure, including the damage or destruction of utilities such as transport, electricity, water and gas. But why England? Why did the IRA not carry out attacks in the rest of Britain?

NORAID would attend St Patrick's Day parades carrying a large banner that read, "England Get Out of Ireland." This was met by howls of derision from Dublin politicians and journalists, who ridiculed the idea that England was in Ireland as misinformed, naive and offensive. Yet, when we speak of British jurisdiction in the North of Ireland, it is not Wales and Scotland who are leading the charge. England makes up 85 percent of the population of the UK and contains 533 of the UK's 650 parliamentary constituencies. It produces nearly 86 percent of the Gross Domestic Product. Tory politicians from England are the most vociferous about retaining a constitutional link with Ireland and the most bloodthirsty in opposing the IRA. Britain has been described as "an imperial euphemism for England." There was little point in bombing Cardiff or Edinburgh.

Donal Gannon and I were of one mind concerning tactics and strategy for a possible attack. We appreciated that the England departments, especially the section under the control of GHQ, were hitting the Brits smarter and harder than ever before. We knew the "ring of steel" in London was a challenge, but there was a way around it. When a banker or financier in Tokyo or Wall Street calls his counterpart in London, it is irrelevant to the caller whether the man or woman on the other end is in a palatial office or a tent. What matters is that they can answer the phone and use the computer, neither of which is possible without electricity.

Active service in England was one of the most dangerous missions for an IRA volunteer to undertake. Donal warned me that operating across the water was like performing a high-wire act with no safety net. If we were undercover agents working on behalf of a national government, we would have the full resources of a state behind us. We would have salaries to come home to and, if we survived, pensions. Professional printers would forge our documents. An industrial complex would manufacture our weapons and explosive devices.

Intelligence services would provide us with critical information. Military specialists would train our volunteers across a broad spectrum of tactics, techniques and procedures. We would have state-of-the-art communications secure from enemy eavesdropping. If apprehended, our government could negotiate to secure our release or perhaps trade us for captured personnel from the other side.

All we had was an idea and the guts to go for it. There would be no safety net and no hope if we were caught or betrayed. We had the military, police and intelligence services of the British government arrayed against us with the unqualified support of their entire population. We also had Garda Special Branch reporting our movements to MI5 and Scotland Yard.

Donal and I agreed upon an operational concept to disrupt the electricity grid in the south-east of England and bring London's economic activity to a virtual halt for days, if not a full week. London alone produced nearly a quarter of the UK's Gross Domestic Product. Using the flight charts, we were able to plot the location of the relevant electricity substations.

Donal picked up the ball and ran with it. He expanded the research by locating a book in England that contained a map of their electricity grid showing powerplants and confirming the whereabouts of the substations. Based on this intelligence, he selected six key substations that ringed London as our primary targets. He received assistance from a sympathetic engineer working for the Irish Electricity Supply Board, who provided information on which transformers to target in the substation so that any devices we planted would have the most effect.

From my demolitions training in the Marine Corps, I knew that electric detonators could explode if too close to high voltage power lines. I like to think we were motivated, but we weren't suicidal. We discussed this with the IRA Engineering Department, who designed bespoke detonators that would withstand proximity to these currents.

Through subsequent research we became aware that hoax devices planted in the substations could be an option that would have substantially the same effect as actual explosives. Power would have to be shut off to the transformers by the British themselves while the hoax 'bombs' were dealt with, giving London a taste of things to come if they didn't get with the programme. From an intelligence source in the Irish army, we learned that marzipan (almond candy dough) looks identical to the plastic explosive Semtex when viewed through the X-ray equipment used by British bomb disposal experts. We were under no illusions that, whether hoax bombs or real, we would suffer the same consequences of death or imprisonment if detected by the enemy.

I am often asked why the IRA leadership sent me to England, mainly because I was a known republican and an obvious target for surveillance. Nobody sent me anywhere. I agreed on a plan with Donal Gannon and volunteered to go because I would never ask anyone to do something I wasn't prepared to do myself. The IRA leadership had nothing to do with it. The IRA Army Council was not in the loop regarding our mission. The operations officer attached to GHQ's England Department supplied us with money and logistical backup. Although he knew we were going for the electric grid, even he did not know the specific targets. Other than that, our ASU organised everything in-house, from conception and planning to execution.

Donal was frustrated that there was no structured vetting process for volunteers being considered for operations in England. Some IRA commanders would send anyone with a pulse, while others would select volunteers with some care. This led to a wide variety in calibre, ability and experience among people arriving in London. Planning and coordination were occasionally slipshod. For one operation in England, weapons were sent over that none of the volunteers waiting there had been trained to use. Their commander insisted that, in the future, volunteers be adequately trained on any weapons required and that specific weapons should be test-fired and kept for the exclusive use of the ASU for whom they were intended.

For our planned operation, I put forward the names of a few IRA men I thought might be willing to come with us. We acquired the temporary use of a home in a plush Dublin suburb and set up an interview suite. Donal brought along a flip chart with a list of Dos and Don'ts to bear in mind while operating across the water. He wanted to get the measure of the men he'd be speaking to and form an opinion on their suitability.

One of the points mentioned on the chart was that any travel by car must be thoroughly thought through. The vehicle would have spare bulbs for every turn signal and brake light. Before every journey, a walk around would be done to ensure the car was in tip-top condition. We couldn't afford to be stopped for something silly like a broken tail light or bald tyres. If we were travelling any distance outside London, we would search the *Loot* magazine servicing our destination and find an item for sale like a racing bike or camper van. We would phone the seller using someone with, or faking, an

English accent and organise a meeting with them at a particular time and date. Of course, we wouldn't show up, but if stopped by police on the way there, we would have a ready and plausible reason for being in the area.

I suggested taking along a small bug-out bag of emergency and survival supplies on any journey in case we had to abandon ship and take off across the countryside. Unfortunately, few of our men could use a map or compass. I also proposed we set up a suitable training centre to instruct men going to England in a wide range of skills from weapons and explosives to lock picking, land navigation, countersurveillance and survival. Donal was up for that, but we didn't have time to do so before carrying out the impending operation against the substations.

The first person Donal interviewed was a former Portlaoise prisoner I recommended who had proven to be a daring resistance fighter in the North. He was highly intelligent but had earned a reputation for having issues with authority. I thought he'd perform well once he understood the strict guidelines and parameters within which we'd have to operate. He was given our address and a time to be there. Punctuality was a major consideration for us. It provided the first clue as to one's reliability.

He was on time, all right, but everything else went downhill rapidly. Peeking out the front window of the house as he approached, I could see that he had shaved his head and was wearing a black leather biker's jacket. *Why the fuck did he shave his head?* I mused. He looked like a thug. Not a good idea in this neighbourhood.

Donal moved in beside me and peered out also. The lad was eating an orange. We were incredulous when we saw him toss the peel onto a neighbour's manicured lawn. Donal looked at me as though I had lost the plot in recommending this guy. He was instantly blackballed. We went through the motions of interviewing him, but there was no chance we would include him on our team. We needed the proverbial "grey man" who would not attract attention. This fellow had warning signs flashing all over him.

As it turned out, nobody we interviewed in that location was suitable. Donal would have to find another way to recruit the best men possible.

I was unemployed and the IRA doesn't pay a salary so, before we left for England in June 1996, I asked Declan Dalton to collect my social welfare payments from the Post Office and keep them for me until I got home. I visited a few close friends and family and said goodbye without actually saying goodbye. I couldn't tell anyone where I was going.

The night before I left for England, there was a lunar eclipse. I drove a motorbike high into the Wicklow mountains to view it without the intrusion of ambient light from street lamps. On the return journey, I stopped at the Killakee view-point. Looking out over the twinkling lights of Dublin, my gaze moved beyond them to settle upon the dark expanse of the sea we would soon be crossing to take the war to England. I hoped we'd get back.

14
THE BELLY OF THE BEAST

DONAL AND I were the first members of our ASU to arrive in London and we hit the ground running. We had a tremendous amount of work to do before the next two volunteers arrived a fortnight later. They would bring the rendezvous details for the following two men. Our operation would require nine IRA volunteers in total, as each target would be attacked by a team of three men—a driver, an engineer to place the devices in the correct position, and a man to act as lookout. Each team would be allocated two substations. I didn't know who would be joining us and I didn't ask. I would find out when they arrived.

We needed to rent three places to stay and buy three cars, one for each three-man team. In the meantime, we stayed in cheap hotel rooms.

There were some lessons the IRA never seemed to learn, no matter how often they were flagged. One was the need for references when renting a property in London. Up to three credible and verifiable references were required to rent a house or apartment quickly and securely without inviting suspicion. At a minimum, these should include a good work reference and a glowing recommendation from a previous landlord. Naturally, we didn't have these.

Had the IRA facilitated operations in England by organising a secure and competent administration to provide these items, it would have been more beneficial to us than almost any other enterprise. In the meantime, we'd have to wing it. We did so by paying cash and using frontmen who were not obviously Irish. I had a false American passport and Donal told me the other man renting properties spoke French with a good accent and held a French passport in a false name.

Unfortunately, the IRA rarely conducted the After Action Reviews a professional army would carry out after an attack. Each IRA operation in England should have added another layer to our organisational learning and built upon a portfolio of knowledge and expertise that could be passed on to the next team going over. The information needn't be circulated to every volunteer but to trusted commanders who had proven themselves on active service. However, frustratingly, this seldom happened.

Moreover, while the operations officer in charge of GHQ's England Department was one of our finest leadership figures, who did the best he could with the human and material resources at his disposal, other senior and middle-ranking figures often demonstrated poor organisational and managerial competence. In contrast, unlike some in the IRA, the Brits learned from every operation and disseminated that to the next generation of security and intelligence officers.

An example of what could be learned from our mission came when Donal insisted that the telephone in each safe house receive calls only. No outgoing calls could be made. This was arranged with the phone company when ordering the phone and made perfect sense. He didn't want anyone being tempted to phone home or contact another safe house. But you can be sure that the Brits would, in the future, investigate any property that ordered a phone with an incoming line only. Also, bank accounts should have been set up and used to pay bills, but we had no means of doing so. The intelligence services watch for clients who pay utility bills exclusively with cash. Almost certainly, this information would not be passed to the next IRA team to go over and they would make many of the same mistakes we did.

There is such a thing as negative security, keeping things so secret that an organisation is effectively paralysed by it. Tell no one and do nothing is an excellent way to stay alive and out of prison, but you won't accomplish much.

Further problems were caused by a lack of adequate planning. Sometimes Volunteers were simply sent to England with arms and explosives, and it was left to their own discretion what operations they carried out. The benefit of this was that the Brits couldn't learn what would happen in advance because the men themselves didn't know what they were going to do until they got there. The disadvantage was that many of these men were poorly trained and some had neither the military ability nor political judgement to pick appropriate targets that would advance the struggle for Irish freedom and not retard it.

About two weeks after Donal and I reached London, it was time for the next two members who would form part of our ASU to join us. I didn't know who was coming but, of course, Donal knew or else we wouldn't have been able to hook up. Donal and I set up a countersurveillance operation at our rendezvous point with them, to ensure that the British security forces weren't following the men. We used the London Underground system to perform this clearing procedure.

There are 270 Tube stations in London. Of those, Donal had chosen Wimbledon Park station on the District Line for our two ASU members to disembark. This is because the District Line is a single line. In other words, trains passing through are not diverting to any other London Underground line. Consequently, when a train arrives at the station, there is no logical reason not to board it. So our men were told at which station on the District Line to embark and to wait until a train arrived, then remain on the platform. Unless the train was packed, anyone else travelling on the District Line would enter a carriage. If not, that was a red flag that the volunteers might have someone tailing them.

We also required a relatively straight stretch of road between two Tube stations so we could keep everyone under observation, which Wimbledon Park gave us. We knew what time the two men were expected to arrive and had occupied a vantage point about half a kilometre away to watch them from a safe distance. The volunteers had been instructed to disembark at Wimbledon Park and walk down Melrose Avenue, cross Revelstoke Road to Elsenham Street and continue towards Southfields station. Anyone whose destination lay closer to Southfields would not be getting off the train at Wimbledon Park. Nothing is foolproof, but this was a simple and effective means of determining whether or not the men were being followed.

The two volunteers who had just joined our team were Gerry Hanratty and Eoin Morrow. Hanratty, known as "Hansey," was a highly experienced volunteer from Andersonstown in West Belfast. He had a history of being at the heart of the struggle for Irish freedom, wherever that struggle led. He served time in Long Kesh Prison in the early 1980s and, in 1988, was arrested in Germany with East Tyrone Volunteer Gerry McGeough for alleged attacks against the British Army of the Rhine. Approximately 70,000 British troops were confined to barracks as a result of these operations. After a two-year trial in which both volunteers were held in appalling conditions and almost total isolation, Hansey was sentenced to two and a half years in prison for possession of AK-47 rifles.

Gerry McGeough became the only IRA volunteer extradited from Germany to the United States where he faced old gun-running charges. In an anomaly that made German legal history, he was extradited to the US a few weeks before the end of his trial and, thanks to the skilful work of his legal team, he was never sentenced by the German courts.

Hansey was repatriated to Crumlin Road Prison and then to the H-Blocks. He was released after the IRA ceasefire in 1994 and immediately rejoined the IRA. He was now on active service in England.

I knew Eoin Morrow from my *Marita Ann* prison sentence; he had been a fellow Portlaoise prisoner. Eoin was originally from Twinbrook in West Belfast but had been living in Dundalk for some years. Eoin, too, was an experienced and dedicated IRA volunteer. He was cool, calm and unflappable. He was also good company. He enjoyed listening to Frank Sinatra and shared my fondness for classic movies such as *Gone with the Wind*. He and his brother Anthony "Dodger" Morrow were among the most well-liked and respected men in Portlaoise. Eoin was the man who would be passing himself off as a French journalist to rent properties.

Gerry Hanratty and Eoin Morrow were married men with families. I thought they showed enormous courage in volunteering for this challenging mission. Had I not been single, I cannot say if I would have done the same.

You learn in the IRA that things can get hairy very quickly. In 1988 Donal Gannon had been in England to meet another IRA volunteer, so he set up a clearing route to ensure the man was not being followed. As Donal waited for the volunteer to arrive, he was passed by an unmarked police car. He wondered if the cops were randomly in the area or on the man coming over from Ireland, who, by this point, was late. But Donal knew that if he walked away, he would miss the contact meeting, so, against his better judgement, he decided to wait a bit longer.

In the extra few minutes he stayed there, the undercover car returned and Donal was arrested on a spurious and completely trumped-up charge of "attempted burglary" to remand him in custody. They could find nothing against him and he was eventually released, but the false burglary charge would be planted in the media to tarnish his reputation. It later transpired that the volunteer Donal was supposed to meet had got lost and that's why he didn't make it on time.

After Hansey and Eoin arrived, our team engaged in a flurry of activity to prepare for the IRA operation against the substations. Tools such as ladders, shovels and bolt cutters had to be bought. Properties had to be rented and cars purchased from auctions. Reconnaissance and dry runs on all targets had to be carried out.

The next two volunteers to arrive were Frank Rafferty and Pat Martin, both from Belfast, although Frank had lived in the South for many years. I hadn't met them before, but

I rapidly deduced they were solid men who would perform their assigned tasks with focus, determination and without complaint.

A total of three properties were acquired. We avoided English estate agents and approached Nigerians and Pakistanis who asked fewer questions and were more amenable to cash. I rented a house in Woodbury Street in Tooting, South London. I told the owner I was from the United States working in information technology. The homeowner was a nice lady who had no reason to doubt my explanation for wanting to live there. I had my American passport in a false name—I have no idea how the IRA obtained it.

Myself and Donal Gannon usually stayed in Woodbury Street. Pat Martin would later join us. This meant other volunteers coming over now had a place to lay their heads until they could find their own accommodation. Eoin Morrow rented a property in Lugard Road in Peckham, where he stayed with Frank Rafferty. A flat was also rented at Verona Court, St James's Drive, in Tooting, where Gerry Hanratty usually stayed. Three more volunteers had yet to arrive and would be lodging with Eoin and Hansey when they got there.

Three cars were bought and carefully checked for roadworthiness and mechanical reliability. They had to be taxed for at least six months and false registration plates obtained. Since a vehicle couldn't be parked indefinitely in one place as it may raise suspicions with residents, we'd have to rotate parking spots at least every thirty-six hours. This was another chore on top of everything else we had on our plates. We were busy men.

I also rented a lock-up garage. This would be used to store equipment we needed to procure for the operation. It would also be used as a workshop to cut down aluminium ladders so they could be placed in the boot of a car and rapidly reassembled at the substations to get us over any fences. In the meantime, the lock-up was empty.

I kept the specifics of the lock-up, including the address, and the name and bank account details of the landlord on a single sheet of cigarette rolling paper. I carried this with me at all times. Every night I placed it on a table beside my bed in Woodbury Street so I could quickly swallow it if we were raided.

We suffered a potentially devasting setback when the components destined for our ASU were confiscated in a garda raid in Clonaslee, County Laois, on 20 June 1996. Four men were later convicted in a Dublin court and were sentenced to twenty years each. Custom-designed Timer Power Units (TPUs) critical to our operation were among the items taken. A TPU is a control mechanism that, in our case, consisted of a wooden box containing Semtex (or marzipan if used as a hoax), the detonator (real or fake), batteries and a circuit board or timer.

Under normal circumstances, the seizure of this equipment would have necessitated a return to Ireland to regroup and reorganise. I got the measure of the men I was operating with when they agreed unanimously to remain in London, purchase 100-hour Central Heating Timers, batteries and other equipment to make their own TPUs, and continue with our operation against the London grid. I was present when the vote was taken and can attest that not a man flinched when this was put to them.

We found ourselves in the most dangerous place an IRA volunteer could be and were being asked to stay for much longer than initially planned with the added complication and hazards of running all over London to purchase equipment to improvise our own TPUs. No one had to stay, yet everyone willingly agreed to do so.

The six electricity substations we were targeting were located at or near Amersham in Buckinghamshire, Elstree and Waltham Cross in Hertfordshire, Rayleigh in Essex, Canterbury in Kent and Weybridge in Surrey. There would be six devices planted at strategic locations in each substation. If our plan worked, it would result in London and most of the south-east of England being plunged into darkness for a considerable period.

Another IRA volunteer to meet us in London was Martin "Spud" Murphy from Belfast. I believe he had once been OC of the Belfast Brigade. Spud, a married man with a family and a fan of Bruce Springsteen, was carrying crucial messages to us from the England Department. The three remaining volunteers who were to be part of our ASU on the mission were still in Ireland making final preparations to join us.

My first suspicion that we might be under surveillance was roused when I noticed a blond man walking towards me while strolling down a residential side street. Something about him grabbed my attention. He walked with a nonchalance that seemed more pronounced than natural. I stared at him as we approached each other in an attempt to catch his eye. There is no way he didn't notice me glaring at him. It wasn't the way he glanced at me but the deliberate way he didn't glance at me that gave me cause for concern. Most people would have given me that "what the fuck are you staring at?" look. This didn't mean I would jump on the first boat back to Ireland, but my radar went into overdrive.

Donal told me that some IRA commanders had treated young volunteers with suspicion when they returned to Ireland before completing an operation because they believed they were under surveillance. "Someone looked at him twice and he ran home with his tail between his legs" was a typical comment. Invariably, it came from men who had never volunteered to operate in England themselves. But there is a fine line between paranoia and reality, and it took a cool head to distinguish one from the other. As time went on, Donal and I became increasingly concerned that we were being followed. There were many clues, some difficult to articulate because they came from an almost primordial sixth sense.

We were leaving a Tube station one day when both of us noticed men in casual summer clothing watching people coming off the train. The man I spotted held a bicycle and was wearing blue shorts. He was scanning every face. He didn't have the appearance of a person searching for a particular individual but of someone looking for a needle in a haystack. We later learned from the book of evidence produced for our trial that the police were performing this exercise at every Underground station in London in the hope of finding us. We slipped by them on this occasion.

"Did you see what I saw?" asked Donal.

"Yeah, those were cops for sure."

We agreed that surveillance was taking place at the station exit but couldn't be certain it was meant for us. There could have been a recent rape or robbery in the area and they may have been looking for someone matching the culprit's description.

Pat Martin and I made a reconnaissance of one of our targets in Canterbury, Kent. We took several trains out to it and walked around the facility. I later learned we were being tailed that day, but they lost us before we got to the substation due to our countersurveillance measures. However, this wasn't much of a setback to the police because we returned to the same house in Tooting that evening. While in Canterbury, we took a quick look inside the magnificent cathedral first founded in AD 597.

As Pat and I stood beside the tomb of the Black Prince and viewed the spot where Thomas Becket was murdered, we were unaware that MI5, the Metropolitan Police's anti-terrorist unit SO13 and Scotland Yard's Special Branch had launched "Operation Airlines" to capture us. Hundreds of police and intelligence officers were on our track.

For example, if one of our team left the house to go anywhere, even to buy a loaf of bread, at least sixty officers would be tailing him. Typically, they were in four teams of fifteen, each team with a mobile command vehicle containing secure communications, wigs, glasses, changes of clothing and other paraphernalia to help in their surveillance activities. All three of our unit's vehicles were bugged and fitted with tracking devices. The enemy also gave us code names. I was "Another Tomorrow." Donal was "Paradise News" and Eoin Morrow was "Bread Board." I believe these names were randomly generated.

Despite their best efforts to remain in the shadows, an increasing number of incidents caused us to suspect the Brits might be on to us. It wasn't just Donal and me who copped it. Hansey and others had their suspicions.

The final straw came while I was watching the television news in Woodbury Street one evening. There was an empty house across the road. Suddenly, my eyes were drawn to movement. I could see the top of a man's head appear momentarily inches above a windowsill. He was crawling along the floor on his hands and knees. Enough was enough. Donal decided to call a meeting of all the volunteers in our ASU at the earliest opportunity to compare notes on our observations and determine if we should pull the plug and abort. As we didn't use phones, this would take time to arrange.

The next night, I stayed in Lugard Road in Peckham with Frank Rafferty and Eoin Morrow. I can't remember the reason for this. It was my first time overnighting at this address. Donal, Frank and Hansey had been making the TPUs in the basement. I didn't go down to the basement, so I wasn't sure how far they'd got with them. It turned out they had completed thirty-seven devices. Six for each substation and one spare in case it was needed.

Retiring for the evening, I saw a single bed in the room and no furniture. There was no table on which to place the paper that contained the lock-up details. The floor was carpeted and I concluded that, in an emergency, I would never find the tiny paper in the shaggy weave, so I had no option but to keep it in my jeans pocket.

Earlier that afternoon, Eoin and I had stopped in a Turkish bar for a soft drink. It was a warm day and we were parched. We each had a Coke with plenty of ice and quickly went on our way. That night, I dreamed that I was back in the bar when I heard men shouting and gunshots. I thought someone was coming into the bar and shooting it up. Suddenly I awoke to the blinding glare of ambush lights shining in my bedroom window, tear gas rounds coming through the broken panes and shots being fired in the house. We were being raided. I believe that listening devices planted in our houses caused the Brits to pounce before we could get everyone together and compare notes on our suspicions.

I sat bolt upright in the bed and placed my feet on the floor. I looked over my left shoulder and saw heavily armed men in black, wearing helmets and respirators, carrying Heckler and Koch MP-5 submachine guns with blinding torches attached. They were pointing their weapons at me and yelling at me to freeze. I knew I had no chance to reach my jeans on the floor and find and swallow the lock-up garage details. Had I moved a muscle, I would have been riddled with bullets.

I was choking from the tear gas and blinded by the lights, which, of course, was their purpose. Because I awoke to shots being fired, my first thought was they were going from room to room shooting my friends dead in their beds. My bedroom was the last in line and I reckoned I was about to get the chop. "Oh, shit!" would have been my last words.

I was thrown to the floor with my hands cable-tied behind my back. Then I was frog-marched down the stairs dressed only in my underpants. The arresting officers were firm but not gratuitously rough. The Irish sailors and police who had arrested us on the *Marita Ann* gave me more abuse than these English fellows.

Two months later, IRA volunteer Diarmuid O'Neill would be shot dead while trying to surrender in a similar arrest operation in a hotel in Hammersmith, London. He was dragged out of the premises with his head hitting the stairs as he was dying. Amnesty International called for an investigation into his death. Brian McHugh from Fermanagh and Patrick Kelly from Longford were captured in the same hotel room.

The volunteers were unarmed. We were separate ASUs and unaware of each other's missions.

I was topless and barefoot. I was led through the house and out the back into an alley and ordered to kneel. Frank and Eoin were placed in a similar position. I shivered from the cold and the rush of adrenalin. The gravel I was kneeling on became extremely painful after a few minutes. The police were crowing with relief and jubilation.

After what seemed an eternity, I was lifted up and placed in a white forensic boiler suit, booties and hood. I was bundled into the back of a small van completely lined with white plastic sheeting. We drove to what I would later learn was Charing Cross police station.

Arriving at Charing Cross, I was fingerprinted and swabbed for DNA. I expected a beating but received no physical abuse. I was asked some questions but refused to answer. A court-appointed solicitor came in to see me. He was an Englishman and a pleasant enough fellow. He told me that if there were an innocent explanation for what I was doing in London, I would have to give it now. I could not use an alibi later in a trial that I did not give upon arrest. I did recall hearing on the news that the law in England had been changed to that effect.

I found myself in a quandary. Had we been in possession of an ounce of explosives or a single round of ammunition, keeping my mouth shut would have been the only and easy option. When myself and another volunteer had discussed the possibility we might be under surveillance, I asked his opinion on what we should do if we were arrested without arms or explosives in our possession. He speculated that we could invent something like stealing cars in London to sell in

Ireland. There were organised criminal gangs that did this. He never told me to give that as an alibi but simply suggested we fabricate an account along those lines. However, he emphasised that we would have to meet up first and get the story straight so that we'd all be singing from the same hymn sheet. We were arrested before we could hold a meeting about our suspicions on surveillance and, consequently, were never able to agree on an alibi if captured without munitions.

I said nothing to the police for two days. All the detectives were English, but I noted many had Irish names. I wrestled with the dilemma of whether or not to give an alibi. Only a moron thinks they can talk their way out of a situation like this, although it wasn't a case of talking my way out but of laying the basis for a defence. I was confident no one else would talk or say anything that would contradict me, so I decided to grasp the bull by the horns and began to outline a defence we could use at a trial. Another factor in my decision was that I had a solicitor present during interrogations and everything was tape-recorded and handed to him at the end of each session, so I couldn't be "verballed" or have my words twisted by the cops as happened in Ireland.

I told the police I was approached in Dublin by someone who asked me to go to London to obtain "ringers." These are cars that are stolen in England and have their identity changed to match another vehicle in Ireland, often one that has been crashed or written off. This is to conceal the fact that the English vehicle has been stolen. I was unemployed and broke and agreed to do so. I said that we were all involved in this scam and the only matter discussed between me or anyone else I was involved with in London was this car theft ring. I didn't like giving criminality as a defence, but two years in jail was better than thirty-five. I did this entirely on my own initiative and I alone was responsible if it backfired.

At one point, they suggested I may have innocently believed I was involved in a car theft ring, but the others were involved in terrorism. This was getting dangerous. They were trying to get me to turn on my comrades by throwing me a lifeline they hoped I would grab to save my skin. I immediately threw it back, saying we were all involved in the car scam and nobody I knew or met with was engaged in "terrorism." If they thought I was making a solo run to get myself out of this, they were seriously mistaken.

I was waiting for them to drop the lock-up bomb. I knew they had discovered the address in my pants pocket. Finally, they asked if I had rented a lock-up or garage. Knowing they already had it and it was empty of anything incriminating, I said that I had rented a garage to change the registration plates and remove the vehicle identification numbers from the stolen vehicles.

I could see this caught them on the hop as they expected me to deny it. I thought denying it would harm the car ringer defence. They pretended they knew nothing about it and asked me if I would come for a drive with them and show them where it was. That was another dangerous moment. To have done so would have transitioned me from providing an alibi to active collaboration with the enemy. I vehemently refused to go anywhere with them.

The next day they told me they found the lock-up and that it was empty. They feebly accused me of knowing it was empty and, furthermore, they believed had anything been in it, I wouldn't have told them about it. Which, of course, was true.

Again, had we been professional agents working on behalf

of a government, we would have been provided with a cover story for just such a scenario. We would have memorised a narrative and had documentation to back it up. But this was the IRA, so no such luck.

After seven days of interrogation, we were charged with conspiracy to cause explosions and remanded to Belmarsh Prison in East London. We were placed in the Special Security Unit (SSU). This is a secure prison within a secure prison. We were brought before the governor and informed that we were considered a serious threat to UK national security and would be placed under the most severe custodial restrictions. He told us the Home Secretary would have to authorise our departure from the unit personally, so if one of us had a heart attack or hit our head off the floor, we would die long before we were given Home Office clearance to be taken to hospital. He smiled, "Welcome to Her Majesty's Prison, Belmarsh."

15
A DIFFERENT AGENCY

THE SSU AT Belmarsh was a concrete coffin designed to bury alive enemies of the UK state. Every device and technique that could be imagined by those specialising in the jailing of men was put to use. One English newspaper described the prison as "Alcatraz on the Thames." Belmarsh was designed to make escape impossible.

The SSU was surrounded by a twenty-foot-high concrete wall located within the main outer walls of the prison. These walls had rounded tops to prevent grappling hooks from snagging securely when thrown over with ropes attached. The SSU had two floors and was split into four wings or "spurs." Each spur contained twelve single-occupancy cells measuring approximately six feet wide and ten feet long. The cell contained a concrete bed with a rubber mattress, a steel toilet, a steel sink and a small steel table and backless bench bolted to the wall. A narrow, opaque window let in light but offered no view.

The concrete in the cells was of a unique tool-proof mixture. The steel bars on the window had tool-resistant cores and internal wiring that would set off alarms if cut. We had to change cells every two weeks within the spur to prevent tampering with a cell. Prison officers were forbidden to speak to us without another officer present at all times to avoid the "grooming" of prison staff. Surveillance cameras were everywhere and we were body-searched and patted down several times a day. Our cells were constantly being turned over.

There was an Irish screw working for the British prison service in the Belmarsh SSU while we were there. His accent suggested he was from Waterford or somewhere in the south-east. My heart fell whenever I saw him on duty. He was a horrible, sneering, snide little toad who believed he could prove to the English how reliable he was by being insufferable towards us. I invariably found that an Irishman working for the Crown was the worst bastard one could come across.

The SSU could hold a maximum of forty-eight prisoners, although it contained only a handful in our time. The inmates did not mix with the main prison population. Food was taken into the unit from the central prison and it had its own exercise yard and gym. The exercise yard was a tiny concrete area roofed by layers of wire and mesh. One never had an unobstructed view of the sky.

We were given "Category Triple A—Exceptional Risk" security status, the highest security status in the UK penal system. At the time, there were nearly 60,000 prisoners in British prisons, of whom only eighteen were awarded this rating. Fifteen were Irish republicans.

English prison officers, many of whom were former soldiers who had served in the North of Ireland, would sometimes ask why we were attempting to bomb England. What had England ever done to Ireland? This was often asked without malice but with genuine curiosity.

Our stock reply was to ask them what they would have done if Germany had invaded England in the Second World

War. They said if they had been around at the time, they would have shot and bombed German soldiers, German police and any other German targets they could get their hands on. We'd reply that we were fighting the British occupation of Ireland. "There's no comparison," they would scoff, "Northern Ireland is part of the United Kingdom."

We were eventually served with the book of evidence. The police and British intelligence services submitted 14,000 pages of material concerning Operation Airlines to the courts. Reading this avalanche of surveillance logs, photographs and forensic analysis, a number of things rapidly became clear.

For one thing, I could see my "car theft ring" alibi was dead in the water. The TPUs were completed and matched the ones captured in Clonaslee too closely to deny. My hope that the Lugard Road basement might contain a bundle of components for which we could attempt to provide another explanation proved to be wishful thinking. Furthermore, we had been followed by British surveillance teams while carrying out reconnaissance of our targets and they had been all over us far too much for us to claim with any credibility we were in London to steal cars.

On the plus side, if one could call it that, we noted from the surveillance logs that on almost every occasion we suspected surveillance, we were correct. We had been alert and tuned in to our surroundings. Had we been able to arrange a team meeting to discuss our suspicions earlier, we would almost certainly have gotten the hell out of Dodge.

I wondered why the British didn't let us continue with the operation and shoot us all at the target sites. Few would have begrudged their security forces the right to do so, least of all their pals in Dublin. The British had an established record of permitting operations to proceed in order to kill IRA volunteers in the act. They had done so at Loughgall, Gibraltar and many other places.

I don't have the answer to that question except to speculate that with secret talks taking place to renew the IRA ceasefire, ongoing discussions we knew nothing about, it didn't suit the British government to add six or seven "martyrs" to the IRA Roll of Honour with the resulting fuss and fallout from the funerals and other consequences. It may have hardened the resolve of some volunteers who voted for the second ceasefire to do otherwise.

Another possibility is that British intelligence, who certainly planted eavesdropping devices in our houses, heard us talking about pulling the plug on the operation and may have been forced to move prematurely before we decided to escape and return home. They preferred to capture us alive rather than not at all.

The Crown prosecution claimed we were some sort of "A-team" dispatched by the IRA leadership to take out the electric grid in England. Fortunately, according to the Brits, we were arrested before we could get our hands on the weapons and explosives required to carry out this mission. Our defence was to admit we were involved in an elaborate hoax operation to shut down the electricity grid for a few days to prove what we were capable of if the IRA decided to plant real bombs. Despite having no explosives in our possession, Crown prosecutors were counting on the bias of an English jury to convict us of "conspiracy to cause explosions."

That might seem far-fetched, but the fact is we were charged with conspiracy to cause explosions and had no explosives. Their forensic analysis could detect no traces either and they could detect a nanogram of Semtex, which is a billionth of a gram.

Our trial was conducted in Court Number One of the Old Bailey, which has held some of the most high-profile and notorious trials in English history. We had a jury of twelve. There were no jury trials for IRA men in Ireland. The trial lasted eleven weeks. I spent my fortieth birthday, 6 May 1997, in the dock. I mused how wonderful it was that life begins at forty.

We gave the prosecution a run for their money. At one point, I was told by one of my defence team, who had been speaking to someone on the prosecution panel, that the Crown was deeply concerned they could end up with a hung jury and a retrial, if not an acquittal. They regretted the sole charge of "conspiracy to cause explosions" and believed they should have added further charges to ensure a conviction.

At any rate, six of us (Donal Gannon, Gerry Hanratty, Pat Martin, Eoin Morrow, Frank Rafferty and myself) were found guilty of conspiracy to cause explosions and each of us was sentenced to thirty-five years in prison on 2 July 1997. It was a ten-to-two majority verdict.

Martin "Spud" Murphy was acquitted because he acted as a courier and was neither part of our team nor the conspiracy. An Englishman who was not part of our ASU but who had met Donal Gannon for some reason I never learned was also charged and acquitted.

After conviction, we were escorted back to Belmarsh for a week or two and then dispersed to various SSUs around England. Eoin, Frank and I were sent to Whitemoor Prison in Cambridgeshire. If one had to be locked into a confined pressure cooker like an SSU with anyone, then Eoin and

Frank were as good as it gets. They were two calm, polite and easy-going men.

The SSU at Whitemoor closely resembled the layout and regime of Belmarsh. In an incredible act of ingenuity and daring, six IRA men and an English prisoner escaped from there in September 1994. They made it outside the prison by climbing over the SSU wall using poles and nets from a volleyball set and then scaling the main prison walls. However, they were recaptured within hours and severely beaten for their troubles.

A consequence of that, for myself, Eoin and Frank, was that security in the SSU was ratcheted up to unprecedented levels. As in Belmarsh, we were not permitted open visits with family members. Visits could only be conducted through thick glass, but we refused to accept visits under these conditions, which was particularly hard on married men with children.

The tiny gym in the Whitemoor SSU had its treadmill removed after the escape. That was the one piece of equipment I wanted to use as it would help relieve the tedium and tension of confinement. We were told it was taken away so that prisoners could not become physically fitter than prison officers in the event of any future attempt. The petty-mindedness of jailers never ceased to amaze me.

I was approached by a senior prison officer on 18 July 1997 and told that officials from the American embassy in London wished to speak to me. I replied that I was a citizen and soldier of the Irish Republic and had no reason to talk to them. He turned on his heels and disappeared. I presumed that was the end of it. He returned about an hour later and said, "The embassy people told me to tell you that you *will* want to meet with them."

This perplexed me. I thought perhaps they would tell me I was being extradited to the United States over the Whitey Bulger case. However, that didn't make sense as I had just been sentenced to thirty-five years in England. I wondered why they were so determined to see me. I was pretty sure it wasn't another offer to attend Annapolis.

I spoke to Eoin and Frank to canvass their opinions. I told them that I wouldn't mind finding out why the Americans were so insistent, because I speculated it was something to do with a legal issue in America. I told the lads that I would decline if they thought it inappropriate to accept the visit. They agreed it would do no harm to meet the embassy officials. What's the worst that could happen?

Entering the visiting box, I was irritated to see it was an open visit—the kind we were not allowed to have with our family members. I was met by a middle-aged, conservatively dressed woman and a greying, distinguished-looking man in a Crombie coat. The man said nothing initially but projected an affable air. The woman had a face on her like a slapped arse. She could barely conceal her contempt for me.

The woman spoke first and introduced herself as a representative of the United States embassy. She said that they provided a consular service for American citizens detained overseas. I replied that I had nothing against the United States but that I held an Irish passport and would be going through the Irish embassy if I required a service of this nature. She asked if I had reading material and was being well treated.

"Oh, yes," I replied. "There's plenty to read and I'm being very well treated."

"Are you getting enough to eat? Is the food of poor quality?"

"You know what? It's the best food I've ever eaten in prison. The SSU in Whitemoor has its own kitchen and there's only a handful of men here, so the meals are top-notch. Also, we can order food in if we have the money and cook it ourselves, which I was never allowed to do before in any other prison. We're eating like champs here."

"Well," she sniffed, clearly irritated, "you certainly don't seem to have much to complain about." I knew what she was getting at the moment she opened her mouth. She expected me to be whinging and whining and begging her to find some way to get me out of there. I wasn't going to play that game. Far from complaining, I was going to pretend that, as far as I was concerned, I had been handed a thirty-five-year ticket to the Playboy mansion.

The man could see his colleague was getting nowhere and interjected. He smiled broadly and reached across the table, shaking my hand. "John," he said. "I'm with a different agency. I've been following your career with some interest."

I interpreted that to mean he was in the CIA. As soon as he said that, I knew what was coming—a sales pitch. It also occurred to me this could be a false flag operation. He could be MI5 or MI6 pretending to be an American on the presumption I might work for the US but not for the UK. I wasn't going to work for anyone but the Irish Republic.

He was suave and professional. He attempted to build a rapport by describing us as honourable soldiers, men who wouldn't wish to inflict civilian casualties.

"John, we know you didn't intend to kill or injure innocent civilians. We can take you out of this prison right now. You don't even have to go back inside. We can leave the visiting box this minute and have you on a plane for a new life in the United States by tomorrow morning. We're prepared to offer you a lot of money." He leaned forward and repeated with emphasis, "John, a *lot* of money. All you have to do is tell the police where the explosives are hidden. That's all. You won't be asked for any information about your friends."

"Are you aware I've already done ten years in prison in Ireland?" I asked.

"Yes, I'm aware of that."

"Good. Then you'll appreciate that although I'm only starting my thirty-five-year sentence, I have been in prison before and know well what is ahead of me. I'm not going to be coming across as the hard man now and begging to see you in another year or two when I realise what a mistake I've made. That's not going to happen. I will never betray my friends or my country. As soon as I get back into the prison, I'm going to phone my solicitor and inform him of your offer to ensure you do not attempt to approach me again with this bullshit."

The two "embassy officials" got up to leave. The woman couldn't get out of there quick enough. I said to the man, "You shook my hand coming in here. Will you not shake it now?"

He reached out magnanimously and took my hand. I grinned and said, "Maybe we'll meet up in thirty-five years for a few drinks and to swap war stories."

He smiled back. "Maybe we will."

"One last thing," I said. "Tell your British friends that I know how to get rid of the Irish Republican Army. Leave

Ireland and allow us to build a national democracy with-out any further interference from their government in our internal affairs. If they do that, I guarantee you the IRA will disappear overnight. Tell the Brits there's no charge for that information."

I returned to the SSU and briefed Eoin and Frank on what had transpired. I then phoned my solicitor's office in London and the republican prisoners' department in Dublin to inform them of the attempt to recruit me. The next day the IRA announced the second ceasefire. I had no idea that was coming. I now understood the rush to see me before I heard about the truce. *Well, that was a slippery move!* I thought.

Shortly after the announcement of the second ceasefire, we were transferred from the Whitemoor SSU into the main body of the prison. The prison officers were stunned by the decision and many resented it. We were still "Category A" but downgraded from "Triple A—Exceptional Risk" to "Double A—High Risk."

It was my first time mixing with common criminals in prison and I didn't like it. In Portlaoise Prison and England's SSUs, I had been in the exclusive company of IRA volunteers. Now I was mixing with drug dealers, rapists, thieves and some very mentally ill and unstable people. Even though this was supposed to be a concession for the ceasefire, I looked upon it as a backward step and would have much preferred to stay in the SSU with the IRA and receive open visits as the concession.

It was in Whitemoor that I first met the "Balcombe Street" men. Joe O'Connell, Hugh Doherty, Eddie Butler and Harry Duggan were captured in December 1975 after a week-long siege in an apartment in Balcombe Street in London. They had carried out numerous shootings and bombings in London and its environs. All were sentenced to life in prison with a minimum of thirty years to serve. These lads were not only legends within the IRA but, I learned, highly respected among English prisoners because of the way they stood up for their right to be treated as prisoners of war and would never allow themselves to be categorised as common criminals.

After a few months, I was transferred to Long Lartin Prison near the Welsh border. While there, I met Pat Martin again, although we were housed on separate wings. It was a reasonably easy regime, despite holding some quite unsavoury characters. Most English prisoners tended to give us a wide berth, although some were sound enough fellows. I liked a lot of the Liverpool and Cockney lads, many of whom had Irish ancestry. Of course, there were other prisoners who were the scum of the earth, for whom a bullet in the back of the head would have provided a valuable social service to their long-suffering communities.

Long Lartin had the smallest cells and the largest exercise yard I had ever seen. I was delighted to be able to run again. I kept to myself as much as possible and wondered where these renewed peace talks I was now hearing about were going. I hoped they were genuinely about peace and not simply about pacification.

Peace would come from political efforts to address the principal cause of the Troubles, which was rooted in the British government's claim to jurisdiction in Ireland. Pacification would result from a counterinsurgency project to infiltrate the IRA, nurture a political leadership fit for purpose and co-opt them into supporting a strategy aimed at achieving an internal settlement on British terms.

I wanted peace as much as anyone but not peace at any price. To hear some republicans speak, one could be forgiven for presuming that the sole purpose of our struggle was to end it. Throughout Irish history, the British have dangled their version of "peace" as a carrot to entice Irish leaderships into a particular course of action. During the Dáil debates on the Anglo-Irish Treaty in 1921, Liam Mellows declared:

> If peace was the only object why, I say, was this fight ever started? Why did we ever negotiate for what we are now told is impossible? Why should men have ever been led on the road they travelled if peace was the only object? We could have had peace, and could have been peaceful in Ireland a long time ago if we were prepared to give up the ideal for which we fought.

Liam Mellows was later executed by the Free State government for defending the Irish Republic and resisting British attempts to impose a treaty that partitioned Ireland and redefined Irish democracy in British Imperial interests.

I was transferred once again to Whitemoor Prison in Cambridgeshire. One day I was sitting in my cell waiting for the one o'clock radio news when I heard a commotion at the door. My heart fell as I anticipated another brutal strip search and the cell being turned over. Instead, a prison officer threw a red holdall onto the bunk and growled, "Pack your gear. You're leaving in an hour."

254

I knew at that moment I was going to be repatriated to Portlaoise Prison in Ireland. There had been rumours of this and news reports it might happen as a result of the ceasefire. Just the day before, an English prisoner told me he heard the reports and reminded me I was as much a criminal as he was and would be treated no differently than any other convict.

I was transferred to the SSU at Full Sutton Prison in Yorkshire. There I met up with the other members of my ASU whom I hadn't seen since conviction. We knew we weren't being released from prison and might never be, but at least we'd be home in Ireland where we could once again see friends and family.

On 15 January 1997, we were brought by a heavily armed convoy to Newcastle airport, where a chartered easyJet plane waited for us on the runway. We were greeted by Portlaoise Prison officers in plain clothes and armed garda detectives. We boarded the flight and took off for Ireland with each of us handcuffed to an Irish prison officer. When I looked out and observed the east coast of Ireland appear in my window, I felt the warm glow of emotion an Irishman who leaves his country feels whenever he glimpses her again, particularly as I had not thought I would see this sight for at least thirty-five years.

We landed at the Irish Air Corps base at Baldonnel, outside Dublin, and were taken to Portlaoise Prison by police and military escort. I never thought I'd be glad to see the place. Entering the prison, we were applauded and cheered to the rafters by the IRA men on the republican landings. We were brought into a recreation area and given a dinner of steak and potatoes with real butter and pepper. I was thrilled. We weren't allowed butter in England, only margarine that tasted like diesel. Nor were we allowed pepper. The food I missed most was a simple dish of potatoes with butter and pepper. It was the finest meal I had eaten in years.

The Dublin government informed us that they had assured the British that our ASU would be treated as life-sentenced prisoners without the possibility of parole. We would not even receive compassionate parole in the event of the death of a close family member, which republicans were normally granted.

From time to time, senior members of the IRA, masquerading as Sinn Féin spokespersons, would be allowed into the prison to brief us on the ongoing talks. We were told to keep our feet on the ground and be prepared to be released or serve the rest of our sentences, depending on the outcome of the peace process.

The Good Friday Agreement was endorsed on 10 April 1998, by all the parties involved in the negotiations. These included most of the nationalist and unionist parties in the North of Ireland. Although Sinn Féin supported it, I was told by a man close to the IRA leadership that a member of the Army Council told him there wasn't a single republican fingerprint on the Agreement.

I didn't read the Agreement, much less study it, and I didn't know anybody who did. We were far too focused on getting released from prison. We trusted the republican leadership when they told us that the Good Friday Agreement was a transitional arrangement that would lead to the achievement of our republican goals. Unfortunately, I did not learn until it was far too late that my goals as an Irish republican and their electoral ambitions as political careerists would increasingly lead our paths to diverge.

16
DOWN THE REPUBLIC!

I WAS RELEASED from prison under the terms of the Good Friday Agreement on 22 May 2000. I had completed four years of my thirty-five-year sentence. Having accumulated forty-eight consecutive years in prison sentences, I served fourteen of them. I am often told that I should be grateful to the IRA leadership for signing up to the Agreement and getting me out of prison. I would be far more appreciative if the IRA had not been riddled with informers and we had completed our mission without being captured.

Shortly after my release, I went to Monaghan to visit a friend. As I walked through Church Square, I bumped into my Irish teacher from prison, Colm Lynagh, brother of Jim, who was killed in action at Loughgall in May 1987. Colm told me he was managing a European-funded project in Clones dealing with republican ex-prisoners and that jobs were available. I was living in a flat in Belfast and unemployed, so I grasped the opportunity. I moved to Clones, rented a house and got part-time work teaching computers to former prisoners and their families. I didn't know anything about computers—we had none in prison—so I had to learn a subject one day and teach it the next. It kept me busy and put a few pounds in my pocket for the first time in my adult life.

I was forty-three years old and had never used an ATM, seen a CD player or spoken on a mobile phone. I could, however, field strip, assemble and accurately fire a wide range of weapons. I could walk into any pharmacy or hardware store and buy the ingredients to manufacture a powerful bomb. I could pack a parachute, navigate underwater at night, organise and lead an ambush team, zero in a sniping rifle, camouflage myself and my equipment in any terrain, and I possessed a wide range of skills and talents that were of no practical use to me now. I had been either a US Marine, a full-time IRA operative or a prisoner of war since I was eighteen years old. The day-to-day realities of ordinary life were mysteries to me.

Just months before my release from prison, our beloved Aunt Alice died and bequeathed me what amounted to 13,000 Irish pounds—a colossal sum for a penniless prisoner. My mother handed me the cheque in Dublin when I got out. I had no idea what to do with it. Somebody told me to open a bank account. I found this daunting. I didn't know how or where to begin.

One day I took it upon myself to amble into the Bank of Ireland in College Green across from Trinity College in Dublin and asked to speak to a manager. I sat in the foyer for some time and, eventually, an attractive woman dressed in a business suit approached and enquired what I wanted. I told her that I needed to open a bank account. I said I was a recently released republican prisoner and that I had no passport or driving licence. In fact, I had no identification whatsoever. I had never held a bank account and I had never paid a utility bill, so I possessed no receipt to prove my address. The only document I had in my possession was a parole docket explaining I was on "permanent temporary release" until the end of my sentence in 2032 and must keep the peace until then.

I half expected her to turn on her heels or call the police, but to my surprise, she smiled and said, "Nobody would walk in here and make up a story like that." She couldn't have been more helpful and I got my first bank account.

While attempting to get on my feet in the civilian world, I was trying to figure out what was going on politically. Like most people, I was being bombarded with conflicting messages. Nationalists and republicans were told the Good Friday Agreement was a transitional stepping stone towards a united Irish republic, while unionists were assured that it secured the union with Britain. British Prime Minister Tony Blair called this ploy of speaking out of both sides of one's mouth at the same time "creative ambiguity."

The British government viewed the Good Friday Agreement as a masterpiece of diplomatic ingenuity calculated to reconcile northern nationalism to British sovereignty while simultaneously reconciling Ulster unionism to the sheer utility of allowing nationalists to become stakeholders in a reformed Stormont. It ended armed resistance to British rule and stabilised the partition of Ireland.

But what of the republican perspective? I attended many meetings, both IRA and Sinn Féin, and could get no straight answers. I was told we had bombed our way to the negotiating table. But we weren't *at* the negotiating table. The Good Friday Agreement was negotiated between the London and Dublin governments.

Of course, there were backchannels and discussions with British and Irish government officials going back years, in which the Provisional leadership was probed and prodded about tackling symptoms of the conflict without addressing the root cause. In the run-up to the Good Friday Agreement, the Provos were routinely consulted on prisoner releases, decommissioning of arms, policing and the Irish language (which most of them didn't speak), but they were on the periphery of negotiations not central to them. Far from being architects of the agreement, they acted as delivery drivers. Meanwhile, grassroots republicans were being breathlessly briefed that the leadership team of Gerry Adams and Martin McGuinness was "running rings around the Brits."

Recalling what a member of the IRA Army Council had told my friend about not a single republican fingerprint being on the Good Friday Agreement, I asked a senior Sinn Féin leader to point out what paragraph, clause or single sentence republican negotiators had inserted into it. I'm still waiting for an answer.

By this time, I had read and closely studied the Good Friday Agreement. It consisted of two closely related documents, the "Multi-Party Agreement" endorsed by most of the political parties in the Six Counties (including Sinn Féin) and the "British–Irish Agreement" signed by the London and Dublin governments. I was deeply concerned about the implications for reestablishing the Republic. The Good Friday Agreement repeatedly guarantees the unionist veto, euphemistically referred to as "the principle of consent," a principle Britain never granted Ireland as a whole.

Worrying implications for the future were flagged up in Section 1, subsection VI of the British–Irish Agreement, which states that all parties to the agreement "recognise that it is the birth right of all the people in Northern Ireland to be recognised as Irish or British or both and that *would not be affected by any future change in the status of Northern Ireland*" (my italics). That means that even in a future united Ireland, people born in the Six Counties, many of whose ancestors arrived in Ireland before the Pilgrims landed at Plymouth Rock (at a time when the concept of Britain didn't even exist), can claim British citizenship in perpetuity. I could only wonder if Ulster Protestants of the plantation tradition are forever condemned to be in Ireland but not of it? Are we never to be a nation? The simple answer is not if London can help it.

My key criticism of the Good Friday Agreement is that it is based upon the principle that the model of Ireland as one nation is a discredited concept. In the accompanying British–Irish Agreement, signed between the London and Dublin governments, we have an internationally recognised treaty that Irish Catholics and Protestants need never forge a joint civic identity. The British anticipate that the republican model of a united, sovereign and secular nation will, at last, be consigned to the dustbin of history. Winston Churchill described the Anglo-Irish Treaty of 1922 as "a great and peculiar manifestation of British genius." I believe the same can justifiably be said of this agreement.

Much play was made of joint referendums held North and South in May 1998 to endorse the Good Friday Agreement. I was in prison in Portlaoise and knew little of what was going on. Because they were held throughout Ireland, they were hailed as a national mandate for the Good Friday Agreement that eclipsed the national mandate for the Republic given by the Irish people in 1918.

However, they weren't quite what they claimed to be. Both jurisdictions voted on separate questions. The North voted on the Multi-Party Agreement and the South voted to amend Articles Two and Three of its constitution, which defined the Irish state's territorial claim to the whole of Ireland. The referendums passed, but republicans were sceptical because, firstly, the English politician in charge of Northern Ireland, Mo Mowlam, said that, whatever the result, only the vote in Northern Ireland would matter to the British government, and, secondly, transforming Dublin's claim to all of Ireland from a legal imperative to a notional aspiration was the *only* binding constitutional change required by the agreement.

Sinn Féin deflected these criticisms by pointing to the "mechanisms for unity" included in the agreement. In order for the Provos to convince their base that they should be pissing out of the tent instead of pissing into it, the Brits were obliged to outline a constitutional path towards a united Ireland. But bear this in mind: only the government of the United Kingdom of Great Britain and Northern Ireland can call a referendum on Irish unity. It will not be a national referendum encompassing the whole of Ireland. If it is ever called, it will be a concurrent vote between two jurisdictions, with the vote in Northern Ireland being the only one that counts in London.

According to the Good Friday Agreement, if a border poll is called, the British government decides the poll's wording and who qualifies to vote. Their parliament in Westminster must approve the final result. So, yes, a path to Irish unity has been outlined but simultaneously constrained by an intricate web of terms and conditions that London alone adjudicates. No Irishman, elected or otherwise, can call an Irish unity poll in Ireland.

The British have played a marvellous hand. Both the SDLP and the Dublin government, by acknowledging that unionists, far from being an integral part of the Irish nation, are, in fact, the British presence, have effectively removed the concept of an Irish nation from Irish nationalism. Sinn Féin has adopted and internalised this subversive trend. In doing so, they have removed the Republic from republicanism.

As the years rolled on from my release from prison in 2000, I had to find a life outside of war and politics. I met the woman who would become my wife. Debbie already had two daughters, Saoirse and Blánaid, and after we married, we had two children, Brendan and Niamh. I found work where I could get it and tried my hand at a number of things. We usually managed to scrape by.

Meanwhile, I did my best, with many others, to defend the republican position in both IRA and Sinn Féin meetings, but the dice were loaded. The decision had been made at the top and grassroots opinion counted for nothing. Meetings were essentially "sussing sessions," not held to test opinion and debate issues but to suss out who was on board and who would need to be marginalised and replaced by "a safe pair of hands".

On two occasions, I was reined in by senior IRA commanders and asked to dial down my misgivings about the direction in which we were heading. I was told that, because of my IRA record on active service and in prison, I was respected by many republicans and needed to "show leadership" by publicly embracing the new departure. I replied that the best way for a republican to show leadership was to have the moral and physical courage to defend the Irish Republic against all enemies, foreign and domestic.

The pro-agreement propaganda from the Provisional leadership became increasingly fraught and could take a nasty turn. Many IRA volunteers resigned in frustration. When asked why someone left the movement, Sinn Féin apparat-chiks would inevitably imply that the defector possessed some intrinsic character fault. Nobody resigned on the point of principle. He was either a knuckle-dragger who only wanted to play with guns, or someone who lacked the intellectual capacity to get his head around the strategy. A whispering campaign would often undermine a volunteer who resigned. He might be accused of being an alcoholic, a wife-beater or a beaten docket. He might be accused of leaving with the sole intention of lining his pockets by cigarette smuggling or fuel laundering. For those who could not be maligned, there was that catch-all phrase, "Ah sure, you know *his* problem." I never realised the Provisional movement contained so many flawed characters within its ranks and how lucky it was for Sinn Féin that these undesirables left the organisation in droves to allow the intelligentsia to beguile us at Stormont.

"What's the alternative?" That invariable battle cry of group thinkers everywhere became the answer to every question.

In 2008 senior republicans Gerry Kelly and Bobby Storey went on tour with an exciting and well-produced presentation about the H-Block escape of 1983 in which both men took part. Thirty-eight IRA volunteers had made a daring break for freedom, with nineteen of them successfully getting away. Three would later be killed on active service.

I attended the production in a packed community hall in County Fermanagh. It was what the US Marines would call "a dog and pony show" and was delivered by Kelly and Storey with aplomb and humour. They told of how they had broken with IRA convention and tradition by engaging with prison officers and doing prison work and maintenance they would typically never do. This relaxed the screws and allowed the volunteers into areas of the prison not ordinarily accessible to prisoners.

The underlying message was that they collaborated with the system to defeat it from within. Sinn Féin would do the same in Stormont. Republicans would enter this regional assembly of the British government to hollow it out and republicanise it. It was a ridiculous analogy with no basis in political reality but made for good entertainment. Events would prove that the only thing consistently hollowed out at Stormont would be Irish republicanism.

The stirring presentation had the added benefit of enhancing the presenters' credibility and esteem among their audience. The IRA leadership required volunteers with the prestige, the clout and the authority to police the new strategy and to be able to question the logic and undermine the motivation of any republican who dissented.

For British policymakers, pushing the concept of a "stalemate" was an important propaganda tool. It gave those within the IRA leadership, who were plotting to flip the script from the Republic of 1916 to the Counter-Republic of 1998, great kudos for having fought the Brits to a standstill. It was a delusional perception lapped up by many republicans because it played into a sense of themselves that they wanted to believe. However, outside of a small enclave in South Armagh, the British security and intelligence apparatus retained a comprehensive dominance and command of the strategic landscape. The fact that the IRA could continue to carry out an occasional shooting or bombing into the foreseeable future could hardly be described as a stalemate.

I was disappointed that two IRA achievements that should have helped win the struggle were being used by elements of the leadership to undermine it. The Great Escape from the H-Blocks was spun into a template for engagement and collaboration with the UK state, while the acquisition of arms from Libya was used to anaesthetise us. The leadership would repeatedly point to the guns as proof there'd be no winding down of the war and that the ceasefire was only a strategic pause to regroup and build political strength for the final push. All the while, they were running the IRA on the principle of planned obsolescence. We were too focused on parochial issues and too trusting of the leadership to see it. Instead of using the weapons to win the war, they used them as negotiating capital to end it on terms acceptable to Britain.

I was embarrassed by the way republican ex-prisoners were paraded before Sinn Féin party activists as a form of moral compass. The line went like this: "If so-and-so spent many years in prison and it's good enough for him or her, then what's your fucking problem?" I believed that going to prison was a sacrifice. When did it become an achievement? Why would anyone presume that a conviction elevates an intellect? Some of the more cogent arguments and analyses I heard came from republicans who had neither been in the IRA nor seen the inside of a cell.

During the course of many meetings, republicans were told by the Provisional leadership that we had to "move on." What they meant was that we had to move away—away from the belief in a united, democratic and sovereign republic; away from the belief that Ireland, all of it, is a separate nation and has the right to defend itself.

At the beginning of political meetings, we would be advised not to utter slogans or spout clichés. These referred to inspirational quotes from republican proclamations and the pantheon of republican icons. We were issued with new clichés, "Get your head around it," "What's the alternative," "Think outside the box." The box, of course, was republican doctrine. We were instructed to think inside a new box designed by the London and Dublin governments.

I resigned from both the IRA and Sinn Féin in September 2008. I wanted to resign immediately after a Sinn Féin Ard-Fheis had endorsed Her Majesty's Police Service of Northern Ireland as a lawful authority in part of our country the previous year. I felt pressured to stay awhile longer out of loyalty to friends and comrades who wanted me to help them continue to defend republican principles from within the movement. After a year of this Sisyphean struggle, I finally concluded that Sinn Féin had become a cold house for republicans and it was never going to change.

The Sinn Féin endorsement of British policing in Ireland was the moment, in my opinion, that the Provisionals officially defected en masse to the counter-republic. Others argue that occurred much earlier with their acceptance of the Unionist veto. The IRA defeated British policing in South Armagh and Sinn Féin was determined to bring it back again.

There was no longer talk of reestablishing the Irish Republic, only of uniting Ireland under terms and conditions defined by the British government. I hadn't joined the United Ireland Army but the Republican Army. That was no semantic or pedantic distinction. It cut to the core of the struggle. Yet, all this talk of reestablishing a united Ireland at the expense of reestablishing the Republic generated a conceptual fog into which many republicans strayed, becoming ideologically disorientated and losing direction. Of course, that is what it was designed to do. I thought back to what the old man who fought the Tans and the Staters said to me in the early 1980s: "There are only two possible outcomes to this struggle. One is the Irish Republic. The other isn't."

Writing in his diary on the first day of his hunger strike Bobby Sands wrote, "What is lost here is lost for the Republic." Later, he passed a note to one of his comrades during a prison mass which, among other things, said, "Don't worry, the Republic's safe with me." Unfortunately, the Republic would not prove safe in the hands of weaker men and women who would claim a share in Bobby's legacy.

As time went by, the Provos continued to lower the bar from the secular Republic to some nebulous entity called "This Island"—neither a country nor a nation but a polity where the sectarian scaffolding comes preassembled by the British government. In so doing, Sinn Féin internalised the conditions, parameters and political architecture of the united Ireland demanded by Britain, should it ever come to pass—a "New" Ireland that may one day contain no international border but will remain fundamentally partitioned between Planter and Gael, a "New" Ireland predicated on all the old divisions.

The Good Friday Agreement awards the British government, for the first time in our history, democratic title in Ireland. By recognising Irish unionists as British citizens in perpetuity, the Irish people must also recognise Britain's right to represent and defend those citizens. The suggestion that an Irish national government cannot safeguard the rights of a minority in its own country is the antithesis of Irish republicanism. It corroborates the ancient English prejudice that the Irish people are incapable of self-government.

It was stomach-churning to listen to those sanctimonious dupes within the Provisional movement who began boasting about their "journey," as if the transition from resistance to collaboration was a measure of personal growth. Guided by the dark hand of British intelligence, they helped transform the Provos from the most dangerous opponent of British rule in Ireland into the gift that keeps on giving.

I soon discovered the sheer futility of arguing the republican position with Sinn Féin party members who had ended up on the payroll of either the London or Dublin governments. It confirmed the truism of how difficult it is to explain something to someone whose salary depends on them not understanding. It also established the truism of George Orwell's observation that "nine times out of ten a revolutionary is just a social climber with a bomb in his pocket."

During the darkest days of the American Civil War, President Abraham Lincoln feared that the Republic might ask more of the American people than they were prepared to give. The support for the Good Friday Agreement suggests that the concept of an all-Ireland republic is beyond the scope and ability of the Irish people either to imagine or to achieve. I do not believe that.

We are told that counter-republics have always commanded democratic legitimacy over the Republic; that Home Rule, the Free State and the Good Friday Agreement have all, in their day, earned the overwhelming allegiance and endorsement of the Irish people. It would take a book in itself to describe the bribery, blackmail, propaganda, conditioning, infiltration and scare mongering required to achieve those results.

I have been in many homes, schools and government offices, and have often seen a copy of the Proclamation of 1916 proudly framed and displayed on a wall. Never in my life have I seen a single page of the Anglo-Irish Treaty or the

Good Friday Agreement exhibited anywhere. Why, if these documents are so democratically precious, so representative of Irish dreams and aspirations, are they not proudly displayed? Why are they not read to Irish school children? Why the 1916 Proclamation—a document signed by seven men in secret and, at the time, voted on by nobody?

The Proclamation of the Irish Republic speaks to the soul of the nation. It speaks to the collective unconscious. It articulates what we could be if we were allowed to be without foreign interference.

The Anglo-Irish Treaty and the Good Friday Agreement were formulated primarily by Britain as tribal settlements rooted in difference—differences the British insist must be given constitutional expression in every accord. Republicanism is rooted in a proposition. That proposition was first enunciated by the Protestant republican leadership of 1798, who called for national unity across the sectarian divide. It was further refined and articulated by the Catholic republican leadership of 1916. The proposition that Britain can be dispensed with and Irishmen and women of whatever persuasion and none can forge a joint national citizenship based upon democracy, equality and fraternity—that's the vision. That is Irish republicanism. That is what I fought for.